## PRAISE FOR *LOSS, SURVIVE, THRIVE*

"Not long after my son died, I realized I had to make a decision. I could listen to the common wisdom that claimed I would never get over his loss or I could choose to create a meaningful life. I didn't just want to survive, I wanted to thrive, and thanks to the support of countless people, I am thriving today. *Loss, Survive, Thrive* is an important book that breaks through common ideas about what grief should look like and shares the stories of families who are creating meaning after experiencing the death of their child. We need to raise these voices and this book does exactly that." ~**Jeannette Maré, executive director/Ben's Mom, Ben's Bells Project**

"We all experience pain and loss as a part of life. The key is to turn the pain into a labor pain and have the curse help us to give birth to a blessing as we learn from the authors' experience and our own. What the contributors share in *Loss, Survive, Thrive* and with their words can help us all to learn from the survivors and ease our own pain." ~ **Bernie Siegel, MD, author of** *A Book of Miracles* **and** *The Art of Healing*

"As an expert with more than 30 years in the field of death, dying, and bereavement, I am delighted that *Loss, Survive, Thrive* exists. With so much grief and loss in the world, this book offers hope to bereaved parents. The contributing authors share their very personal stories of how they pulled themselves out of the abyss of pain, and found the strength to keep on going. This wonderful book will be an invaluable guide to others who have lost a child." ~ **Virginia A. Simpson, PhD, FT (Fellowship in Thanatology), award-winning author of** *The Space Between: A Memoir of Mother-Daughter Love at the End of Life*

"When someone has to face the tragedy of losing a child, I am glad *Loss, Survive, Thrive* is available to help them get through it. The stories offer hope and role models. My own grandmother gave up on life after her eldest son was killed in WWII and she died not long after. As bereaved parents trudge through the darkest of days, the stories in this book show they are not alone and give them hope that life can go on." ~ **David Feinstein, author of** *Rituals for Living and Dying*

"This is such an important book! When people are faced with a major trauma, like losing a child, they feel they are out alone in the middle of a deep, dark ocean with no land in sight. That's when they need a life preserver and compass to not drown in the intensity of the emotions of grief. Every story in *Loss, Survive, Thrive* demonstrates how a bereaved parent made it out, each with a different roadmap. This book will be treasured by not only the grieving parents, but also their support people who don't know how to help." ~ **Robin Trainor, trauma specialist**

"The passing of a child does not mean you need remain forever bereaved. This treasury of healing stories, collected by a woman who shares your journey, will show you an alternate path. Savor every word as you learn to celebrate the continued presence of your child's light in your life." ~**Suzanne Giesemann, author of** *Messages of Hope*

"As a trauma therapist, I have seen how a major loss can lead to a lifetime of suffering. I also know that even the most devastating trauma can be healed under the right conditions. However, most people never find the quality of support that's needed, and this is especially true in the case of the death of a child – an immeasurable loss on many dimensions, which strikes at the core of our identity and trust in the goodness of life. Meryl Hershey Beck has a rare ability to unflinchingly share her journey, showing how it is possible to honor a life cut short with an ongoing relationship that is fully open to love. This message could only be delivered by someone speaking from her own experience. I highly recommend *Loss, Survive, Thrive* to bereaved parents and those who care about them, and for anyone who looks for reassurance that we can emerge from the depths of grief to rebuild a life of strength, compassion, and undiminished joy." ~ **Kate Hawke,** director, Trauma Transformation Network

"It's deeply sobering to know how much parents suffer when a child dies. The not being able to cope, the dropping down into addiction, the loss of health and even life. Tragedy as a result of tragedy! *Loss, Survive, Thrive* is such a gift for those who feel shattered and do not know where to turn." ~ **Maureen Morley, professor of English (retired)**

"We honor Meryl Hershey Beck for taking the time and energy to publish *Loss, Survive, Thrive*, and we are grateful to have a mention therein. To experience a loss and then to slowly but surely begin to survive and even thrive, is a challenge beyond measure. However, please know that there are resources to help. This book will no doubt be an excellent resource, as is Helping Parents Heal. Wishing you the best and *Namaste*,"
~**Ernie Jackson, board member, Helping Parents Heal**

"I have lived through the grief of losing many loved ones. Reading these stories of loss of a child, extreme grief and healing has affected me greatly. Each chapter broke my heart wide open again. Each chapter became a salve of healing again. The grace and courage it takes to dive into unfathomable suffering and not only drift through but fight and kick through to resurfacing into acceptance, hope and joy became another level of healing my own heart wounds. I recommend it to anyone who has a heart." ~ **Ellayn B McBroom, CHt, MA, miracle mentor**

"Hope. Such a simple word that holds so much promise. When one loses a child, they also lose hope and without hope, it's hard to survive. I applaud Meryl for creating a book of inspirational stories of survival by others that have navigated the aftermath of losing a child." ~ **Kelly Farley, bereaved father and author of *Grieving Dads to the Brink and Back***

"Being a mother who endured one of the most devastating events in life, I searched and searched for a resource that would give me life after death, something that would bring light into my dark, dark world. *Loss, Survive, Thrive* brings the grieving parent hope, inspiration, and a sense of belonging. We are not alone, and there's a place for us in this world."
~ **Rebecca Hendricks,** founder, Fight the Flu Foundation

"*Loss, Survive, Thrive* is a much-needed book—to give bereaved parents a sense that life can go on and it's possible to not just survive, but to thrive. I personally experienced the excruciating pain of losing a child, and my daughter's dad was unable to recover and drank himself to death. I wish he had had a book like this during those dark days. I used my pain to begin Healing Hugs, which now has over two million followers. Having a book like this would have helped us both immensely."
~**Tamara Gabriel, LMT, founder of Healing Hugs**

"For those of us who have lost children, navigating the road back to a 'normal' life can be difficult if not impossible. Like those who have gone through other tragedies, the weight of our grief is lessened when we find others with whom we can share our experience. When we share our journey with others, we walk alongside those who really do understand. I enjoy reading about others who have survived the loss of their child and learning how the experience changed their lives." ~ **Wayne Carroll, business consultant and musician**

"When people are grieving, they want to be heard and understood. They're not looking for advice or suggestions — though we mean well and want to offer support, often the words we say contribute to more pain instead. The best support I can imagine is to give this book to anyone who has experienced the loss of a loved one. They will receive profound sympathetic understanding by reading and relating to the stories in this book of pain and loss and hope and thriving. Within these pages are profound, heartfelt stories that will touch its readers to the depths of their souls and uplift them during these tough transitions." ~ **Sylvia Haskvitz, author of *Eat by Choice, Not* by Habit and Center for Nonviolent Communication certified trainer/assessor and communication consultant**

"For those bearing the unfathomable pain that attends the loss of a child, reading Meryl Hershey Beck's collection of narratives on loss and recovery will feel like witnessing a miracle. In the early stages of grief, it is nearly impossible to imagine ever feeling a spark of joy or fulfilment again, yet these inspirational accounts of triumph over the immense weight of grief will bear witness to the contrary; that it is not only possible but within the grasp of every human heart to embrace life and happiness again, even as one lives with the daily reality that will forever remain a part of life. I know Loss, Survive, Thrive will provide the inspiration so many need to deal with the difficulties of life." ~**Marla Grant, Helping Parents Heal Tampa affiliate leader**

# Loss,
# Survive, Thrive

# Loss, Survive, Thrive

Bereaved Parents Share Their
Stories of Healing and Hope

Meryl Hershey Beck

Edited by Mary Langford

Foreword by Susan Whitmore,
Grief Counselor, Founder/CEO of griefHaven

ROWMAN & LITTLEFIELD
Lanham • Boulder • New York • London

Published by Rowman & Littlefield
An imprint of The Rowman & Littlefield Publishing Group, Inc.
4501 Forbes Boulevard, Suite 200, Lanham, Maryland 20706
www.rowman.com

6 Tinworth Street, London SE11 5AL, United Kingdom

British Library Cataloguing in Publication Information Available

**Library of Congress Cataloging-in-Publication Data**

Name: Beck, Meryl Hershey, author.
Title: Loss, survive, thrive : bereaved parents share their stories of healing and
   hope / Meryl Hershey Beck.
Description: Lanham : Rowman & Littlefield Publishers, [2019] | Includes
   bibliographical references and index.
Identifiers: LCCN 2019011972 | ISBN 9781538125236 (cloth : alk. paper) |
   ISBN 9781538125243 (electronic)
Subjects: LCSH : Grief in parents. | Bereavement in children. | Children—Death.
   | Parent and child.
Classification: LCC BF723.G75 B43 2019 | DDC 155.9/37085—dc23 LC
   record available at https://lccn.loc.gov/2019011972

To all our angel kids—our Shining Lights—and
the courageous parents who shared their stories

*Erika* • *Nijhoni* • *Katie* • *Noah* • *Aiden* • *Zia*
*Lucas* • *Elizabeth* • *Garrett* • *Ryan* • *John*
*Travis* • *Janna* • *Quinton* • *Gabriel*
*Jon* • *Anthony* • *Leslie* • *Garrett* • *Austin*
*Doug* • *Jonny* • *Brennan* • *Hunter*
*Suliman* • *Susan* • *Mike* • *Shane* • *Nicole* • *Ryan*

Those who have suffered understand suffering, and thereby extend their hand.

—Patti Smith, American singer-songwriter

# Contents

# Foreword

## By Susan Whitmore

"*Y*ou won't always feel the way you do now, I promise. One day you *will* know happiness again."

After the death of my daughter Erika, such advice came readily from many. Yet, as helpful (and unhelpful) as much of that well-meaning advice was, it was those two sentences, coming from another mother who had lost her child seven years prior, that I fervently held on to as I grappled with intense sorrow and hopelessness every day. *How could it possibly be true? My life is over. I will never know another day of joy or happiness.*

Or so I thought.

In 2002, my daughter and only child, Erika Whitmore Godwin, died from an extremely rare sinus cancer. Just prior to her diagnosis at thirty-one, Erika was thrilled to be starting a new chapter of her life: planning her wedding and working toward her teaching credential. My daughter was my best friend, and I had never seen her so happy. Yet, barely one year later, surrounded and held by those whom she loved most, Erika succumbed to cancer and died. It wasn't until my sweet girl's memorial was over, and everyone else had gone back to living their lives, that my real grief journey began.

Mark Twain, always a master at painting pictures with words, was left utterly speechless when attempting to express how he felt after the death of his twenty-four-year-old daughter Susy. He wrote, "To do so would bankrupt the vocabulary of all the languages." To this day, that is the best description of grief I have come across.

As I searched for meaning in Erika's death, and a new sense of purpose for moving on without her, I wondered what my life would hold now that I had no child. Hoping to find some answers, I sought out the type of grief support I knew I needed—but didn't find any. That's when I got the idea to make a documentary film about grief, and also to create a true haven where people from all over the world could visit, at any time of the day or night, and find many facets of grief support. That is how griefHaven was born.

It is through my work over the past seventeen years, as a grief specialist, grief researcher, and founder of griefHaven, that I have had the privilege and honor to meet some of the most beautiful and caring people from around the world.

Regularly contacted by those who either want to honor their loved one in some special way or want to help others who grieve, Meryl Hershey Beck came into my life because she wanted to do both. Through *Loss, Survive, Thrive*, Meryl gives us an anthology of hope that is more than just a glimpse into the life of each contributor's grief journey; rather, she offers us a full view into the hearts of twenty-seven parents who have lost a child, and shows us precisely how they made their way from hopelessness to embracing life once again.

Why does that matter? Because it is through the heart of stories that we, too, can find and grab hold of our own lifeline, when we come to realize *if they can do it, I can, too!*

*Loss, Survive, Thrive* is no ordinary grief book. This is a melding of broken hearts who provide insight and direction by allowing us to delve deeply, with them, into their own very personal stories.

Author C. S. Lewis wrote, "We read to know that we are not alone." These stories hold universal threads of truth that weave us together and unite us, heart to heart. I hope as you read the words in *Loss, Survive, Thrive*—words carefully stitched together by each loving parent who shared, each mom or dad who, no doubt, shed many tears as they recalled their own painful healing journey—that you will know you are not alone, and will take to heart the offerings herein that can help you. Whether you are the griever or the person looking to help a griever, this is my wish for you.

In the end, the initial vow made to me by another grieving mother turned out to be true. I no longer live with feelings of hopelessness and despair, and I *have* come to find happiness again. It's my promise to you that if you immerse yourself into the following stories and climb aboard the life rafts offered by these brave parents, you will not only survive, you'll thrive—and you will come to find happiness again.

\* \* \*

**Susan Whitmore** is an international pioneer in the world of grief. In 2003, following the death of her thirty-two-year-old daughter, Erika, from an extremely rare sinus cancer, Susan founded griefHaven (www.griefHaven.org) in Los Angeles, California. Her work includes grief research and creating new grief support methods using the latest scientific research on the grieving brain. Susan's unique and educational approach to death and grief has been the subject of her many keynote presentations, workshops, TV and radio appearances, and educational seminars. This comprehensive grief support organization/facility/website provides support groups, private support, workshops, newsletters, articles, podcasts, special events, professional presentations, and more. Susan lives in Pacific Palisades, California, with her husband, Wendell. They enjoy gardening, movies, and spending time together in nature.

# Acknowledgments

*G*reat big thanks to so many angels who made this book possible . . .

First of all, the **angels on earth,** beginning with a big shout-out to dear friend Robin Trainor, the catalyst for writing this book. She told me that she met some parents who had lost a child and wished she had a book to give them. Furthermore, she said that she sees me as a *wayshower* for bereaved parents (because I succeeded in not allowing my son's death to ruin my life), and that I *had* to write a book to give bereaved parents a sense of hope. So . . . thank you, Robin, for loving me so much, for being the impetus to get this book written, and for always being my cheerleader.

I am so very grateful to all the amazing, courageous contributors who were willing to dig deep remembering the past as they shared their stories, showing that life doesn't need to end when your child dies. My life has been enriched getting to know them and working with them on their stories. Much appreciation, also, to Sandy Peckinpah for all her time, love, and energy in getting this project started.

A gigantic thank-you to my hardworking editor, Mary Langford, who is a magical wordsmith. She worked on the manuscript (for hours and hours every day!) for at least seven months, as we cheered each other on and enjoyed a wonderful collaborative relationship. The contributors and I continue to marvel at her ability to take the author's original words and craft them into a polished story while retaining each one's voice. You, dear Mary, are a treasure.

And I am also grateful to all the other editors who stepped in to help finish up a story or two, including Jan Henrikson, Linda Mallory, Janet Graves, and Sarah Coolidge.

Thank you to all the people at Rowman & Littlefield who've made this book possible, especially the acquisitions editor Suzanne Staszak-Silva and senior production editor Elaine McGarraugh. And, appreciation also goes to Jeff Herman, my literary agent.

Also, as always, so much gratitude to my wonderful friends and family who "get me" and continue to shower me with love, energy, and support. A special acknowledgment to my awesome daughter, Alison Hershey Manes, who has loved, championed, and believed in me for many, many years and has graced me with the joy of being a grandma and, the lineage continues, a great-grandma!

Finally, it goes without saying . . . so much appreciation to **our heavenly angels,** our Shining Lights—all the kids whose lives (no matter how brief) appear in these chapters. As their stories *and* their parents' love for them reverberate through the pages, they live on.

> Gratitude unlocks the fullness of life. It turns what we have into enough, and more. It turns denial into acceptance, chaos into order, confusion into clarity. . . . Gratitude makes sense of our past, brings peace for today, and creates a vision for tomorrow.
>
> —Melody Beattie, *The Language of Letting Go*

# Introduction

## By Meryl Hershey Beck

*Broken. Shattered. Devastated. Hopeless. Lost. Afraid. Empty. Over-whelmed.*

These are some of the words I used to describe my feelings in the days, weeks, and months following my son's suicide. Other bereaved parents use those same words and more, whether they lost an infant or a grown-up child, and whether the death came from a miscarriage, a neonatal death, an illness, an accident, a homicide, or drugs.

We, the bereaved parents, all know the hell of grief. We feel fractured, our hearts ripped out. None of us is prepared for the loss of a child. No one is. It feels completely unnatural for children to predecease their parents. We, the bereaved parents, share a common bond that creates a sisterhood and brotherhood of the heart. We are members of a club that nobody wants to join.

Many of us say we felt "isolated and alone" in the grief process. Well-meaning friends and family members usually rushed to our side . . . in the beginning. There's a bustle of activity filling the void, like planning the memorial service, going through memorabilia, telling stories, looking at pictures, and figuring out what to do with the physical stuff that is left on this earth by our beautiful, precious child. Once the floral arrangements have wilted, and the dinners from caring friends have diminished, there really isn't much that can be said or done to bring comfort, especially if those friends haven't lived through this horror themselves. And so often, they say the wrong things.

Unfortunately, there is a widespread belief that says, "You'll never get over the loss of a child." This is one of the most destructive assumptions

1

for those parents living the nightmare. They give up. They see themselves as victims and assume there's no life after this kind of loss.

It's true that life will never be the same. But we, the bereaved, can and must continue to live . . . and do it to honor our children. In the process, we can heal, grow, and evolve. And we learn to create a new normal.

It *is* true that some people never recover from the death of their child. Some fall into a deep depression and never climb out; others turn to alcohol or drugs, or emotionally sabotage themselves in other ways. And sometimes, the bereaved get sucked into the addiction of grieving. A beast inside takes hold and spreads its nasty tentacles, never to let them free. These people won't allow themselves to feel happy, believing that to do so would somehow dishonor the life of their now-deceased child. They are addicted to misery, addicted to feeling bad, addicted to grieving.

People say, "Time heals all wounds," but that is simply not true. Time doesn't fill the hole in a parent's broken heart. Time, however, does give us the opportunity to commit to our own healing and forge ahead. Healing from the loss of a child is hard work. There is no timetable. It takes as long as it takes.

Those who face the loss head-on are willing to feel the full impact of the grief process. It's no picnic. It sucks big-time. Although feeling the feelings can take them into a deep pit of despair, they don't need to stay there. Pain doesn't last forever. It's simply the very first step.

Best-selling author Harold Kushner reminds us, "We can endure much more than we think we can; all human experience testifies to that. All we need to do is learn not to be afraid of pain. Grit your teeth and let it hurt. Don't deny it, don't be overwhelmed by it. It will not last forever. One day, the pain will be gone and you will still be there."[1]

The next step is to make a choice to recover and find ways to heal. Bereaved parents can choose to honor their child's memory by living as full and as rich a life as possible.

The contributors to *Loss, Survive, Thrive* are such parents. Here, they share their personal, heartfelt stories and offer a lifeline of hope and help. The chapters are designed to be uplifting: inspirational stories written by parents who have experienced the deep, deep pain of losing a child, have reclaimed their vitality, and are now enjoying a fulfilling life. These are ordinary people with the same message: *If we can survive and thrive after the horrors of this unfathomable death, you can too.*

We, the collective authors, reach out through these pages to hold hands with those who are suffering this profound loss. Your life does not need to end when you lose a child. We know your pain, and we know how to survive. Our stories are here to lend comfort and support during the darkest days and provide a road map for moving beyond loss into thriving.

As you read our stories, you'll discover how we each found our way toward reclaiming our lives. There's Rukiye, who shocked everyone when she faced her son's murderer and then gave him a hug in the courtroom (the viral video produced by Humankind has attracted more than forty-four million views in America alone, and has been translated into six other languages worldwide). And there's Sandy, who became a Grief Recovery Specialist and wrote an award-winning book to help other suffering parents. Personally, my son suicided, and I have been commended for being a role model to help other bereaved parents rebuild their lives.

Then there's Kelly, whose loss of two children spurred him to write a book to help other grieving fathers and found the Grieving Dads Project. And Alice, who attributes her becoming a licensed Five Element acupuncturist to the lessons she learned from her son's passing. And there's Tamara, who took on her healing journey in a very big way—she helps others through her nonprofit community Healing Hugs (her Facebook community has grown to more than two million followers).

Also, there's Jo-Anne, who discovered firsthand the brutality of losing a child and then, after learning to love herself again, became a contributor for the websites Glow in the Woods, Courageous Mothers, and Still Standing Magazine. And Ernie, whose loss opened his perception to a whole new world.

As you turn the pages, you will meet these brave souls plus many others.

Everybody suffers losses; everybody grieves. It's part of the human condition. Perhaps you haven't experienced the death of a child, but the death of a spouse, sibling, or parent has torn your heart apart and battered your soul. This book offers comfort no matter the nature of your loss.

Maybe it's not your own personal loss, but a friend or relative who is grieving. Sharing this book with the bereaved can help them see that it is possible to not only live through their tragedy, but also actually find happiness again.

The following stories all abide by the same simple format: *Child dies. Parent suffers. Parent chooses to heal and rebuilds his or her life.* Although the formula might be simple, each person is unique, each story different.

*Loss, Survive, Thrive* is one giant step toward healing the grieving heart. It offers a cultural awakening to the true nature of grief and gives suggestions as to how to best navigate through it and get to the other side.

Read this book cover to cover, or pick out the sections that most apply to your life. Our wish is that our stories give you hope and faith that you *can* recover, that life *can* go on, and that you *can* live a great life filled with promise, purpose, and joy.

> Deep grief sometimes is almost like a specific location, a coordinate on a map of time. When you are standing in that forest of sorrow, you cannot imagine that you could ever find your way to a better place. But if someone can assure you that they themselves have stood in that same place, and now have moved on, sometimes this will bring hope.
>
> —Elizabeth Gilbert, *Eat, Pray, Love.*[2]

## NOTES

1. Harold Kushner, *When All You've Ever Wanted Isn't Enough: The Search for a Life That Matters* (New York: Fireside, 2002), 168–69.

2. Elizabeth Gilbert, *Eat, Pray, Love* (New York: Penguin Group, 2006), 79.

# I

# BABY LOSS

Grief is not something that you can hide from, it is not an illness, and it is nothing to be ashamed of, but it is something that you need to nurture.

—Jo-Anne Joseph

## • 1 •

# It Takes a Village

### By Vickie Bodner

$\mathcal{I}$had always dreamed of being a mom. From the time I was a young teen, I used to say, "These hips were made for babies." That's how sure I was that I'd have children.

Growing up, I babysat a lot and loved being with youngsters from infants to middle-schoolers. Looking back, I can see that I was groomed to be a caregiver from a young age by a certain dysfunction in my family, and that somehow provided me and my life with a feeling of purpose and meaning.

There was always a lot of chaos and craziness in my home, and the years before my parents' divorce (when I was nine) were painful and challenging due to the tension and constant fighting that took place between them. My mom definitely had her challenges, and I became like the little grown-up watching over my younger sister, even though I was just a kid.

From the ages of two to four, I was hospitalized frequently due to multiple inner ear infections and several very serious life-or-death mastoid surgeries. I'd hear a noise in my ear, which felt like a tiny little man pounding on the (ear) drum, very loud and painful, and my mother would spend hours rubbing my head and temples while I cried in pain. She would take me repeatedly to the emergency room at Marymount Hospital in Cleveland, Ohio. I was there so much that when I'd come into the ER, the nurses would often greet me by name! Even today, I have to be very careful to protect my ears in order to avoid serious pain.

While in the hospital, I wasn't allowed to be around other children (so as to not contract an illness or infection that could lead to threatening complications), so I spent a lot of time by myself. My little heart

7

would break after each of my mom's visits, as I watched out my hospital room window as she walked back to her car to go home to take care of my newborn sister.

The playroom down the hall from my room became my saving grace, and you'd find me there many hours each day. As that curious young girl, I felt like I was connecting with comforting spirits such as Mother Mary (looking back on this now, it seems only natural, since it was named Marymount Hospital) and what appeared to be angels. I always felt safe and loved in their presence, which was truly a blessing.

Even though I always knew that someday I would have children, once I was an adult, I chose to focus instead on my career, self-healing, and travel. In my late thirties, I met a man whom I'll call "Mathew," my husband-to-be, and at the tender age of forty was shocked to find myself pregnant! I couldn't wait to become a mom, and I could not contain my excitement.

My husband, however, felt unprepared. Mathew was eight years younger than me and was still in the process of career searching when he decided to go back to college. His quiet ambivalence over me and the baby was apparent, and while he was focused on finding himself, I felt very alone.

My career as a graphic designer ended suddenly, when the company folded. Afterward, I had sessions with a psychotherapist and began attending twelve-step support group meetings for codependents (codependency is putting other people first at the expense of your own needs). Also, although my family knew only Western medicine, I became interested in Eastern (Chinese) medicine, and planned a trip to China to study introductory Chinese medicine and herbs.

A few days after hearing the great news of my pregnancy, I journeyed to Beijing, China, on that planned trip to immerse myself in my studies. I left the US feeling joyous, regardless of my husband's ambivalence, because I was pregnant for the first time in my life and loving every minute of it.

Upon my return from that wonderful nine-day trip, the doctors felt I should be watched closely due to my advanced age in pregnancy. They surmised that I was about eight weeks pregnant and scheduled an ultrasound for a few weeks down the road.

Approximately two weeks before the ultrasound was to happen, I had two very upsetting dreams that my baby had died. Panicking,

I shared the dreams with some of my close friends, who assured me that this is a normal occurrence during pregnancy and not to worry. However, it was hard to ignore such visceral dreams that had felt so real in my body.

In spite of the dreams, the day of the ultrasound found both Mathew and me feeling upbeat, eagerly looking forward to hearing our baby's heartbeat for the very first time. Mathew had finally accepted and was beginning to embrace fatherhood.

About halfway through the ultrasound procedure, though, the technician's demeanor radically changed. She said she could not continue the appointment since the machine had stopped working and was broken. Her energy was suddenly so agitated, I knew something was not right. I began to panic and asked her if something was wrong, and she said she could not discuss anything and that only the doctor had that privilege.

I left that appointment feeling extremely distressed. With super-high anxiety, I spent the next two days awaiting the doctor's call, doing my best to keep my mind from driving me crazy with fear of the worst-possible-case scenario.

Finally, the doctor called. And in a matter-of-fact voice, he told us of the loss of our baby, and said that he wanted to schedule a D&C procedure immediately.

I was in such shock, I could hardly formulate words. I knew I wasn't anywhere near ready to let go of my baby, so after a moment I told the doctor I wanted to wait and allow the process of the miscarriage to happen naturally. I had been so thrilled with the pregnancy, and though I was only nine or ten weeks pregnant at that time, the loss of my only child was way too hard for me to accept.

Since learning of my pregnancy, I had been going to Womankind, an amazingly supportive pregnancy care center for women without insurance. They had been able to see me on a sliding-scale fee basis, which allowed me to have good health care and counseling from the early stages of my pregnancy. I was—and always will be—very grateful to this organization and, with their support and guidance, I believed I could safely allow the miscarriage to happen naturally.

It was September, and as I approached my twelfth week, the pain in my abdomen became unbearable, so I called to set up the D&C procedure for the following Tuesday. The weekend was scary, though, and unbearably painful, so in a panic I called the emergency room at my local hospital for advice. They told me to stay home and not come in since the ER was overloaded with patients and there was not much they could do to help me anyway.

I rested as much as I could through the remainder of the weekend, and on Monday begged the nurse at my pre-op appointment to take me in for the procedure that day, as I was sure I would not make it until Tuesday's scheduled appointment. I guess those same angels of my youth were watching over me because even though my doctor was off on holiday, his associate was available that day to perform the D&C.

Meeting this new doctor, I immediately sensed his compassion, kindness, and gentleness, which felt like a huge blessing to me. As I prepared for the surgery, my labor began. Then the pain increased even more because the miscarriage was finally progressing. I knew it was time to surrender, to somehow accept and let go of my lifelong dream of being a mother. Although quite sad, I was grateful to feel the sense of peace that accompanied my decision to let go. There was also a level of comfort knowing that the process was happening naturally and in its own time.

Already in excruciating pain, I felt tortured as the nurses attempted to insert the IV—since I was dehydrated and very stressed, they were unable to get a needle in my arm. After five unsuccessful tries, they brought in the anesthesiologist, and he was able to insert the IV needle relatively quickly. As they wheeled me off to the operating room, my husband sat in meditation and prayer, which held a lovely healing space for me.

In a strange sort of way, I felt like everything was exactly as it was meant to be. As I awoke from the anesthesia, my eyes were immediately drawn to the most beautiful sunset I've ever seen. It was on the TV screen, and the sunset was being shown during the weather segment of the local news. Gazing at it gave me a sense of deep peace. Later, as we drove home, I viewed the actual sunset and it affirmed for me, once again, that all was well, and everything was in divine order.

Although this was the same hospital where I had spent so much time as a toddler, the layout had been reorganized, so it was somewhat disorienting. The pediatrics and labor/delivery floors had been switched. And, even though my procedure was originally scheduled to take place in a traditional operating room on one of the lower floors, there were none available that evening. As such, the doctor reluctantly did the

D&C in the labor and delivery room on the maternity floor. Since he did not want me to hear the cries of newborn babies while my baby was no longer viable, this floor was not the kind doctor's first choice.

To my amazement and in full-circle fashion, I realized that the procedure for my miscarriage actually took place in a room that was formerly the hospital playroom where I had spent so many hours and days as a young child!

This was the same room where those loving and supportive spirits took care of me when I was left all alone as a youngster. And apparently, they were also there in the operating room that day, supporting me and loving me during the loss of my baby, which was evident in the overwhelming sense of peace that I felt as I awoke.

Once back on my feet, I chose to attend grief counseling in order to allow my process its own time and the stages of grief to naturally unfold. The hospital bereavement groups for parents who had experienced the loss of their child through miscarriage or stillbirth were especially helpful because my husband and I met other people who shared our deep sadness.

We also participated in a memorial service held at the hospital chapel, which honored all who had passed during the month of September. Then during the holidays, we attended several other memorial ceremonies, including one where we placed our baby's name, Nijhoni (which means "beauty" and "harmony" in Navajo) on a Christmas tree in her memory.

After the D&C, I discovered that the hospital was planning to treat our baby's remains as biohazardous matter. Outraged, I wrote letters and met with the hospital chaplain to rewrite the hospital rules to allow a miscarried baby to be treated as a person and buried in a cemetery, if that is the parents' wish.

It took a great deal of time and effort to get this accomplished, but it has been well worth the fight in the end, because the loss of our baby daughter changed the rules for all other baby losses that have followed at that hospital. Nijhoni was buried with the other infants who died in that same hospital, under a tree, in the very cemetery where most of my family is also buried.

At the time of my pregnancy, I had been working for many years as a massage therapist. Doing chair massage at a company's headquarters in Cleveland, I felt a very friendly connection to some of the employees.

Even though I'd wanted to shout out my excitement when I learned I was pregnant, I waited about six weeks to announce it, and they were all so happy for me.

After the miscarriage, one can only imagine the devastation I felt as I responded to each person's inquiry as to how I was doing and what I thought would happen for me in terms of any future motherhood. As each person learned of my news, I felt grief, loss, and even embarrassment as I watched their faces fall with shock and horror. My only consolation was that some of the gentle women offered to share with me how they survived their own challenging miscarriages.

To my amazement, after hearing of my loss, multitudes of women opened up to me about their own miscarriages and baby losses. Many of my friends and relatives had known about my pregnancy, and after I lost the baby, several seemed to come out of the woodwork to share with me about miscarriages they had also suffered.

When it happened to me, I felt so alone at first, but I found comfort in knowing that miscarriage is much more common than I had ever realized. Very often, I quickly learned, women keep the secret of losing their babies sacred and to themselves, like they belong to some secret exclusive club—that is, until someone they care about ends up suffering a similar loss.

I was certain I didn't want to hold my loss as a secret, and soon discovered that it's only in sharing it that true healing can finally begin.

It took me about two years of deep grief and sadness to come to a place of rage. After a full-out screaming session with God, I felt ready to let go entirely and embrace the precious gifts of my life, knowing with 100 percent certainty that all is in divine order, even now. Both of my grandmothers had died before I was born, so I have always considered the ocean to be my grandmother. To help heal, I spent time with my favorite grandmother, in Cancun, Mexico, and she gently reminded me to go with the flow and gave me the courage to move beyond my pain.

Lots of women have miscarriages, but many have other children. There are just a few of us who desire a child but are never able to give birth to one of our own to raise. It's a smaller club I'm in—getting pregnant, having a miscarriage, and no future children, even though there's still such a strong desire to have them.

In my twenties, my health care professionals insisted I'd never get pregnant because of certain past medical issues. But it happened, it really happened, and I enjoyed those precious few weeks of pregnancy with all my heart. I later found out that during my pregnancy, I had been ill with Hashimoto's disease, which affected my thyroid and other organs, and perhaps that contributed to my miscarriage. I guess I'll never know what happened for certain.

It is said that it takes a village to raise a child. Although I was never blessed with a child of my own, I am proud to be an integral part of that village for others. Children have always been very important to me. My calling is clear now—to support all parents as best I can and to love all children everywhere, as they always bring the world so much joy.

I love children and want them to know they are truly loved for the special human beings they are, and I will spend the rest of my life encouraging people everywhere to enthusiastically love *all* children— including the child that still resides inside each of us.

These precious children are our future, and they have so much to teach us if we are open to learning from them. After all, they are the most beloved part of the village that's helping to raise them.

\* \* \*

**Vickie Bodner,** a Reiki Master, has been a licensed massage therapist since 1996, in private practice. Her specialties include therapeutic and relaxation massage, craniosacral therapy, and energy bodywork, all of which increase awareness and relationship of the body, mind, spirit, and emotions. Vickie believes that by creating a safe, nurturing environment physically and emotionally, the body may heal itself given the right circumstances, and she supports others in choosing to make their good health—and their children's (if they are blessed to have any)—a priority.

## · 2 ·

# Then and Now

### By Kelly Farley

*I* grew up in a typical blue-collar Midwest town where working hard was a way of life. Men were expected to "toughen up" when things became rough. You had to push through. There wasn't room anywhere for "weakness." And nobody talked about the pain they might be carrying regardless of its severity.

These important lessons I learned from my dad, and I strongly suspect he learned them from his dad. Every other male figure in my life lived by these rules. Rules that I was taught and later subscribed to. I just assumed it was the right way to deal with things.

Looking back, I now realize that alcohol and other forms of self-medication had played a major role in helping these men cope with their pain. Interestingly, I do not remember seeing a grown man cry until I was well into my thirties.

Although I found my way out of that blue-collar town, I still carried many of these life lessons with me when I moved to Chicago with my girlfriend, Christine, after college graduation in 1994. Both freshly equipped with engineering degrees, we were ready to take on the world. We didn't have the luxury of taking time off after graduation to enjoy the fruits of our hard work—we had financed our way through college and the loan repayments would be starting soon—so we went straight to work.

Christine and I were fortunate to find great jobs and success in our new profession. Climbing the corporate ladder became important to us, since we were the first in each of our families to graduate from college and wanted to prove that we were successful. With close family and friends surrounding us, we were married in the fall of 1996 in our home state of Iowa. She and I both came from working-class families and were responsible for paying for our own college and wedding, so we continued to focus on climbing the corporate ladder to pay off college debt with the hope of saving enough to someday buy a home. We accomplished both of these goals in late 2000. However, we kept telling ourselves that if we worked a little longer and saved more money, we would be in a good financial position to have children. We became so busy being busy that we put off starting a family.

In 2003 we decided that it was finally time to have a child. However, we soon found out that just being ready for and wanting a child doesn't necessarily mean a child will arrive when you want. We were planners, and not being able to conceive when we wanted to was not part of our plan! Then, after a series of fertility treatments, we finally conceived our daughter Katie.

I had never been that guy who knew, without doubt, that he wanted kids; yet, after two years of living with the emotional roller coaster of fertility treatments, we were excited to finally be parents. Having grown up with two brothers, I knew if I had a child, I wanted a daughter to spoil, and I longed for that father-daughter relationship.

Sadly, in the fall of 2004, all those exciting dreams of watching my daughter grow up and everything that went along with them slipped away and turned to sorrow when, seventeen weeks into the pregnancy, we lost Katie. My very worst nightmare became a reality.

In the aftermath of Katie's death, I did what I had been taught to do growing up in that blue-collar town: I toughened up and pushed through my pain. I did what every "man" is supposed to do: I focused on helping my wife through this tragic event. I buried my pain and grief somewhere deep inside and never talked about it with anyone. Instead of turning to the bottle, I turned to seventy-hour workweeks in an effort to take my mind off the agony. I didn't want to think about it, and I was certain that if I stayed ahead of the pain, I could outrun it.

About a year later, Christine and I decided we would try to conceive again—also with the help of fertility treatments. This time, we were expecting a boy, and we felt blessed that little Noah was going to be a part of our lives. Katie's little brother was going to be the answer to our pain. We had made it through all of the key early milestones of the pregnancy and felt relieved. But then, during week twenty, we were told that our son was struggling and would not survive.

In June of 2006, at twenty-two weeks, our little Noah passed away in utero and was born still the very next day. The eight hours I spent with his lifeless body was the best day of my life and the worst, all wrapped up into one gigantic nightmare. I knew, like with Katie's passing, my life would be changed forever, but this time I was certain I couldn't bury the pain nor hide from it. If I had any hopes of surviving, I would have to learn to grieve and allow myself to process the pain of losing first Katie, and now Noah. But that's not the route I chose because, like it or not, I was still trying to live up to the "tough guy" persona that I was taught was the one that mattered.

I never wanted to get out of bed and for the most part I didn't, at least for the first three months. All the pain from the loss of Noah, coupled with all the pain I'd buried deep inside after the loss of Katie, rushed to the surface, nearly crushing me. I was barely functioning, and the fog of grief was thick.

For a short period of time I tried to fight the pain, but the burden was so heavy and unrelenting. I wanted to run away from everything, but didn't know where to go. I was too devastated to forge my escape. Instead, I would sit in my office searching for information and clues as to what might be the matter with me. My doctors told me I had depression; I didn't believe them. I told myself, "Something else must be wrong with me." I thought my upbringing had equipped me to handle anything, but I could not control my response to this overwhelming pain.

After months of despair and finding myself on my hands and knees begging God to relieve the pain, I realized I needed help and finally surrendered. Reluctantly, I decided to meet with a counselor. Within the next week, I found myself sitting in the waiting room of her office. Embarrassed that I wasn't "tough" enough to fight through this pain on my own. Embarrassed that someone I know might see me at this office. Then, when it was my turn to go in, I walked inside her office and sat down in the appointed chair. When she asked me what was going on, it all started releasing uncontrollably. I sat there for an hour and bawled like a baby. Not just a few tears streaming down my face, I was sobbing. I had finally given myself permission to let out all the pain, and the pain was taking the opportunity to do just that.

After several sessions with the kindhearted counselor, I was referred to a psychiatrist, who diagnosed me with not only depression, but also with post-traumatic stress disorder (PTSD). Though the diagnosis made sense, I refused to give in, and I was determined not to allow this to define me.

There were days I could have easily given up. I could have dropped out of society—walked away from my job, my house, the life I'd worked so hard to build. And many days I thought about it. It was truly the first time in my life that I didn't care if I lived or died. I wasn't suicidal; I just didn't care. But somehow, I managed to hold on just a little longer.

After I surrendered to the grieving process and allowed myself to be vulnerable, I noticed there were a lot of people around who were willing to help me: strangers that I had met in baby loss support groups, a Stephen Minister from my church, and others that I had shared my story with over general pleasantries. These people had no agenda; they just listened and wanted to help a grieving dad deal with the enormous pain he was carrying. These kind folks didn't judge or become uncomfortable when I started to cry while telling them my story. Rather, they held a space for me in which I could safely feel.

These people embraced me, checked in with me, and took my frantic calls regardless of what they were doing at the time. They provided me with compassion, sympathy, and hope. They never told me to "toughen up" or "fight through it." Instead, they taught me perseverance and how to handle the loss in a healthy way. Their gift of compassion allowed me to release the pain, grief, depression, and despair ever so slowly.

The first couple of years after the loss of Katie and Noah, I found that getting out of bed was a daunting task, never mind making plans for my future. However, deep down I knew I couldn't go back to being the man I had been before—but I also didn't know who I was going to become. If I was to survive, I knew I had to re-create myself. To evolve.

Early after the losses, I was evolving, but not in a healthy way. I was spiraling out of control, and I knew it. I just didn't know how to stop it. Eventually, I started grasping at things that I thought could help me. Some did, some didn't, but I kept at it until I found the one thing that finally pulled me out of the pit of despair—which was reaching out to other grieving dads. I went from barely surviving to something closer to thriving. Yet, I wouldn't say that everything is always great or that I am beyond the losses.

Thoughts of Katie and Noah enter my head every day. The difference between then and now is that I no longer let thoughts of my children impact me negatively. Now, thoughts I have of them make me smile.

Although both of my little angels' lives were cut short, each encouraged me to live a life that I know would make them proud of their dad.

As challenging as some of the years since the losses have been, learning new lessons and new truths has helped mold me into the person I am today. Lessons that are much different than the lie that *big boys don't cry* that I was told while growing up in that blue-collar town. Lies that caused a lot of avoidable pain.

All of the new lessons I've learned about life and the compassion I received from complete strangers gave me the strength I needed to help others. Strength I didn't realize I had. But the one thing that gave me hope was the fact that I made a promise to Katie, Noah, and myself that once I was strong enough, I would reach out to other dads that have lost a child and help them find their way back from the brink.

It became evident to me while going through my own grief and pain that men do not have many resources when it comes to dealing with the loss of a child. So, in late 2009, I decided to do something about that. I began a blog called the Grieving Dads Project, which was nothing fancy, but it provided an outlet for me, and also proved to be a valuable resource for the men who grieved alone and suffered in silence.

To my amazement, within just a few weeks I started to hear from other men from around the world that they, too, were looking for something, anything, that could give them some sort of insight into what they were feeling.

Soon after starting my blog, it became apparent to me that I needed to do something more. I decided I'd write a book. Since I wasn't a professional writer, I had no idea where to start, but I knew it had to be hard-hitting, honest, raw, and—most importantly—transparent. I began traveling around the United States and conducting face-to-face interviews with dozens of men who had suffered horrible losses like I had.

Thousands of other stories from grieving dads worldwide started showing up in my inbox. I knew I was on to something profound. Something that was really going to make a difference, that would give permission to men where it never existed before. Permission to grieve their losses and feel the unbearable pain. Pain that must be processed, not tucked away into a dark corner of our innermost selves but faced head-on. We can't run from it, nor can we hide from it, try as we might.

*Grieving Dads: To the Brink and Back* was published in 2012. I had no idea when I wrote this book that it would be so far-reaching and have the impact it has had on so many. I'm told it has inspired others to take action to find a purpose in their loss, and to go on to honor their beloved children. *Grieving Dads* has created a ripple effect, a movement that says, *It's okay for me to feel, to hurt, and to share my emotions.*

One thing that became obvious to me as I have navigated through my own losses is this: It is an absolute must that we allow ourselves to become vulnerable, transparent, and authentic. We must learn to let it out, all of it. Even the darkest stuff that has happened to us, that we never thought we could share. If we are to have any chance of thriving after our loss, the pain must come out.

It is hard to believe, but it's been seven years since *Grieving Dads* was published, and I know it has helped tens of thousands of grieving dads and moms through the aftermath of losing a child. I hear from more grieving dads every week who continue to struggle through this journey, as well as the brand-new members of this horrible club none of us ever wanted to join.

I am both honored and inspired by the response and feedback to my work that I receive. It helps me realize that life is much bigger than me and my problems. It's about having the strength to reach out and pull as many people as possible out of despair and help them find hope, as well as discover the purpose in their loss that will ultimately change the course of their life for the better.

I will never be the person I was before the deaths of my children. But I realize that I can live a life of meaning that helps others and also honors the lives of my Katie and Noah. I try my best every day to make those two kids proud of their dad.

\* \* \*

**Kelly Farley** was caught up in the rat race of life when he experienced the loss of two babies over an eighteen-month period. Like many men, during these losses and the years that followed, Kelly felt like he was the only dad that had ever experienced such a devastating loss. He discovered during his journey that society, as a whole, doesn't feel comfortable with an openly grieving male. That realization inspired him to start the Grieving Dads Project (www.grievingdads.com) and to write his book *Grieving Dads: To the Brink and Back.* Kelly has a passion for helping people "pick up the pieces" after experiencing a profound life event. He currently lives in the suburbs of Chicago with his wife, Christine, and his four-legged friend, Buddy.

## · 3 ·

# Embracing Hopelessness

### By Shoshana Garfield

*I* had the privilege of growing up in a poor neighborhood in Rego Park, New York City, USA. The privilege came, in part, from having so many neighbors with blue number tattoos on their arms identifying them as Holocaust survivors.

There are many firsthand accounts publicly available detailing the horrors of all those death trains. You hear about the suffocations, being without food or water for days, packed in with corpses rotting in summer and those who froze alongside living bodies in the ice-cold months of winter. What you don't hear about so often are the fart jokes.

It's irreverent, right? Yes, it is. Yet, there is an important distinction between irreverent and disrespectful. For many people, that boundary line is blurred. One ought not dare to bring lightheartedness into grief unless one is willing to face accusations of betrayal and not being loving. That sensitivity to the judgment of others is why those stories haven't made it out into the general public, despite the fact that the people who lived those stories have every right to make those distinctions.

Personally, I think being able to have a laugh in the truly abject misery of those death trains is an immense accomplishment, at least as a way of coping, and at best a genuine triumph of the human spirit.

I had no idea how useful and nourishing that distinction—secretly and lovingly passed on to me by my neighbors and other Jews I knew as a child—would be when I was in my early forties, the age some of those unfortunate people had been on their own journeys to mass extinction.

Getting pregnant with my firstborn, Aliyah, was an understated affair. It would be more accurate to say that the actual getting pregnant part was quite fun, but receiving the news of the actual pregnancy was

20

the understated bit. After all, how excited could I let myself get after having had ten miscarriages over the years? Chances were, this one wasn't going to stick either.

For some reason, though, I had a great feeling about this pregnancy, so I cheerfully indulged in baby name searches once we passed the hurdle of my first trimester.

I nevertheless had a very anxious pregnancy, with the shadows of all the previous, withered attempts hanging around in corners. I knew the stats for my age, late thirties, and part of me was waiting for complications. The medical care from radiologists, midwives, and the rarely spotted doctor (here in the UK, antenatal care is mainly in the hands of midwives) were cautiously reassuring. I did my best to encourage things along with very, very strict, healthy eating, that is, loads of lentils and vegetables, and no caffeine or refined sugar.

It took months to find midwifery care that I felt I could really trust. Finally, at seven months, I was assigned Lucy, who had decades of the sorts of expertise I could lean on. Finally, I could relax and enjoy the pregnancy . . . just in time to be really terrified about childbirth.

When my water broke at eight months and two weeks, I felt like a horse urinating on my bedroom floor. Gross. I did everything my gorgeous Lucy, and the Internet, told me to do as a laboring mom (luckily the same advice—long walks, massages, spicy food, raspberry and nettle tea). Nothin'. . . no contractions whatsoever, not even a twinge.

Two and a bit days and many discussions and Internet consultations later, I had a scheduled C-section on April 10, 2004.

My stunning baby girl was on the light side, just a few ounces above what would have put her in the premature category. What did I care? Aliyah was here! Yay! When she looked at me, I felt like she saw my soul. It might be a cliché, but I tell you, that was really, truly, totally my experience. Even remembering this now makes my eyes water up with happiness. I have told her all her life that she was my miracle baby and is my miracle child.

Now, at fourteen years of age, she rolls her eyes when I say it, but at least she smiles when she does it. Sometimes I even get a warm hug.

I had applied for a PhD course in England, where I was living, just after I got pregnant and before I knew how things were going to work out with my wee fetus (not yet a baby; I couldn't bear thinking of her as a baby yet). I had already worked in the field of domestic abuse for many,

many years. By that time, I had been a caseworker in various refuges in two countries, was the manager of the first refuge in all of Europe to cater to religious Jewish women, and was on the management committee of another refuge.

There were so many delightful and important topics that beckoned to me as a focus for my PhD. My deepest curiosity was in wanting to know what was happening on the other side of the fence, in the treatment programs for domestically abusive men. So, while pregnant with my first successfully planted fetus, then with my baby Aliyah, who dutifully turned into a toddler, I interviewed several violent men and traveled all over the country for the privilege.

George, my husband at the time, was particularly amazing in the first few months after Aliyah's birth. As I was stuck recovering from a C-section, he had to do most of the heavy lifting—literally. He changed all the nappies, did all the laundry, brought me brekkie in bed, the lot.

When I started getting better, though, things changed dramatically in a way I found hurtfully confusing. George apparently thought Aliyah's nappy stage was an overall share, and he had successfully completed the majority of his contributions in the first few, bed-bound months. By the time Aliyah was a year old, George had retreated immensely (yet innocently; he was trying his best) in a way that we never quite got over.

Between studies, a baby, and a marriage, I had to stay really focused. There were months later on where I worked from home, up at 4:30 a.m. and at my desk by 5:00 to transcribe the interviews with these violent men. When Aliyah would start to wake about 9:00 a.m., I would put the recordings away and turn into mommy for the day. I loved it all—well, everything except the exhaustion.

George didn't get why I was sticking to my schedule so hard when it obviously tuckered me out. My bursary for my doctorate had a shelf life of three years; if I didn't finish on time, I might never be able to afford to finish. Three years it would be, then, to complete the PhD, sleepy or not, and that meant cohering to the overall plan with all its deadlines.

Over the next few years, Aliyah grew up, and George and I continued to grow apart. I had supported him through his MSc in computer science, so had thought his support of me through the PhD would be similar. I think we both gave it our best shot. We even intermittently took relationship courses, argued, and made up. We wanted this to be forever-after, so . . .

George and I thought (dumb in retrospect, I know!) we would try for another kid. I was entering the last stretch of my PhD, Aliyah was awesome, and maybe it would be just what we needed. I also thought my chances of pulling off a successful pregnancy were much better. You would think a PhD student with training in statistics would know about "regression to the mean"—the statistical likelihood of an event following the usual course rather than the immediately previous exceptional outcome.

One is not statistically "on a roll" if one wins at the roulette table or the craps table; that lack of logic is what allows casinos to make piles and piles of cash off of people's doomed, illogical fantasies. I was right in there with the high rollers! Between my marriage and my pregnancy, I just stuck my fingers in my ears and went "La-la-la."

Just like with Aliyah, I got pregnant first try, and I followed my same recipe of the careful diet: no caffeine, loads of lentils and green vegetables, folic acid supplements, you know the deal. Lucy, my previous midwife, had moved to another hospital, and I was immediately set up with Ida, who was, incredibly to me, even more gorgeous than Lucy.

Yes, I was in my early forties by then, and the statistics were a tiny bit grimmer, but a 3 percent chance of a stillbirth seemed pretty low. *Fuggetaboutit. La-la-la.* After my first-trimester sonogram cleared baby Aiden of any noticeable health issues, I just got on with being pregnant. I did my best to have more fun with it, especially as my marriage with George was going so far south we were beginning to see penguins.

Fast-forward to my last trimester. By this time, I had gracelessly faced the depth of the unhappiness and loneliness of my marriage, and had asked George for a divorce. No more la-la-la, at least with George. It takes *a lot* for a seven-months pregnant woman and mum to a lively toddler to ask for a divorce.

Although it looked crazy from the outside, it still felt right to me. *So* right. Once I told him my decision out loud, believe it or not, I relaxed. I had spoken my truth, and committed to what I knew in my heart was right. *Ahhhhhhh.* I had *no* idea what was coming next, but I was open and finally at peace.

I spoke to my protruding belly regularly, and made sure Aiden knew that the conflict with George had nothing to do with him (Aiden), that I loved and wanted him dearly. My PhD was almost done. Aliyah was coming up to three and a half, and she was doing well despite the unhappiness around her and George's continued withdrawal.

I was having a model pregnancy, confirmed yet again at my midwife visit on Tuesday, April 24, 2007. For some reason, neither of us felt inspired to listen to the baby's heartbeat, something we had both delighted in on my previous visits.

That night, Aiden died.

I could not, however, face what deep down inside I already knew. The la-la-la track was *still* running, just for one more day. Aiden and I had a routine. He would wake me between 3:59 and 4:01 a.m.—seriously, it was that precise. When I awoke Wednesday morning, having slept peacefully all through the night, I told myself, "Well, he's allowed to sleep in. Hope he does more of that once he's out." *La-la-la.* At just over eight months pregnant, on the 25th of April, I had only two days of work remaining before submitting the final amendments to my PhD and starting maternity leave.

As the midwife appointment had gone so well just the afternoon before, I convinced myself I had nothing to worry about. At the end of the day, that night of the 25th, I told myself I hadn't felt him kick during the day because I was just too busy. One more day to go, and I was done with a massive work chapter of my life, on the verge of a new life as Dr. Single Mum. I didn't mind at all, I was just happy to be on what felt like, seemed like (smelled like even) the right path.

When I awoke the morning of the 26th, having once again had a full night's sleep, my denial cracked, but full acceptance was still a way off. Part of what was keeping the confusion intact was that both George—who had not yet moved out—and I could feel energy pulsing out of my abdomen. It felt like such a strong and vital force, but I hadn't felt any kicking for over twenty-four hours. This could not be good.

George called Ida, and we were rushed in for an emergency sonogram. The radiologist kept her face carefully neutral when she looked at the screen that we couldn't see and called in for a second opinion.

My baby's death, technically at full term, was confirmed. George and I could still feel that vibrant pulsing, but neither of us said anything at the time.

When I called my father, Eddie, in New Jersey to tell him the news, he had just checked in at a conference where he expected to make connections resulting in many freelance jobs. Being a loving and supportive dad, the minute I told him about Aiden, he left the conference, ran home to grab his passport and a few clothes, and was without exaggeration on the very next plane to England.

My dad arrived that first evening and helped take care of Aliyah, that night and through it all, including drawing happy faces on her toes and my toes, and on all of our fingers, accidentally using three different colors of permanent marker. We felt so loved.

I was meant to get Aiden delivered at various times that day, the 26th, but, fair enough, mums with living babies in crisis took priority. His delivery was rescheduled (for the fourth time) for Friday, the 27th, at 11:00 a.m.

That afternoon of Thursday, the 26th, I felt a cold sore start to rise up on my face. Not just on my lip, but over half of my upper lip, on the right, and up past my nose onto the real estate of my cheek. It was, horrible pun intended, the mother of all cold sores. My face was swelling up as if I had been punched, and I could feel the slicing razor blade sensation in my face from the inside.

I was quite scared, to be honest (What kind of monster scar will *that* leave? I'd never even *heard* of a cold sore that big), and I asked the nurse on duty for some meds. She took one look at my face, swelling up by the minute, and said, "I'll get it for you as fast as I can."

I suddenly remembered, "Der, I have skills. And der, this must be related to my son's death." By this time in my life, I had studied various forms of energy psychology. I did the preparation I usually do and asked my guides for assistance in figuring out the place of most leverage to heal these razor blades. I immediately heard, "You are punishing yourself because you feel guilty about your son's death and responsible for it. You think you should wear that shame on your face."

I immediately did some healing work for myself about both the shame and the belief that I had to outwardly mark myself with it for all to see.

By the time the nurse came back with the drugs an hour later, the swelling was already gone, and the sliced-from-the-inside pain had disappeared. *Phew.*

I was fortunate enough to be in a hospital that had private rooms on the maternity ward for us grieving mothers (in the UK it is almost always wards only). The morning of my rescheduled C-section, I took in the fact that my room had a deep bath in it. Pregnant women aren't supposed to take very hot baths, and oh, how I love a scalding hot bath. Obviously, I hadn't had a bath since I became pregnant.

I filled that gorgeous porcelain thing up with the hottest water I could bear. As I levered my full-moon body into the delicious warmth, I was flooded with gratitude. Gratitude for the privacy, gratitude for the bath. I became aware that I was grateful, even while I was so over-whelmed with crushing grief. And I was so grateful for the capacity to be grateful in these moments. And then I was grateful for being grateful for being grateful! It kept cascading, and in moments, I had one of the most deeply spiritual experiences of my life.

I felt like I was being buoyed up by numerous hands of angels rather than the nourishing water. I *knew*, right down to the warm bones of me . . . I was hearing it in words in my head and feeling it somehow with words unspoken: *"All is well. All is well."* Over and over. I wept for joy.

I knew my life would be forever different in ways I couldn't even begin to comprehend. Nothing could ever erase that knowing. It wasn't that the grief in any way was even lessened by the joy of knowing all was, and is always, well. It was just that the grief was so completely *held*. I honestly can't explain it in words, try as I might.

I opted for a C-section birth because I wanted to hold my little son not squished and misshapen by a vaginal birth. He weighed a pound more than my daughter did when she was born. Apparently, and with all later tests confirming, he was a healthy baby, just a mysteriously dead one.

Our midwife, Ida, was also distraught on our behalf. She only told us a year later how she almost dropped Aiden after he was born. She said, "I've put off telling you because I've never felt this before or since in all my decades as a midwife. It's hard for me to tell you now, because frankly you might think I'm bonkers. When Aiden was born, the sur-geon rested him on a towel and handed him to me. He was clearly dead, limp, with his macerated skin (a technical way of saying that because his corpse had been soaking in amniotic fluid for more than two days before he was born, much of the skin had sloughed off). I hugged him to my chest, and I felt his beating heart. I swear, Shoshana, I felt a heartbeat. It was so shocking, I almost dropped him."

I then shared with Ida the pulsing that George and I had felt right up until the time they had wheeled us inside for that horribly too-silent birth. Neither of us knew quite what to make of it, but it was comforting to share the experience. The pulsing Aiden had gifted to Ida was his last.

After the operation, by the time he was in my private room so I could hold him, Aiden was, as one might expect, a tiny armful of a corpse, who happened to have the very same carroty-red hair I had when I was born. Due to my *Bathtub Moment*, I was never angry at God, or Source, or whatever you might want to call it. It helped me keep my grief clean, though in no way did it erase the intensity of my loss. I used Emotional Freedom Techniques (EFT) and other psychology methods to rinse away any further guilt as it emerged—for not being functional, not being the mum Aliyah needed, etc. Of course, my world was stitched through with the foreverness of his absence.

I spent a significant chunk of the next six months on the sofa, doing EFT tapping, talking occasionally to friends, and watching Massive Attack's "Teardrop" video over and over (the one with the in-utero baby). After six months, I still wasn't ready to get off the couch, but my supervisor compassionately urged me to complete my doctorate before it felt too far away to ever finish. It took me two weeks to complete that last day of work.

My graduation was too close following Aiden's death day; I couldn't make myself go.

I learned to separate the experience of grief from suffering it, a subtle but critical distinction. I was rocked by pain that was practically physical. The grief was like a bomb, a massive bomb that would go off repeatedly. The shock wave of the large-scale explosion compressed things around me, made everything flat, and hard to hear, and gray. Then the immeasurable pain would crash through, over and over again, and that continued, with decreasing intensity, over the next four or so years.

In the beginning, I noticed detachedly that people really do wring their hands in grief. I watched my own hands, which seemed like someone else's, do so, too. I would put food in the oven and forget to turn it on, or turn the oven on and forget to put the food in. Taking care of my daughter was so hard, but I did my best, pretty much on my own.

Aiden's death had taken the momentum out of my divorce. Everyone was telling us not to make big decisions right now. As it turned out, George and I had very different ways of coping and healing, and we pushed each other even farther apart. The tectonic shift of our paths finally rent us asunder about a year after that.

Fast-forward again, about four years more this time, to the summer of 2012. I'm happily with a different man, Sasha, and we are still together now, happier year on year. We've moved, and I started my own coaching business specializing in the sorts of issues my PhD had included—healing from abuse and learning to be happier and kinder in relationship. This wasn't just about the clients; I worked on my own temper, too.

In the summer of 2012, I'm in our private back garden, resting between clients, and it is a rare, stunning summer's day in Wales, UK. The apple trees are flowering, the birds are singing, and the sun is delightfully warm on my skin in a country that rarely hits seventy degrees Fahrenheit, even in August.

I was aware that I was happy. I was happy even though Aiden was absent, and I was really accepting that both his absence and my happiness coexisted. I floated in that for a spell. And then I suddenly realized, with a force that literally sent me to my knees, weak with joy, that I couldn't possibly be more joyful even if Aiden were alive. I wept in a way I had never wept in my life to that time but have since.

*All was well. All is well. Always.*

It was another one of those life-changing moments.

"Hang on," you might say. "Is she *really* as happy in that moment as she could be if her son were alive? *REALLY?*"

Well, yes. If all is well now, then, not to put too fine a point on it, all is well. I might not understand why that is so in any particular moment. I forget that "all is well" at least once a day. But that's OK. Because, duh (compassionately), all is well.

It isn't a platitude; it's a paradigm.

If all is well, there is cause for happiness no matter the circumstance. Even emotional neutrality has a quiet joy to it upon closer inspection. If I look hard enough even when I am down, I can see a glimmer of it. There is always a glimmer, a sparkly, fairy-dusty, glittery glimmer. That is part of what my Aiden taught me.

I don't need to "la-la-la" my way through anything unpleasant or even dreadfully, horribly unwanted anymore. "La-la-la" was a defense against emotions and pain I didn't think I could handle, a defense against a reality I thought I could not bear.

Well, first of all, I can bear it, whatever it is. Secondly—and this was a tricky bit for me to get my own head around—when I am resting in the epicenter of "all is well," that knowing is like a soothing balm.

I'm not physically capable of feeling the despair I used to be able to feel before my *Bathtub Moment*, because that depth of despair was based on a paradigm of the world and of life where things can go wrong.

It is my understanding now that things don't go wrong; they just don't go the way I want sometimes. Ergo, it follows logically that if nothing can go wrong, not really, because all is always well, always, then I never really have anything to worry about.

Nothing can happen in my future that shoves me into a world different than "all is well." I can accept whatever comes my way, with more grace than I ever had before. Moreover, although I'm free to make plans, even joyfully so, I don't really need to prioritize one particular outcome over another. In other words, I don't need to hope for something in the future to work out "right." Everything is right, right now. All is well.

Hope is redundant within the "all is well" paradigm. Hope is a cheerful sticker on top of worry. It's doubt and fear with a smile in the front window. Think about it—isn't it? Hope is about a future that hasn't arrived, that takes you out of the present possibilities of joy and noticing all that glimmering. Hope says, "Don't think about how doomed you are if things don't work out the way you want. Look at me. Stay focused on me. Don't worry about the doom. Visualize to materialize, baby!"

That is way beyond the borders of "all is well." Since there is nothing to fear, and nothing to need, there is nothing for which to hope. However things turn out, it's OK. Not fun sometimes, horribly painful sometimes, but OK. In the most delightfully possible way, I do my best to live joyously, cradled in the arms of "all is well." Hope doesn't fit in anywhere.

Aiden has been dead ten and a half years at time of writing. I don't feel double-kicked in the chest and stomach by a donkey anymore when I meet a child the age he would be, or a child of any age with his carrot-colored hair. I still miss him, at times with an ache of sadness, but the days of being rocked by grief are complete.

Pam Altaffer, one of the founders of Ask and Receive, often ends sessions with this blessing: *Thank you, that part of my being that gave me this healing today. I know that I am never alone—that you are always with me, in me, below me, above me, and around me. Thank you so much.*

Thank you, my sweet Aiden, for pointing me down a joyously hope-less path. I am so grateful to you, my angel.

And thank you, death train survivors, for all the fart jokes.

(Blessings to my weekly Monday Energy Psychology group— we had a lot of laughs talking about this precious topic of death and "death." *Thank you* for all your contributions.)

*    *    *

**Dr. Shoshana Garfield, PhD,** lives in England with her best friend and beloved Sasha. For years, her clinical practice was focused on severe trauma recovery, including torture. She presents and teaches internationally on 100 percent responsibility for self-leadership, and her first book is cheerfully entitled *The Smart Person's Guide to BIG FAT LIES on Stress, Suffering and Happiness,* soon to be reissued as two smaller books. Her second book, *A Cup of Happiness: One Journey of Torture Recovery,* is almost complete, and an additional book, *Self-Leadership and What Torture Recovery Has Taught Me,* is under way. Shoshana volunteers for two international charities: She serves on the executive board of EFT International and is a consultant for MISSING, a charity in India doing public education to reduce abduction of teenage girls into the sex slave trade. Since Aiden's death, Sasha and Shoshana gave up on having a child together after a miscarriage left her ill for the better part of a year. Furthermore, Shoshana has recovered from cancer and was hit by a car in an accident that left her somewhat brain damaged. Never mind— she still believes *All is well.* Shoshana considers her greatest and most important accomplishment to be that she is abidingly happy. Visit her websites, www.shoshanagarfield.com and www.notjustacontract.com.

## • *4* •

# I Am Still Standing After the Fall

### *By Jo-Anne Joseph*

*At* twenty-nine years old, I felt on top of the world. I was married to the man I loved, and we had a beautiful toddler son whom we adored. I was in a thriving career I enjoyed, and my husband Brian and I had just bought our second home. It was truly the home of our dreams.

Complete with a large backyard garden, it had three large bedrooms—and more than enough space in which our three-year-old son, Braydon, could play. Braydon was our little ray of sunshine, with his chocolate-brown eyes and adorable mop of curls. We were a happy family living an adventurous life in Johannesburg, South Africa, and things were falling into place for us beautifully. As a young couple, we could not have asked for much more.

The icing on the cake arrived in December 2012, with news of my second pregnancy. It was entirely unexpected, but the prospect of a second child came as a welcome surprise. Brian and I had spoken of having another child, but only in passing. Still, that news could not have come at a better time. There were so many exciting new things to look forward to, and those bright pink lines on a stick were a declaration of how blessed our life truly was.

Braydon would soon have a sibling, a playmate he'd enjoy growing up with. News of my pregnancy brought with it hope and bliss. Looking at our son, we already knew what an incredible blessing and honor it was to have a child, and we could not wait for our new baby to arrive.

The following few months were terrific—the anticipation of the new baby, especially finding out, after several exciting and often eventful doctors' visits, that we were having a girl. There was never a dull moment during those visits, and we built an amazing relationship with

31

our obstetrician. It took three scans to discover the sex of the baby, as she was often curled into a ball, her genitals hidden from us. My doctor swore she wouldn't rest until we knew the sex of our baby. The day we finally learned we were having a girl, my son burst into tears demanding that he wanted a brother. My obstetrician and I watched in amusement as my husband huddled in a corner comforting Braydon. Boys will be boys.

To me, it was incredible news, the chance for me to have a mother-daughter relationship and do all those girly things I didn't get to do with my son. I wanted to give my daughter all the things I had longed for when I was growing up.

It didn't take long for Braydon to warm up to being the big, protective, older brother. He would often ask me when the baby was coming, and I would always smile at him and say, "Soon."

In early July 2013, I began to fall ill. It was nothing too serious: a cold here and there, migraines and backaches. But that made me more attentive to my baby's well-being and, especially, her movements. I contacted my doctor a few times and found myself going to the maternity unit twice in one week for a checkup, in addition to my scheduled appointments.

I also booked two separate fetal movement monitoring sessions for myself, and both times I left relieved. My baby was healthy and her movements were regular. But for some reason, I couldn't allow myself to relax. I was concerned and edgy. The feeling of foreboding kept me up at night, and my anxiety levels were at an all-time high.

On July 13, I felt her movements lessen, but I'd been told that babies' movements usually decrease as they near full term. I didn't want to continually worry my husband or put myself under undue stress, so I waited till July 16 to go for another checkup at the maternity ward.

It was a cold winter's day, and I can still hear the painful words spoken by a doctor who was, unfortunately, not my own.

"I am sorry, there is no heartbeat."

Those are words no parent should ever have to hear. Earth-shattering words which changed my life forever.

I nodded. What else does one do in a situation like that? You accept the prognosis. The doctor knew best, I supposed. There are moments of sheer disbelief that cripple you, and that was mine.

The doctor asked if there was anyone to call. I said I would call whomever I needed to. It hadn't hit me yet, the thought that I was about to call people and announce that my baby had died. After eight-plus months, she was gone, just like that. In the blink of an eye, everything changed. It was all over.

I remember the doctor saying he didn't know why these things happened and that my own doctor would be notified. He left, and I never saw him again. I can't even remember his name, just the feel of his cold hands holding mine as he spoke. At the end of it all, our little Zia was gone, and what was the point of anything after that?

Just days before, I'd been making lists of things with my sister that we needed to buy and do and plans for the baby's room with my husband. I had even hired a nanny. I'd shopped for some new baby things I needed, and now everything sat in the spare room untouched, the room that should've been Zia's. Suddenly, it all became unimportant because our precious baby girl was dead.

We eventually learned that Zia had died of birth asphyxia. The cord had been wrapped around her tiny neck three times. There was nothing that could have been done to prevent it, and there was nothing I could have done any differently as her mom. I had done everything according to the pregnancy rule book. I ate healthily. I didn't drink alcohol. I went to all my obstetrician visits, scans, and checkups. My doctor was brilliant, and she took great care of me during and after my pregnancy.

Numbness overtook me that day; everything faded in and out of perspective. I don't know what did or didn't happen at times. The only truth was that my daughter was gone, and I would soon be holding her tiny, lifeless body in my arms and bidding her good-bye.

The experience of delivering a baby I knew would not live is something that is difficult to put into words—the silence in the hospital room, the looks on the faces of the nurses, doctors, even your husband are all torture. Nobody knows what to do or what to say, and neither do you. You're bringing death into the world. And when they wrap death and place her in your arms, she doesn't even utter a sound. She looks like a bluish-purple baby, who has my husband's face and the tiniest hands, but a real baby, nonetheless. I held her still, lifeless body in my arms and kissed her sweet forehead.

"She was really a girl." Our doctor laughed. An inside joke, just the three of us knew, since it had taken forever to determine her sex.

"Does baby have a name?" the anesthetist asked.

"Her name is Zia," I answered.

"It's always good to have a name."

Those are the most painful experiences a mother should ever have to endure.

The hospital room was quiet, and my husband and I had some time alone with our child. It was not a lot of time, but it was time, and I spent much of it staring at her in his arms. I was shocked by what I was witnessing. He would say things to Zia. He would sing. He would look lovingly at her. He would talk. He would talk to her and to me, and I would answer, but I didn't know what was happening because I was caught in the place between here and there, and I couldn't really decipher what he was saying. There was a dead baby in the room, and she was mine, and I was her mother.

The family came in to see Zia and kissed her good-bye. The coroner showed up a few hours later. After we kissed Zia good-bye, we watched in disbelief as that stranger took our little baby away in a cot that was far too big for her little body. We watched as she fell to the end of it, in a pile, and we wondered if we would ever forget. I guess we never will.

Family and friends tried to comfort my husband and me, but it did nothing to ease the pain. In fact, their comments were far from helpful. Some said that God would give me so many more babies that I would never be sad again. Others said that they were not really sure if the baby had a soul anyway, at that tender age. And a few said that there were bigger plans for the baby's life and that she was with God now and I should not mourn, but rejoice that the baby was with the Lord and not born sick or with disabilities.

I nodded and thought how strange a thing to say to a mother when her baby had just died. A child was a child, and I loved mine. I would still love her with all my heart, even if she was sick or born with disabilities.

Though my baby had long since been carried away, I had to stay in the hospital for three days. When my husband was with me, my parents and sister took care of Braydon. When Brian left the hospital after visiting hours, it felt as if he were taking a part of me with him. But I was glad he was able to be home to take care of our son.

Being in the hospital that first day, away from Braydon, was very painful. I wanted to hold him and reassure him that everything would be okay, that his dad and I were still here, and that we all still had each other. When my son did visit, he was cautious. He asked about the baby, and I told him she'd gone to the sky to be with the angels.

When I eventually went home, I noticed the sadness in Braydon's eyes for the very first time. Losing his sister was his first experience with death, and though I know he felt the loss deeply, he was so young, he barely understood what had happened.

We had a funeral for Zia. We chose not to let Braydon attend it. We wanted to protect him from the sight of death; we knew all too well the trauma it had caused us. A cousin of Brian's stepped in to care for him.

As Brian and I walked into the cold, dark mortuary that morning, we couldn't have cared less about the other dead bodies in that room. It was agonizing seeing our daughter in an unkempt room, surrounded by boxes, and wrapped in a plastic linen saver. The parlor did not even have the decency to prepare her body, like they promised they would. Instead, they discarded her like she was not a real human being. There are no words that can honestly describe the disgust I felt and still feel toward the funeral parlor that handled Zia's funeral. It was evident they had no care and compassion for grieving families.

I was a zombie. It was like an out-of-body experience for me. My husband told me to hold my baby, and I did. I held her close to me, and I smiled. I kissed her and ran my fingers over her smooth, powdery forehead. She looked so much like my husband, and her small hands reminded me of a doll, as if we were there playing dress-up.

Later, as I sat in the pews, I kept thinking that I needed to be more of a mother to Zia, but I didn't know how. I wanted someone to tell me what to do, but nobody did. Looking back, I see that was an impossible task.

Then the mourners arrived, and I had to nod and smile and not say a word, as they started saying they were so sorry—and I was sorry, too—that the baby had died.

The funeral was small, with just our immediate family.

Sadly, I watched my husband carry his daughter's little white coffin in his arms, his head low. I could feel the heaviness of his heart.

To this day, those memories still haunt me, and my heart still breaks as I think of that awful day. While sitting in that chapel, I envisioned my husband standing over a white crib, instead of the tiny coffin. It helped me to see anything but the truth before me. That day will always remain one of the hardest days of my life.

Zia was a beautiful baby, and I long to turn back time so I could spend more time with her. I'd hold her a little bit longer, maybe sing her a song, and tell her I love her more.

It was hard to find hope after Zia died. I fell into a deep depression and I didn't know who I was for a very long time. I lost myself when I lost her. I lost the parts of me that used to believe in happily ever after and the goodness in life. It is hard to imagine anything else after what we'd experienced.

When I looked in the mirror after I lost Zia, I only saw a shell of the woman I used to be. I didn't want to go out anymore. I didn't want to participate in family functions or any kind of events. It was too hard to be the person everyone wanted me to be because the person they expected me to be did not exist anymore.

There was a dark cloud hanging over me. I carried it with me wherever I went, and I was too afraid to let it go. It was as if letting go of the tragedy of Zia's death was letting my baby go altogether. I was breaking, and I didn't know whether I could ever return from this nightmare. I couldn't stand to be around other babies or pregnant women. I became someone even I didn't quite recognize.

Then after a while, I tried to suppress the sadness, thinking somehow that would make me feel better. I wanted to keep my sorrow at bay because it didn't look good, but even more than that, it didn't feel good, and no one wanted to be around someone so severely broken.

Unfortunately, my plan didn't work. Doing that only caused me more pain and anguish. And then, in time, I realized that the only hope I had was to acknowledge the sadness, acknowledge that I'd lost a significant part of myself and that I would never be the same person again. I couldn't pretend to be okay because I wasn't. I was utterly and completely incomplete.

Brian was my pillar of strength. He took time off work to care for our son and gave me the love and understanding I so desperately needed. We eventually decided that he would home-school our Braydon for a while, and that he'd work from home while he did that. Our decision made sense to us. I became paranoid, afraid to let Braydon out of my sight. The thought of sending my son back to nursery school again was frightening. I didn't want to lose him, too.

To say that there were very few baby loss support groups in my area for face-to-face support would be an understatement. There was and still is a need for more groups of this nature. I felt all alone for those first two months, nearly drowning in the ocean of my grief.

I knew people who had lost children, and there were Compassionate Friends meetings, but for some reason I just never felt like anyone understood what *I* was going through. It seemed to me at that time that baby loss was, in a lot of ways, minimized—not quite acknowledged as being valid. I saw a counselor twice during that time, but I quickly became restless. Her methods were just not working for me. I could not understand how standing in the middle of a girl's aisle in the clothing store talking to my daughter, who'd passed on, could help me find comfort. I could not imagine myself going into shelters offering to bathe babies to get back a moment I lost with my own baby. Her methods may have helped others, but it was unimaginable to me.

Family and friends pulled away, not completely understanding what I was going through, and that left an even larger cavernous hole inside my heart. Even religious leaders could not offer the kind of comfort I was seeking. I wanted to talk to someone who had lost a baby the way I had. Someone who would understand the pain and anguish I was in. Someone who would not tell me to get over it and that I can always have more children. I did not want more children. I wanted my daughter Zia.

I turned to online resources, and one night I came across a website called Glow in the Woods. It is an online baby loss community with such heart that it immediately called to me. I had no idea then that I would eventually come to refer to this community as my saving grace, because in many ways, that is exactly what it is to me. I read through other bereaved parents' stories, and suddenly I didn't feel so alone anymore. I related to what they were writing and sharing. I could see myself and my own experiences through their words.

I later found healing through capturing my own thoughts and feelings about my loss in words and sharing them with other people who had experienced the same or similar losses. I finally found the support and understanding I had been longing for in those various forums.

I deeply appreciated the bereaved parents who were willing to share their methods of coping and finding hope in their lives again, and soon I discovered my own path. I learned that grief was a journey and that everyone experiences it differently. I was encouraged to share my story and my emotional state and not to bottle up what I felt, especially from my husband, who was always so wonderful.

It helped me open up to Brian about what I was going through, mentally and emotionally, and it helped me understand how he felt and how he was coping. This communication strengthened our relationship, which at times felt like it had been on the brink of despair.

The Baby Loss Community also helped me understand how to acknowledge the different ways in which other people grieved and mourned. I learned ways in which to include my daughter in my life that had never occurred to me earlier.

I started documenting my journey through poetry and stories on my personal blog. I came to a realization that Zia was a part of me, she exists, and I was her storyteller. I was the one who would bear witness to her young life.

Regularly, I'd blog capturing my life with and without Zia. I noticed positive changes in me. I was becoming more aware of my own needs and how to meet them. I was becoming more willing to talk openly about my loss. I stopped feeling guilty for being alive, and in time, I came to accept the new me, my new normal.

Before my daughter died, I had no real understanding of what child loss truly meant. I knew it was sad, and my heart went out to those who'd experienced such tragedy, but losing Zia opened my eyes to the pure brutality of having your child die. No parent should have to bury a child, and as I was able to move beyond some of my grief, I wanted to reach out to other bereaved parents on a deeper level. I wanted them to know they were not alone. That we walk this path together, hand in hand, despite the distance and our differing circumstances.

In the early days, the guilt wore heavily on me. No matter how hard I tried, I could not shake it off. I also found myself turning away from the religion I'd practiced my whole life, as it did not support my healing process. But that wasn't so bad because I found hope in understanding myself as a human being and the gifts of being in touch with that feeling. I'd always been a compassionate person, but I became a more empathetic human being. I learned to love myself again and not blame myself for the death of my baby girl.

I will always love Zia because love is infinite, but I now know that I do not need to suffer to display that love, nor do I need to ignore the fact that I have a child who is no longer with me.

Today I enjoy writing for the websites Glow in the Woods, Still Standing Magazine, and Courageous Mothers as a regular contributor. These sites provide insurmountable support and resources for grieving parents. Writers from all over the world share their words and experiences in different stages of the grief and healing processes. The need to express myself through words burns deep within me, and being a part of these publications is a great honor.

In July of this year, five years after Zia passed away, I published a collection of poetry, prose, and artistic expression in collaboration with other bereaved parents across the globe, titled *Footprints on the Heart: A Remembrance Anthology*. The following is an excerpt:

Time

*By Jo-Anne Joseph*

The years have passed quickly,
time, after all, is a slave to no man,
"Let time pass," I say bravely.
It will not diminish my love for you.
I feel your absence like the skin ripped off my body,
I feel it like an ache in my bones and muscles after a long day,
it eases and returns,
eases and returns,
there were days when I was crippled by sadness,
days when I was drowning in madness,
I reached for anything that could steady me,
I fell several times and got up again, wobbly,
but I realized that the unsteadiness I felt wasn't foolishness,
the only folly was denying the absence I'd grown accustomed to,
I am a crippled happy fool now,
I smile, and I laugh because I live in harmony with the pain,
The pain is real,
The joy too,
It is as real as I am,
I cannot exist without either.

In addition, I am a pen pal volunteer for Grieve Out Loud, which is a pregnancy and infant loss support network. I am deeply grateful to be able to be a part of the loss community in a more positive way because I understand how much it is needed, and I hope to continue to support others who are in my same or similar situation.

Often I am asked how it is that I am able to still be so involved in the loss community. Some have even asked me whether it is not an unhealthy way of coping, and I always answer in the same way: Grief is not something you can hide from. It is not an illness, and it is nothing to be ashamed of; rather, it is something you need to nurture.

I choose to live out loud and embrace each day, whether it is a stressful day where the shadows creep in or a good day filled with making new and happy memories.

It was not easy; it took a lot of self-reflection and a lot of falling down before I could pick myself back up again. But the one key thing I learned was that the more I fought the sadness, the harder it was to live life again. For me, it was like denying that my world had been altered. It is because of embracing my grief and the loss of my child that I am stronger now than I have ever been; I look at myself, and I feel proud of how far I have come.

Today I am standing, and I am honored for the time I got to spend with my baby despite how brief it may have been. You don't need a lifetime to love and bond with your child. Love is not measured in that way, at least not in the way I gauge it. Those eight months Zia lived within me were a profound honor. I was her only home, and I am deeply grateful for that time. Our precious time. I have learned to separate the sadness from the good times and memories I have from those months I carried my daughter and the milestones she achieved in utero, and now they coexist harmoniously.

I try to enjoy life and find meaning in everything I do. There is so much goodness in life, and I choose to live in such a way that I am able to see it every single day. I am able to appreciate my son Braydon as he grows into an intelligent young man who continues to reach his own milestones in life, without the guilt I once felt for my daughter's absence.

Today, I am a better mother than I ever was; my family life is thriving, and so is my son. We speak openly about Zia, Braydon included.

I am a mother to two beautiful children: one that I get to share my living days with and watch grow into an incredible little man, and the other one I hold in my heart until we meet again.

I realize there is no reason for what happened, and I have stopped trying to find one. Love is what drives me to do more and do better for my family and for the loss community every day.

Today, I want to make every second count, to stand tall after the fall.

\*    \*    \*

**Jo-Anne Joseph** is a contemporary romance, dark romantic suspense, psychological thriller, and poetry author. She describes herself as a dreamer, a doer, and an artist with a flair for creating stories that leave you on the edge of your seat. Along with a passion for writing, Jo-Anne is an avid reader and enjoys painting and coloring. She has published six novels and a novella, as well as contributed to three anthologies. Jo-Anne is a business professional by day and also writes on a volunteer basis for the websites Still Standing Magazine, Glow in the Woods, and Courageous Mothers. She lives with her husband and nine-year-old son in Johannesburg, South Africa; her daughter Zia lives in her heart. Visit her website at www.joannejosephauthor.com.

# II

# ILLNESS AND DISEASE

My son's death was the birth of my new life . . . learning to
live with his loss, and rising up to be the woman I am today.

—Sandy Peckinpah

# A Gift of Light

## By Alice Adams

*Lucas*

*This is the story of a young boy named Lucas, whose name means "light" and who went into the light, thus leaving me, his mother, an illuminated path to follow. And while the details of his leaving are not of much consequence now, they seemed of great significance to me at the time.*

In the fall of 1975, at the age of twenty-two and after an uneventful pregnancy, I gave birth to my second child, a son. With a short and easy labor and delivery, Lucas Daniel came into the world, two years to the month after his sister Rachel. And like his sister, Lucas had a lusty cry and healthy appearance, and both my husband and I were grateful and very happy. While in the hospital, our pediatrician examined Lucas and informed us he'd heard a heart murmur. But the doctor was quick to point out that sometimes newborns have them and they resolve spontaneously in the first hours or days of life. Somehow, even then, I think I felt a sense of foreboding.

45

We followed up with the pediatrician in his office a few days later and were told, "No, unfortunately, the murmur is still there." This beautiful, perfectly normal-looking newborn would need to be seen at a large teaching hospital to be more adequately assessed. In the next couple months, Lucas ate, slept, and developed like a seemingly healthy newborn. But before his third month of life, he needed to be evaluated by the pediatric cardiologist.

Living just outside Baltimore, we had access to Johns Hopkins, a well-known teaching hospital. After a long day of examinations and testing, I was told that Lucas had congenital heart defects and would require a couple of cardiac surgeries to repair them. I remember carrying my infant out to the parking garage, and then I sat nursing him in the car, bawling my eyes out.

This sad day was the beginning of our foray into the world of pediatric cardiology. Although only a high school graduate at that time, I dove headfirst into learning the intricacies of Luke's diagnosis and proposed treatment. He was to have more advanced diagnostics (a cardiac catheterization) in a few months, when he would be a little bigger. Then he would have his first palliative (a word I learned meant "helping, *not curative*") surgery at about eighteen months of age. If all went well, a couple years later Luke would have corrective surgery.

When Lucas had his cardiac catheterization, a different diagnostic picture emerged. The anatomy of his heart was far more complicated and defective than the doctors had originally thought. At that time in 1976, there was no corrective procedure available for the treatment of his complex heart defects.

All along I had thought, *This is horrible, but he'll have those surgeries and be all fixed.* To now hear that Lucas had such complicated anatomical defects that had no solution astonished me to no end, and I felt completely shell-shocked. I had never even entertained the idea that my son would actually die because of these defects.

All anyone knew to do now was proceed with palliative surgery as originally planned, and hope that medical science progressed toward a new corrective procedure as Luke got older.

In the first couple years of his life, Lucas had two palliative heart surgeries. He recovered well from them and continued to grow, develop, and live as a joyful, inquisitive, fairly active toddler, then preschooler and kindergartener. Luke went to a progressive private school affiliated with a local university and received some testing in his preschool years for what was observed to be somewhat delayed language and poor fine motor skills.

Despite the frequent medical monitoring and hospitalizations, Luke was always a cheerful, gregarious child. In his earliest years, we lived in the country, and that always made him so happy. Luke loved animals and was frequently outside, soaking in all the beautiful surroundings. He never learned to read independently, but loved being read to by his sister and by me.

After several years, Luke's father and I separated. Due to our frequent interactions with the medical field, I had become quite interested in science and medicine, and I decided to further my studies. Once I completed all the college prerequisites, I enrolled in nursing school.

When I graduated as an RN, I got divorced and moved with the children into the city (Baltimore). As it happened, I went to work in the same large teaching hospital Lucas had been visiting regularly since he was a baby. Even though he had poor physical endurance, Luke was self-limiting: He stopped and rested when he was tired and took no cardiac medications. In spite of his short supply of endurance, Luke learned to ride a bicycle—and it quickly became one of his most favorite things to do.

Lucas was my joyful, exuberant, seven-and-a-half-year-old son when he cardiac arrested while riding his bicycle on July 26, 1983. Despite severe and complicated congenital heart defects, Luke had been quite physically active and loved riding his bike so much!

On that summer night, his nine-year-old sister Rachel called me at work from the babysitter's to tell me the paramedics were doing CPR on her brother in the middle of the street. Although he was only minutes away from Johns Hopkins, Lucas did not survive the ambulance ride to the hospital.

There really are no words to describe what I felt as I ran down those two flights of stairs from my unit to the pediatric ER—hoping against hope that Lucas would survive.

But that was not to be. When I arrived, the ER physician informed me that Lucas was gone, and the staff gently guided me into a room where his small body, wearing a hospital gown, rested on a gurney. I was asked if I wanted to stay with him a while, and I said yes.

Could they call someone to be with me? they asked. I don't know how long I stayed in that room holding Lucas's tiny hand. I don't know how my two dearest friends, Anna and Jane, got there, but they came and took me home.

Six months later I wrote to Lucas in my journal: *I remember so vividly the night I had to walk down that long hallway (in the hospital) without you, my friends on either side of me, so close at either elbow, they were buoying me up, keeping me from sinking. And I drew myself in like a turtle in a shell and I just kept putting one foot in front of the other. . . .*

After the immediate shock and chaos of arrangements and the funeral, condolences and well-wishing, I settled into the first few months of what I now think of as "the dark time." The dark time was punctuated by the need to know *why* and characterized by *shoulda, woulda, coulda,* and ultimately *didn't,* culminating in self-judgment and blame. It was a journey into my history as Lucas's mom, an attempt to discover what I had done wrong that could possibly have resulted in his being taken from me.

In those early days and weeks, I vacillated between lethargy and a frantic, almost panicked need to find Lucas. Whenever I was driving, I would picture my little boy in my mind's eye, sitting on the curb, just around the next corner, *if only I could get there in time.*

Then, a little over four months after Lucas transitioned, so did my father. Although eighty years old, my dad was a very active and vital man, still driving and golfing. Lucas and Rachel were his only grandchildren, and he was very close to both. He had driven them back and forth to school every day since they were old enough to attend. My brother Bob found my dad at home in his bed, reading glasses still on, newspaper still on his lap, dead of an apparent heart attack.

Several days after my father's passing, I had a comforting vision— *my dad in his bed propped up with two pillows, the bedside lamp on. Glancing up from his newspaper, he saw Lucas standing at his bedside. Surprised, he heard Lucas say, "Come on, PopPop, it's time to go." He reached out and took Lucas's outstretched hand, and he was gone.*

That vision was a great comfort to me, and I wrote about it in my journal. I also had sporadic "visitations" from Lucas in the form of dreams with such clear, lucid remembering that on awakening, I was certain he had truly been there.

Following my son's and my dad's passings, I did not seek any professional support. Neither did I take medications, attend support groups, or get counseling. At the time, I found I could not emotionally handle returning to my nursing job in the Neonatal Intensive Care Unit (NICU) and was fortunate enough financially that I didn't need to.

I made several brief forays into other types of work that did not involve patient care, including being a vintage clothing shop owner, but all these were ultimately unsatisfying. Through it all, Anna and Jane, also single moms, were an invaluable support system for me.

My son's only sibling, his sister Rachel, had significant coping issues and strongly resisted the bereavement counseling I urged her to attend. Over the next couple years, her acting-out behaviors escalated, and with me still in my own "fog," the chasm between us grew wider. Those behaviors (like skipping school, staying out late, and inappropriate and disrespectful language), while sometimes present in preteen years, became overwhelming to me. Rachel's own complicated grief over the deaths of her brother and grandfather and my divorce from her dad were further exacerbated as I sought solace in new relationships and dating. At age twelve, Rachel went to live with her father in another state, almost eight hundred miles away.

Now I felt truly alone—an orphan (my mother had died in my teenage years) and a mother without her children! I did a lot of artwork and writing, including poetry, although my artwork was rarely seen by anyone and my writing was never published. While my creative process was invaluable to my healing, my most profound assistance came in a way I would never have anticipated.

## LUCAS'S GIFT

In a way, my story really begins here, because this is the tale of the true gift Lucas gave to me, and how I have been sharing it with others ever since, whenever I can.

In the fall of 1986, in a loving and heartfelt attempt to support me, Anna and Jane suggested that I have acupuncture treatment. At the time, steeped in Western (allopathic) medicine as an RN and knowing very little about acupuncture, I retorted, "Acupuncture! Why would I want to have *acupuncture?*"

Both of them were patients of the same acupuncturist. They looked knowingly at each other, nodded, and said in unison, "We really think it will help you." They knew I wouldn't buy it, though, so they tried a backdoor approach and suggested I see the acupuncturist for treatment of my severe allergies.

I had recently become suddenly allergic to my cats, causing me to awaken often at 3:00 a.m. with horrendous eye itching, coughing, and congestion, after which I could rarely return to sleep. I grudgingly agreed to try it and booked an appointment for the following week with the office mate of their acupuncturist because theirs had a waiting list several weeks long.

This acupuncturist and I shared the same first name, and I was pleased to discover that she was also an RN. Both acupuncturists practiced Five Element Acupuncture, and I was soon to learn that this style of acupuncture is an ancient Taoist form of healing, truly body-mind-spirit medicine. The focus is on the patient's constitutional strengths and vulnerabilities, always incorporating the mind/emotional component rather than merely treating the physical symptoms.

My first visit, a two-hour history taking and then treatment, explored my current health issues first, before delving into various aspects of my history, all the way back to my earliest memories.

This felt to me like *psychotherapy meets alternative physical medicine.* But my new acupuncturist was quick to point out that she was not a psychotherapist, and that acupuncture is a form of energy medicine aimed at finding the cause of physical symptoms while balancing the patient's energy on all levels—body, mind, and spirit.

I wasn't sure what any of this meant and was embarrassed to be crying within the first five minutes of the history taking, but I left her office after my first treatment feeling strangely calmer and even lighter. So, I was game to give acupuncture a try.

Healing doesn't often happen overnight, but my allergies did go completely away after eight to ten weekly treatments. In addition, I quit smoking spontaneously, which I had never even intended or tried to do, and many other aspects of both my physical and emotional health started to come beautifully into balance. Best of all, I felt hopeful for the first time in years.

After being in treatment for about nine months, I asked my acupuncturist if she thought I could learn to do this. "Of course," she said.

Consequently, in the spring (season of beginnings) of 1987, I began Five Element Acupuncture school at the former Traditional Acupuncture Institute (now Maryland University of Integrative Health). It is the oldest degree-granting acupuncture school in the United States.

In 1990, I graduated with an M.Ac. (master of acupuncture) degree and became a licensed acupuncturist in the state of Maryland, practicing there until 1993. Then I moved to Tucson, Arizona, and established my private practice in acupuncture, which continues to thrive to this day.

Over the past twenty-nine years, I have treated a wide array of physical and emotional issues. Although my practice is not exclusive to patients who are grieving, I often attract patients with some physical complaint only to find that grief and loss are at the heart of their imbalance.

I remain deeply blessed and honored to do this work, which I feel is as much of a gift to myself as it is to my patients. Looking back, I can only say that Lucas's birth and death are two of the greatest gifts I have ever received. I would not have reached this beautiful place in my life were it not for my terrible loss, and I'm grateful each day for new beginnings.

I will not try to tell you who have lost a child—you mothers and fathers, siblings and grandparents, aunts and uncles—that your missing them ever goes completely away, whether the child was an infant, an adult, or anywhere in between. But I will say that their coming, their time here, and, yes, even their leaving can be a great gift, especially if you extend to others what you learned from that gift—in the sharing of your memories and your journey through grief and beyond.

Perhaps that is your child's legacy. And that is the grace and the healing.

\*   \*   \*

**Alice Adams** was working as a registered nurse in a large East Coast hospital when her son died suddenly of congenital heart disease in the early 1980s. In addition to practicing acupuncture, she continued working part-time in hospice nursing for over twenty years. In 1993, Alice moved to Tucson, Arizona, where she gave birth to another daughter. The relationship with her first daughter, Rachel, has been healed and Rachel has gone on to thrive as well. Alice is currently in private practice as a licensed Five Element acupuncturist and Qigong instructor in Tucson.

# · 6 ·

# Brandon's Gifts

## A Father's Story of Love

*By Robert (Bob) R. Burdt*

*Bob and Brandon*

There's a hole in my heart and a wondering that will never leave, and yet, I have had a great life.

His name was Brandon Robert Burdt, and he was my son, my first child, the one who made me a father. This was his first gift.

Brandon was born August 27, 1977, and died less than two years later on Good Friday, April 13, 1979. He never lived to see age two. His birth was the happiest day of my life, and every day for the first six months, my joy and love grew beyond what I could have imagined was possible as I watched this sweet, good-natured baby smile and blossom.

No words can come close to describing what it meant to me to be there for my son's birth; holding him moments after his birth, giving him his first bath, and loving every second of those early days of his life. Of course, like any new parent, when the nurse first placed Brandon in my arms and said everything was great, I checked to make sure he had all the right number of fingers and toes. He was perfect.

52

Brandon's bright blue eyes, framed by long lashes, reflected a surprising depth for someone so new to this world. And a bonus for me, my son was my spitting image.

My heart expanded in those early days as I felt Brandon fall in love with me, and my love for him opened me to a depth of emotions I'd never known. Only then did I begin to realize what my father and I had missed.

It was World War II and my father was overseas fighting for our freedom. Our one connection was the miracle that his army unit threw him a party celebrating my birth on the day of my actual birth—a coincidence they could not have predicted because communication home was so rare. My father and I didn't meet until I was fourteen months old.

He and I never got to experience the everyday things most parents take for granted: holding your newborn child and watching him grow; being held and nurtured by your father; sharing the joy of your entry into parenthood, and the wonder of your baby with your friends and family; and falling in love with each other as you delight each day in this new world of exciting discoveries.

Brandon was an easy baby with a smile so broad and contagious that friends who visited would fall under his spell of joy and tell us how happy his smile made them feel. Unfortunately, and with little warning, when Brandon was six months old, his almost nonstop smile disappeared. He began to cry more than normal, couldn't sleep, and no longer wanted to eat. Whenever he did eat, he'd throw up.

We took Brandon to his pediatrician, who referred us to a local hospital, but they didn't know much about caring for small children. They referred us to Children's Hospital in Oakland, California, which was about thirty miles from our home in Benicia.

After several tests were performed, my wife and I heard words no parent ever wants to hear about their child: Brandon had an inoperable heart defect.

If I said the earth under my feet collapsed and my world shattered, I would not even be coming close to expressing the devastation I felt. It was worse than plummeting to the ground after being thrown out of an airplane without a parachute. The doctors prescribed several heart drugs, and also taught us how to insert tubes through Brandon's nose and position them into his lungs so we could remove the continuous buildup of fluids. We wanted more.

Hoping for a cure, we searched for specialists and found a revered surgeon who was a pioneer in the heart transplant world. After his examination, the tears staining Dr. Shumway's cheeks and the crack in his voice told us what we absolutely did not want to know: Nothing he could do would prevent the inevitability of Brandon's death. How could this be possible? Our little boy was only six months old.

My joy in being a father was overwhelmed by fear and a sadness more profound than I'd ever known or could have ever imagined. I felt powerless. I would have given anything to find a spell or a cure. I bargained with God, offering my life or anything else, if He would let my son live. And yet, despite the pain, my love for this beautiful little guy continued to grow. As I fought to save my son and make every day of his life the best it could be, I discovered a courage within myself I hadn't known existed. That was Brandon's second gift.

We never gave up trying to save his life. Brandon spent the days, weeks, and months prior to his death in and out of Children's Hospital in Oakland. When he was home, we had to drain the fluids from his lungs every four hours to keep him comfortable. I physically felt every grimace of pain with him. Those times when he felt well, his contagious smiles and giggles brightened my days. This was his third gift. Brandon taught me that when life is going well, celebrate and don't hang on to yesterday's pain.

Maybe his real lesson was that pain teaches us to celebrate any chance we have to experience happiness.

Brandon never walked on his own. Because his heart condition stopped his body from developing the way it should have for a child his age, he had to rely on his baby walker to walk. When Brandon felt good, nothing could stop him. With a pure joy smile, he'd be in his walker dashing all over the house. We called him "Our Little Tough Guy."

On his good days, I'd often take Brandon to the local small airport to watch the planes take off and land. Whenever we'd arrive at the airport, I'd look through the rearview mirror at Brandon, perched in his car seat, and be gifted with the gleam of his glowing blue eyes and huge smile. As I unbuckled him from his car seat, his body would sway back and forth and up and down with excitement. My son couldn't wait for me to hoist him onto my shoulders.

Once up there, he'd grab onto my hair with both hands. When he saw a plane taking off or landing, he'd release my hair from his grasp and point his little finger up to the plane in the sky with a happy baby giggle and squeal. Moments like those were special and gave us all a chance to breathe—even if for just a few moments. An angel and airplane are engraved on our tough guy's tombstone.

Although Brandon didn't talk much, it feels good to recall those times he had called me *dada*, his eyes filled with love, and with surprising strength he wrapped his bony little arms so tightly around my neck.

We never gave up hope for a miracle, and even tried a session with a highly recommended faith healer. His visit to our home was magical. He went outside and raised his hands to the heavens and prayed. As he moved his hands over my son's heart and chanted, for the first time in a long while, Brandon's agony seemed to disappear. With a smile, he fell quietly into a peaceful sleep.

This small window of hope didn't last long before we were plunged back into despair. Brandon's discomfort returned the following day. Having no control over what was most important to me was beyond hard!

Brandon was extremely uncomfortable his last night on Earth. He was agitated and cried nonstop. Draining the fluids that had built up in his lungs offered little to no relief. I spent the rest of the evening pacing throughout the house with Brandon in my arms, kissing and praying. But I knew . . . somehow, I knew.

The next morning, we revisited the faith healer, hoping his healing hands could again do their trick and bring comfort to my little son. I watched as this kind man moved his hands over Brandon's chest. It took all my will to keep standing when I saw the deep sadness and tears in this man's eyes because I knew what his silent sadness meant.

Brandon died in my arms later that night at Children's Hospital in Oakland. We stayed with our tough little guy for hours, not wanting to leave our baby. We only left after he was removed from the room and the hospital told us it was time to go. We returned to our home, where the only thing left of our son were his toys, clothes, bed, scent, and forever silent laughter and voice. My heart splintered into pieces.

I couldn't save my son and felt guilty that I hadn't done enough to help him live. There are times I still feel that crushing sense of guilt, despite eventually realizing, many years after he died, that I did everything that was available at the time. But that's my logical side. As his father, there will always be a place in me that believes I should have been able to save my son. I think all parents feel that way about their children—we're supposed to protect them and keep them safe always.

Brandon died thirty-nine years ago, and as I write, my body still shudders as it recalls those days and nights I spent helplessly watching my baby suffer as his life was being stolen away from us. Until Brandon became ill and died, I had never experienced grief. Grief was just a word, something that happened to other people. Once he was gone, my grief felt like I lived in a barren forest destroyed by fire. No beauty to be seen no matter where I looked—just total, unrelenting devastation. Being a man, I was expected to stay strong, and while I could pretend to anyone looking from the outside, inside I was a mere shadow of the man I'd been.

When Brandon was undergoing treatment at Children's Hospital, his mother and I didn't want him to ever be alone, so one of us was always there with him. The hospital had no accommodations for us or other parents, so I would spend each night sleeping under his crib in order to remain close to my boy.

I was not alone. Many parents I met at the hospital, who were able to stay with their children, also slept under their child's bed, or in the waiting room, or in any corner they could find so they could remain close to their child. Like mine, their misery was heartbreaking. They needed a place to rest and cry—everyone does.

There were only one or two rocking chairs available where I could sit and hold my son. I often wondered why there weren't more. After Brandon's funeral, we were gifted with money from many friends to help pay for the services. We used the money left over to purchase additional rocking chairs with Brandon's name on them in addition to five rollaway beds. But we knew that wasn't enough.

Although my grief was all-consuming, I believed Brandon's life had to have meaning beyond the still unimaginable fact that he was gone. Shortly after his death, I met with a few other parents I'd met when we were at the hospital, and together we decided to raise money for a home so that parents would have a place to stay close by.

We held many fund-raisers and meetings with hospital executives and local businesses. Our goal was to establish a Ronald McDonald House like the one Stanford did in Palo Alto, California. Unfortunately, due to restrictions that were in place at Stanford, we were not allowed to call our home Ronald McDonald House.

We were able to raise enough money to buy a three-story Victorian home near Children's Hospital in Oakland. After improvements were made to the structure, Children's Hospital Family House opened in the early 1980s, providing a very low-cost place for families whose children are under care at Children's Hospital. It has sixteen bedrooms, two kitchens, a common living room, playroom, exercise room, and laundry room. It is still going strong now, thirty-five-plus years since first opening its doors.

Getting involved and knowing I was doing something to help others helped me cope with my grief in the light of my precious son's death. My forest was devastated, but I began to see new trees and flowers and noticed the birds singing for the first time in a very long time. This was Brandon's fourth gift: He added meaning and purpose to my life and to the lives of many others.

Brandon gave me the gifts of fatherhood and love, and his courage enabled me to reach out to others, knowing it was more important to do something that would honor Brandon's life rather than sink down forever in a hole of depression. I wanted the joy of his life to mean more than the pain of his loss. Brandon lived, and because he did, I learned to celebrate life whenever there's an opportunity, and to be a better father to my two sons who came later. Sadly, they never knew the love of their older brother.

I will always miss my little tough guy, Brandon, but because of him I learned compassion, love, and how to listen to others when they are hurting without having a need to fix, judge, or change them or anything about their circumstances. That was his fifth gift: Brandon made me a better man, husband, father, and friend.

These were Brandon's lasting gifts: Live with joy, laugh often, be kind, show compassion, focus on what's good, love with all your heart, and celebrate life as often as possible.

\* \* \*

**Robert (Bob) R. Burdt** became involved in charity work after Brandon's death and eventually became a father again with the birth of his sons Justin and Evan. Bob's philosophy is "We're not here for a long time but we're here for a good time." He currently lives in El Dorado Hills, California, with his wife, Virginia, and Shelby, their golden retriever.

# Losing Elizabeth and Gaining in Love

### By Lucia Maya

Lucia and Elizabeth

$\mathcal{O}$n Friday, November 4, 2011, my world was forever changed. My older daughter Elizabeth, twenty-one, called me just as I had finished taking a Qigong class. She was in tears, having trouble breathing, and I knew at once something was wrong. Elizabeth was in severe pain again and was headed back to the Student Health Center on the University of Arizona campus.

I knew this was serious, as this girl never cried, and she also had a very high pain threshold. I assured her I'd meet her there, and immediately jumped in the car and headed toward campus. I tried everything I could think of to center and calm myself as I drove, but with little success.

Elizabeth was multifaceted (like we all are, but more so!) and full of contrasts. At times, she could be the sweetest, most appreciative daughter. I have a collection of handmade cards and notes from her marking various occasions—for Mother's Day, my birthday, or simply notes of gratitude that I was her mother. Since she was eighteen, Elizabeth made sure we had a weekly coffee date, where she loved to ask about me and the details of my life.

On what would turn out to be her last Mother's Day here on Earth, Elizabeth was out of town, but she was sure to set up another time to meet me for lunch so we could celebrate the holiday that was one of our favorites. I was delighted when the day for our lunch finally came, and my daughter blessed me with thoughtful gifts of special lotions and a beautiful card.

But Elizabeth could also be pretty "bratty" (her word), manipulative, and good at getting her way, or making everyone around her miserable if that didn't happen.

One time we were in New York trying to get out the door for my aunt's memorial service. Elizabeth had been taking much longer to get dressed and ready than the rest of us—a common occurrence, given the many outfits she would always try on and the constant need for the best-looking makeup and perfect accessories.

My mother, who was with us, was anxious to get out the door on time, as it was her sister who had passed, and Mom had made the arrangements for the gathering. When she headed out the door, I followed because I felt she needed support on that difficult day. Moments later, Elizabeth had a complete meltdown; she was crying and bitterly angry with me that I hadn't waited for her before leaving the house.

Elizabeth could also use this same level of emotion and honesty to be very direct and insightful. For instance, she'd sometimes show me painful, yet true, aspects of my life or close relationships that were out of balance, or where she felt I hadn't been taking good care of my boundaries.

Before she was even old enough to speak, I noticed that whenever Elizabeth was expressing anger through a tantrum or tears, often *I* was actually feeling angry (about something unrelated) but hadn't tuned in to my own emotions enough to notice or express them. Once I had the insight, Elizabeth would calm down quickly. This is just one of the many ways in which my daughter was such a great teacher for me.

Elizabeth was incredibly smart, a writer, poet, and visual artist. She was also very sensitive, and a deeply spiritual being from a young age. She was always an honors student and in college started a women's group to discuss feminism and sexuality.

Elizabeth was also a badass. She loved to hang out and drink at the downtown bars in Tucson, dressed in heels and red lipstick, embodying the sexy and gorgeous young woman she was. She liked dating men who were slightly (or very) dangerous. She smoked cigarettes and yet was a vegetarian who ate organic food and loved yoga.

To put it mildly, she was a study in contradictions.

At age thirteen, Elizabeth had blue dreadlocks, was hanging out in punk rock clubs in San Francisco, and had already seen several friends die from drug overdoses. At age fourteen, she loved to sit in spiritual circles, offering gems of wisdom that would have been remarkable even from someone decades older than she, but was extraordinary for someone of her tender age.

So, when I walked into the Student Health Center to find my beloved—albeit unconventional—daughter, the kindhearted and concerned campus doctor was urging her to go to the ER at a nearby hospital. We asked if she could go home, drop off the car, and pick up a few things, and he said yes, but said not to delay any further than was absolutely necessary. The doctor also called ahead to the hospital, and made sure Elizabeth knew to tell the folks in the ER that she was having chest pain, to ensure that she'd be seen quickly.

Apparently, the doctor had a strong suspicion that Elizabeth had mediastinal non-Hodgkin's lymphoma just from looking at her, as her face and neck were quite swollen, and a large tumor that was wrapped around one of her veins was causing the swelling.

Elizabeth had been having pain in her right upper chest for weeks that another doctor had dismissed as allergies and treated with prednisone.

We didn't learn of my daughter's precise diagnosis until after her biopsy a couple days later, on Monday. However, within hours of arriving at the ER, Elizabeth's chest X-ray revealed a large mass in her chest, about the size of her fist, just to the right of her heart.

It was shocking to see and so frightening. Elizabeth was always so healthy—she'd rarely ever been sick and had been treated with homeopathic remedies throughout most of her childhood. She also ate organic whole foods, was a vegetarian since age fourteen, and had been a dedicated yoga student for much of her life. How could she, of all people, have a mass in her chest the size of a fist? How could my precious and strong-willed Elizabeth have cancer?!

Our dear friend Ann Marie, Elizabeth's doctor, came to sit with us as we waited hours for her admission. I walked outside with Ann Marie at some point and started to sob on her shoulder. "No, no, no, no, no . . . !" I cried. I could not believe this was happening.

I was feeling overwhelmed with worry about all kinds of things—from Elizabeth's limited insurance cap versus the staggering cost of the yet unknown cancer treatment, to whether or not she'd be able to complete her semester as a junior at the U of A, to how she would cope emotionally with the diagnosis of cancer. But I did *not* think she would die. That was not in my world of possibilities at all. I couldn't even begin to imagine my world without Elizabeth in it.

Elizabeth had been my firstborn, and although I was only twenty-six when I had her, I'd been ready to be a mother since I could remember and couldn't wait to have the first of what I was sure would be two daughters. Elizabeth was wanted and deeply loved. From the moment of conception, I was thrilled by her very existence.

My elder daughter and I were very similar, and we were also quite close. This meant Elizabeth knew me extremely well—and that made her teenage years incredibly challenging for both of us. Elizabeth's need for absolute independence, combined with a desire to be the number one priority in my life, was difficult, especially once I was in a new relationship with a woman I deeply loved. Elizabeth adored my new partner yet competed wildly with her for my attention.

This created a great deal of stress between mother and daughter, including a devastating time when Elizabeth was sixteen and had grown very unhappy living in our new home of Tucson, Arizona. She had been making my partner and me miserable and convinced us that she needed to move back to Berkeley, California, and live with her father.

Oddly enough, once the arrangements were set, Elizabeth changed her mind. I insisted she go anyway, but the transition didn't exactly go smoothly and my daughter wound up deeply depressed. Even though it turned out to be only four months before she was back, it took us years to rebuild our relationship, and for me to win back her trust.

Had I known she wouldn't be around for the rest of my life, I'm certain I would have made a different choice. But I didn't, and I still regret the years of distance those four months apart put between us. I'm so grateful that the time we spent together when she was sick made us acutely aware that we wanted to resolve our past hurts. Elizabeth and I moved forward into forgiveness *now* and we were both thankful we did.

Our family was moved very slowly and gently into the possibility of Elizabeth dying from this cancer—and then the reality of it—and for that I am deeply grateful. For the eleven months we had together after the fateful day in the ER, nine were spent believing and trusting she would fully recover and live a long, healthy life; while the last two months were spent with Elizabeth at home, in hospice, knowing her death was inevitable—I am eternally grateful.

Every moment I had with my daughter was a blessing, and Elizabeth and I did a lifetime of healing in those final months. She lived fully and richly, and in the end, she somehow became love itself. She showered us all with pure love, and lived in a state of grace that I'm blessed to have experienced in this lifetime.

I believe that every experience in my life that led up to this one had been preparing me to move through *this* unimaginable experience with grace and peace. The death of my dad when I was three, the illnesses I've lived with and healed from, my many spiritual teachers, my partner and friends, and my Reiki training and practice for fifteen years prior—all of these were drawn from on a daily basis while my girl Elizabeth was living with cancer, when she died, and in the six years that have passed since.

Remarkably, Elizabeth was one of my first and foremost spiritual teachers. She was just two when she told me she could "see" the spirit of my dead grandmother. When we came home to Berkeley from my grandmother's funeral on the East Coast, that night at dinner Elizabeth looked just past me and said, "Bama's here!" (what we called my grandmother). I could tell that she saw her clearly, and though it would be many years before I could feel the presence of spirits and hear messages from them myself, I fully believed her.

Elizabeth also sometimes knew things were about to happen before they seemed possible to even predict. One example of this is a time she told me that her preschool teacher wasn't going to be there that day and described in detail who the new teacher would be instead. I argued at first, as her teacher had never been absent, and the woman she described was entirely unfamiliar to me. It turns out she was right, though. Elizabeth's teacher had become unexpectedly ill, and her description of the substitute teacher was completely accurate.

After a few more similar experiences, I learned not to argue, and would respond, "I didn't know about that, sweetheart, but thank you for telling me. And let's see what happens!"

After Elizabeth's death, in rereading her poetry, it became clear that at some level, she "knew" that she would be leaving us at a young age. Not consciously, but at a soul level, she knew and this, in itself, was a great comfort to me. My daughter had lived a very full and rich life in her brief twenty-two years. We were incredibly close and connected during her life, as I mentioned, and still are, even in her death.

This poem was written by Elizabeth in 2010, over a year *before* she was diagnosed with cancer. I found it on her computer the morning after she died, and I felt compelled to share it with the world.

### Bird's Nest

Five days ago I watched two birds mate.
Yesterday I watched as they began
in unison
to build their nest.

Today it occurs to me
that I will be gone
by the time they lay eggs
and the eggs make way
for the new life
within them.

Today it occurs to me that I will be gone.
The lines between body and land have blurred
and the land will miss my body.
Perhaps it will be lonely
I think it will weep.
I think it will miss me
more than my body or mind
could miss it.

Something
today
made it real.
That is something today brought the actual
lack of myself
in Tucson
on this porch
into the forefront of my reality.
I'm ashamed to say
that it hadn't occurred to me before
the breathtaking absence
of myself.
my body

my flesh and blood holder of humanity
would cease to exist as it has for so many years.
In a desert where wind is a promise
and rain the greatest solace.

Elizabeth Blue, © 2010

For the memorial service held three weeks after my daughter's death, I had this poem printed on 5x7 cards laid over an image of the "heart with flowers" tattoo that had been started on the back of her right thigh, but never filled in with color due to her cancer treatment. When Cailin, a close friend of Elizabeth's, asked me for a copy of the image after she died so she could get the very same tattoo on her body, I was delighted. Even more so when she had her tattoo filled in with color.

There are three primary gifts that have helped me maintain a sense of peace and find joy in life, even with my beloved older daughter gone: the practice of staying in the present, made possible in part through The Work of Byron Katie; my deep faith in the divine and the consciousness that continues when we leave our bodies; and being in service to others with gratitude.

## STAYING PRESENT

There were so many times during the two months Elizabeth was in hospice when my mind would go to "This shouldn't be happening. . . ." Yet, she never did that. Elizabeth never tried to be anywhere other than where she was. She lived each day with quiet strength, in a state of incredible grace.

I, however, was not. In time, I would notice that I wasn't actually *with* her, even though she was still in front of me, because of thoughts swirling around in my mind. So as soon as I finally caught myself, The Work would go something like this:

I'd have this thought: "Elizabeth shouldn't be dying. She's only twenty-two!" I'd ask myself, "Is that true?" and if I said yes, I'd then ask, "Can I absolutely know that is true?" And the answer was always no, I couldn't know that she shouldn't be dying. That would always begin to shift things and my perspective. . . .

There are more steps to The Work,[1] but the practice is one of continually bringing myself back to the present, noticing that it's only my story about the past or the future that is creating my suffering. When I'm in the present moment, I am *always* okay. Maybe feeling incredibly sad, maybe on the floor sobbing, but as the emotion moves through and I'm present with it, without a story, I can allow it to be fully expressed without judgment or holding back, and I'm okay. I am at peace.

## FAITH AND DIVINE PRESENCE

I'm grateful that for years I've been successfully using The Work for myself and my clients, as it helps immensely. I have been a Reiki Master since 2001, and this channeling of healing energy, with my work as an intuitive guide, has kept me in deep connection with the Divine presence. Reiki is an ancient form of energy healing in which the practitioner channels Universal or Divine healing energy to promote relaxation and help relieve stress in another. It can help with symptoms of emotional stress and physical pain. Though much remains unknown about just how it works, I've seen amazing transformations in myself and my clients who receive Reiki treatments, especially in moving into acceptance and having a sense of peace. This is true even when life presents us with "impossible" challenges, like the unexpected death of a child.

Using Reiki on myself and others helps me feel closely the Divine with me. It has also helped to soothe and quiet my mind and leaves me feeling balanced and clear—physically, mentally, and emotionally.

In my intuitive work I now receive messages from those in spirit. The messages and physical images I communicate have been validated as accurate by their loved ones so many times that I wholeheartedly trust they are real. It brings me great comfort to know that there is a consciousness, a soul that continues to exist even after we leave our bodies.

After Elizabeth died, I was worried initially about her being happy, the same way I'd worried about her all her life! I've since heard over and over from Elizabeth, including in several readings with various mediums, that she is happy, that she is doing wonderful work where she is—more than she could have done while in her body—that she is exactly where she is supposed to be and where she *wants* to be.

I feel my daughter's presence with me often, bringing healing energy through me—in the form of a golden light—in addition to the Reiki energy. I believe she has been guiding and protecting those she loved while alive, especially her sister Julianna, who was three years younger than Elizabeth, and just nineteen when Elizabeth died. I have been told Elizabeth also helps comfort and guide new souls (especially young ones) when they have recently transitioned out of their bodies into the afterlife, and this feels very true and real to me.

I have many stories of Elizabeth showing herself to me when I've needed confirmation from her that she is around. One of the most remarkable happened soon after she died, when I was missing her terribly. I was floating in the ocean, looking at the sky, which was filled with puffy round clouds. I asked her to *show* me that she was present and immediately the clouds shifted to form a huge letter *E* in the sky above me!

Another way Elizabeth lets me feel her presence is through music. When I'm alone in the mornings, especially in the months after she died, I play Pandora on shuffle, with about twenty different stations selected. This means there are many thousands of possibilities of songs that could play.

On mornings when I desperately wanted to know her spirit was close, I'd ask Elizabeth to show herself. Each time I made this request, the next song that played was one of a handful of songs that she and I had both loved, that had particular meaning to both of us, and that *did not play* any other time than those times I asked. It brought me to my knees in tears each time—simply overwhelmed with emotion and deepest gratitude.

## SERVICE AND GRATITUDE

The third aspect that I've found essential to having a life of peace and joy is being of service and feeling grateful. I was able to take time off work during the weeks Elizabeth was in hospice, and only slowly started seeing clients again in the months following her death. I am so blessed that I love my work as I do, and that it's nourishing to me, too, while I'm supporting others in their healing journeys. I have always been blessed to work with people during their times of great transformation, and now especially, those dealing with grief and loss of all kinds find their way to me, too.

In my own healing journey, I have found writing—blogging (www .luminousblue5.com) in particular—to be immensely helpful. It serves as a way of processing my experience and emotions while at the same time having a forum to share Elizabeth and her writing. It's also connected me to an online community, through other bloggers and Facebook, which has brought so much support, love, and nourishment. The more vulnerable and authentic I am, the more authentic the connections and friendships are I have received. It has felt like an offering, something coming through me that serves me and hopefully many others.

I find that six years later, I still need more time alone than ever before. I need time to just be, to meditate, to connect, to listen, to not answer to anyone . . . and I need to balance that with living a life of purpose, doing the work I came here to do.

Every day, I feel Elizabeth with me, joining me in serving others, and I believe that living my life as fully and joyfully as possible is the best way I can honor Elizabeth's life and death. I take care of myself in every way I know how, and remember how blessed I am.

I do my best to focus on all the gifts in my life—twenty-two years of having Elizabeth as my living daughter and the rest of my life with her as a spiritual companion; another amazing daughter, Julianna, now twenty-five, very happily living and working in New York; a home on Maui and a thriving practice with clients all over the world; and a marriage to my partner of sixteen years that supports me in so many ways.

I am blessed. I am grateful. I am present.

## NOTE

1. See Byron Katie, *Loving What Is: Four Questions That Can Change Your Life* (New York: Harmony Reprint, 2002); www.thework.com.

*     *     *

**Lucia Maya's** work as a Reiki practitioner, teacher, mentor, and intuitive guide brings her great joy and peace, as she supports others in their transformation and healing. She lives and works on Maui and Molokai, Hawaii, with her loving and supportive wife, Zelie Duvauchelle, and her younger daughter, Julianna, is thriving in New York City. Visit her websites, www.luminousblue5.com and www.luminousadventures.com.

# Honor Your Child by Healing

## By Sandy Peckinpah

*Garrett*

*I* remember walking the red carpet at the Emmys long ago, and thinking, *My life is a fairy tale.* My husband David was nominated as writer/producer for a hit television show that actually *was* a modern-day fairy tale, *Beauty and the Beast,* starring Linda Hamilton and Ron Perlman.

I thought of the years David and I had envisioned and dreamt of this very day. The night was so alive with glamour, expectation, and sheer excitement. It represented an achievement, indeed, but enchanting nights like these often veil the common thread of human experience; these are real people with real lives, sometimes filled with glitz and excitement. And sometimes, great tragedy.

My husband and I had a lot to be grateful for, especially our growing family. Our two young sons, Garrett and Trevor, were at home on this special night, anxiously watching television for a glimpse of Mom and Dad on the red carpet. And be-

68

neath the soft fabric layers of my gown was the roundness of yet another child just beginning to show.

I was caught up in the magic of fairy tales, believing that love conquers all, and everything I ever dreamed of could come true. On that very magical night, no one could have told me that our beautiful family would one day be ripped apart by the worst thing that could ever happen.

Just a few years later, in 1993, without warning my life changed in an instant. My sixteen-year-old son, Garrett, came home on a break from school complaining of a headache and fever.

I whisked him to the doctor, who said, "He's got the Type A flu. Take him home and put him to bed. Have him drink lots of fluids. Tylenol and ibuprofen should control the headache and fever. He should be better in a few days."

I did as the doctor ordered. That night, I made a big batch of chicken soup. Garrett ate a little, and wanted to stay up to watch *Saturday Night Live*. I put the other children to bed and settled into a chair in his bedroom beside him to watch the show. Sometimes we laughed, and sometimes I'd watch him doze off. He complained again of his head hurting, so I gave him what the doctor ordered—Tylenol and ibuprofen.

When the show ended, Garrett asked if we could go gift shopping as soon as he felt better. It was just six days before Christmas.

"Of course, sweetie," I said. "I love you. You'll feel better in the morning." I kissed my son on the forehead and went to bed.

As soon as I woke up Sunday morning, I headed downstairs to Garrett's room, expecting to see him awake and feeling better. At least, that's what the doctor had said. As I headed toward his room, I suddenly felt this incredible, indescribable fear. Even without seeing him, I knew something was wrong. I ran down the hall, into Garrett's room, and reached for him in his bed. He didn't move. I screamed for my husband to call 911. I jumped on top of Garrett, pressing his chest, blowing air into his mouth, but there wasn't one breath of life left in his beautiful body. I looked up, defeated, to see my husband holding our newest baby, and our other two children standing beside him, all in shock . . . and sobbing.

It took forever for the ambulance to arrive.

The doctor's misdiagnosis was a deadly mistake. The autopsy showed Garrett had died several hours before, while I slept, apparently afflicted with one of the deadliest bacterial infections there is—bacterial meningitis. It killed him while he was sleeping.

I heard someone say grief isn't a life sentence; it's a life passage. It's the one common human experience we all have at one time or another. But, we did not expect it to be the death of our child, did we?

If you're reading this, it's likely you've lost a child or been affected by the loss of a child. You're no doubt discovering that this kind of grieving is the hardest thing you'll ever have to endure. I couldn't believe this happened to *me*, to *my family*. I thought I was immune from bad things happening. I had a fairy tale life, remember?

Have you ever felt such incredible emotion as losing your child? It's an unimaginable loss, feared by all parents. Unimaginable—until it happens to you. People refer to it as "the worst that can happen," and that's precisely what it feels like.

I used to believe the cliché "Everything happens for a reason," but with this kind of tragedy, it doesn't make sense at all. It defies the natural laws. We aren't supposed to outlive our children.

In the days following my son's death, I discovered that no matter how great my loss or how deep my grief, the world never stops. In fact, it intensifies.

I remember thinking, *How can I ever be happy again?* I felt as though my pain was visible to everyone, and I would forever wear grief as a mask and a tagline: *I'm Sandy Peckinpah, and I've lost a child*.

Then, a friend gave me a journal and said, "Write, Sandy. Just write." The first blank page was so difficult. I could only manage one sentence: *My son died and my life will never be the same*.

The next day I wrote a paragraph, and each day after that I found words started to come more easily. My journal became my safe haven to empty the well of my sorrow, pouring tears of ink onto paper. And for a little while, I could let my emotions rest.

I *had* to survive this. My husband needed my support. We were a team. I had three living children who needed a whole mother!

I kept writing. Words pulled me and pushed me. As weeks went on, I'd read back over the journal entries and I began to see something remarkable: I'd actually survived another day, another week, another month. I was growing stronger, and the words rising up from the pages illuminated my way, reflecting my own hope back to me.

There's no magic secret to starting a journal. Just pick up a pen and begin with one word or sentence. *Keep writing.*

I tried to picture my life without the pain of losing my son. I'd write that very question, *What would it be like to feel peace around Garrett's death?* Then, I'd close my eyes and visualize myself without the heavy veil of sorrow that draped me. And for a very brief moment, I *could* actually feel the peace.

Some days were better than others. Grief felt as big as the sky; it was everywhere I turned. There was no escaping it.

What surprised me most was the absence of joy. Before my son died, I had never known what that felt like. I woke up each day feeling joy. But after, it was like a kick in my gut, and every morning I'd relive his loss. Another day, another hour, another minute of more unrelenting grief.

I was exhausted.

One morning, several months after Garrett died, I awoke to the sounds of my youngest child giggling. Jackson was just a year old. He was laughing at the sun as it poured into his room, and every time he looked at it, it made him sneeze, one right after another.

I burst into laughter and the sound of my voice shocked me. I hadn't heard myself laugh in so long. I realized then that you can have two emotions living in the same body, and you can choose to focus on one or the other.

Each morning after that, I woke up with that choice, *happy or sad?* I began to learn how to choose "happy," even through the veil of my grief. The choice was mine. The tears were *not* gone . . . just allowed to be tucked away now and then.

> You may not control all the events that happen to you, but you can decide not to be reduced by them.
>
> —Maya Angelou, *Letter to My Daughter*

Healing from the death of a child is not on a timetable. In fact, time doesn't fix this loss. Healing comes from taking steps to resolve the negative effects of grief, accepting the new relationship with your child, and actively pursuing life again. The sadness will come and go, but you don't always have to let it take away your day.

As mothers, we always wonder if we could have saved our child if we'd done things differently: *If only I'd slept in his room that night*, or *if only I'd taken him to a different doctor. What mistakes did I make? Could I have saved my son?*

There will come a time when you'll make peace with knowing you did everything you could with what you knew at the time. I know I did everything I could, and it still happened. My son died. Sometimes loving your child more than anything isn't enough to save them.

You have a choice. You can remain stuck in depression and despair, or step into the next act of your life and declare that your child did not die in vain.

> In some ways suffering ceases to be suffering at the moment it finds a meaning.
>
> —Viktor E. Frankl, *Man's Search for Meaning*

Give your child's life meaning. Some parents plant a memory garden, some create a foundation, some write about it and share their story, while others feel the calling to just sit and hold the hand of those newly struggling. The moment you recognize how powerful it is to share your experience is the moment your grieving will shift.

Keep returning to your journal, and after a while, you'll look back over your words and no longer recognize the person you once were. You'll see how strong you really are and what you're made of.

Many years after Garrett's death, I became inspired to finally write the book I knew had been welling deep inside of me for quite a while. Drawing from my personal story, I shared the healing steps I took to restore my life in my book *How to Survive the Worst That Can Happen: A Parent's Step by Step Guide to Healing After the Loss of a Child*. Not only was this a way for me to help other parents struggling with loss, it was also an opportunity to give meaning to my son Garrett's untimely death.

As my book went out into the world, I found more and more parents were asking for my help. It inspired me to return to a program I had explored when Garrett first died, the Grief Recovery Method. I enrolled in the Grief Recovery Institute and achieved certification through their training. Because of it, I've been able to help other parents and connect in a meaningful way.

It's been more than two decades now since my beautiful son left this earth and sometimes the tears will surprise me. The hard work of healing has brought me a harmonious blend of resolution and comfort as my heart joyfully connects with the sweet ballad of my beloved son's memories.

Healing doesn't mean you'll never feel the sadness again. It means you'll be able to have memories without being pulled back down into despair.

I chose resilience, and writing was a big part of helping me restore my vitality and spontaneity again. My journal was my safe place to form a new relationship with my child. As I recalled stories and sweet memories, I felt the joy I once had when Garrett was living.

Now, I look at the life of my son and marvel at the sixteen years, three months, and ten days that I had with him. He was the first to call me *Mom*. As the years go by, I've learned a mother's love never diminishes; in fact, my love for my son has grown just as it would have if he were alive. I am still Garrett's mother, he is still my child, and my love for him grows with each passing year.

Garrett's death was the birth of my new life . . . learning to live with his loss, and rising up to be the woman I am today. He taught me to love harder and appreciate every single day. He taught me to reach out to others and begin sharing my story in the hope it could reassure other heartbroken parents that there really *is* life after loss.

No child dies without a legacy and a purpose for those that are left behind. It's up to you. Honor your child by healing. He or she wouldn't want it any other way.

\*    \*    \*

**Sandy Peckinpah,** a Certified Grief Recovery Specialist, is the author of four books, including the multi-award-winning *How to Survive the Worst That Can Happen: A Parent's Step by Step Guide to Healing After the Loss of a Child.* Her articles on resilience are featured in the *Huffington Post* and Thrive Global. Sandy became a single mom to her three surviving children, Trevor, Julianne, and Jackson, when their father died just twelve years after Garrett. She remarried a wonderful, supportive man, Jim de Girolamo, and they currently reside in both California and Arizona. Learn more at www.SandyPeckinpah.com and www.HowTo SurviveTheWorstThatCanHappen.com.

# · 9 ·

# My Journey from Grieving to Grateful

## By Tina Zarlenga

*The brutal winter of 1993 epitomized the depths of my anguish as life became frozen in a haze of tragic and unrelenting grief. Solemn doctors spoke medical terms I was sure were intended for someone else. As I sat there among the chatter attempting to assemble my thoughts, I finally heard what the doctors had been leading up to. "There is no brain activity. He will not survive." In the course of only two days, our cherished five-year-old son Ryan is gone. I will never hear the sweet sound of his voice again.*

*Just like that, the world as I knew it unraveled. And I could not have imagined the life that would emerge in its place.*

In the middle of February 1993, a winter flu bug has made its way through our family and Ryan is the first to recover. It's a Friday, and Ryan's three-year-old sister Chelsea is on the couch, still feeling pretty miserable. Always the adoring big brother, Ryan does his best to help little Chelsea feel better. He refills

9          Ryan

her sippy cup with ginger ale, tucks her little blanket around her, and pops *Fern Gully*—their favorite movie—into the VCR.

On Saturday, Ryan again gives up his favorite spot on the big couch to Chelsea and sleeps on the loveseat beside her. Both doze on and off while watching TV until it is bedtime, and our still drowsy kids toddle off to bed to get some more sleep. None of this feels startling to me in the aftermath of the flu.

By Sunday morning, though, his dad Joel and I are concerned because Chelsea, who had gotten sick a few days after Ryan, is already bouncing back, and Ryan is not back to normal or anything close. By Sunday evening, we notice that Ryan stares off into space whenever we talk to him and it is hard to keep his attention. We ask him to count to a hundred and to recite his ABCs—both things he loves to do—but he can't, and tears begin to rush down his face. Ryan does not want to go to the hospital, but we insist, and reassure him he'll feel much better if he goes. Joel drives him to the ER at Southwest General Hospital in Cleveland while I stay home and look after Chelsea.

After several long hours, the doctor releases Ryan with barely a glance and a prescription to fill for an ear infection he has diagnosed.

Ryan is happy to be back home. He pours himself a glass of water and asks if he can lie down on the couch and watch some TV. I agree and lie with him a while until he closes his eyes and I am sure he is fast asleep.

Monday morning, as soon as I'm up, I check on Ryan and discover that he had vomited at some point during the night. He is shaking, and within minutes he begins convulsing and is rendered unable to speak.

Panicked, I dial 911 and Joel, who had already left for work. Fear threatens to submerse me until denial assures me everything will be okay. I grab Ryan's winter jacket and climb into the ambulance. As we are rushed back to the hospital, I stroke Ryan's tiny hand gently, though I'm certain it was more for my own reassurance than his.

Joel and I wait in the emergency room as doctors feverishly review the previous night's charts in search of an explanation. After another examination, a spinal tap is performed on Ryan to check for meningitis. Even amidst all the chaos surrounding him in the ER, Ryan remains unresponsive except for a single tear that rolls down his emotionless face. I will never know what prompted his tear, and that has haunted me since then.

It soon becomes clear that Ryan's condition requires a level of care not available at Southwest General, so he is life-flighted to Metro General, where he is quickly whisked away to the Pediatric Intensive Care Unit (PICU).

Joel and I arrive at the hospital an hour later and are relieved to learn that Ryan's condition—viral encephalitis—is common, and like any other virus it would just have to run its course. Finally, we can breathe a huge sigh of relief.

During the evening, amidst the distraction of family and friends, Joel's mom arranges to sit with Chelsea at home. Now we can focus all our attention on Ryan. Once our visitors are gone for the night, Joel and I retreat to the family lounge to get some much-needed rest.

Early Tuesday morning we are startled awake as a nurse informs us of Ryan's decline. Still in the PICU, he has taken a turn for the worse, and Dr. Pope orders another round of testing while Ryan's small body struggles to fight this virus. The tests, we are told, will take some time, and they convince us to get breakfast in the cafeteria since it was certain to be a long day.

I shuffle the food on my plate, unable to establish an appetite. Smothered with fear, I remain too nauseous to eat. Joel and I speak quietly of our worries, each looking to the other for reassurance; yet the grip of unease clings to us both. Unable to stave off our panic any longer, we return to the PICU in search of answers.

Hospital staff had been waiting for us to return, and usher us down the hall into a cramped office with a polite invitation to sit. My stomach gurgles with worry as I arrange my fears in neat little rows, attempting to stifle unease. Several specialists quietly enter the room. A discussion ensues between Joel and the various doctors, and I am lost in a fog of uncertainty when I hear Dr. Pope explain that there is no brain activity, his brain is still swelling rapidly, and Ryan will not survive. Silence floods the room as I struggle to absorb the words. Then, just as quickly as silence fell, chaos erupts.

Unable to be consoled, I fumble out of my chair and bolt from the room screaming. In my wake, Joel explodes furiously at the doctors but I refuse to stop or look back, as if fleeing will somehow change the course of this nightmare.

Sheltered in a quiet place all alone, I immediately begin dialing my parents. Tethered to a phone on the wall, my trembling hands misdial repeatedly. Frustrated, I force my hand steady as the call connects. When I hear my mother's soft-spoken hello, I slink down the wall to the floor. Immediately I howl wretched sobs and she knows—as only a mother can—and begins sobbing with me as the weight of my grief pulls me under.

Joel and I sit with our young son's motionless body while a twist of machines keeps his tiny figure alive, both of us praying desperately for a miracle. Our parents and siblings return, and updates on Ryan slowly trickle to the outside world.

My father's fear becomes anchored in questions as he tries hard to assess the situation—his feeble attempt at control. He is stern but calm and I borrow his grit as I step from the room seeking solitude. Each of us dithers between stillness with Ryan and the need to get up and move as we somberly await the results of one last definitive test.

After wandering the drab halls of the hospital for what seems like hours, I am distracted by a foreign sound emanating from somewhere up ahead. Moving closer, I detect an echo of violent sobs and find my siblings pacing in the family lounge while trying desperately to calm our inconsolable father. He is broken in a state we have never before witnessed, and his inability to fix what's wrong with his only grandson swallows him whole. Nobody can save our precious boy, and the last seeds of hope slip away.

Joel and I watch in shock as the nurses unhook all the tubes and cords that had once kept our baby alive. As the hum of machines is extinguished, a piercing quiet blankets the room. I am seated beside Ryan's bed while a tenderhearted nurse gently rests our precious boy in my arms. One by one, family reenters the room to say their good-byes and to hug Ryan one last time. The stillness of his body weighs heavy, and silence is only broken by muffled cries.

Overcome by the gravity of our loss, I have no idea how much time lapsed before they urge us to leave, but eventually Joel and I choke out our final good-byes as a nurse lifts Ryan from my arms.

Feelings of betrayal consume me as we vacate the hospital to the backseat of my parents' sedan. Cold gray skies mirror my heart and a blinding snowstorm obstructs our path as we inch away from the city to our rural address. Weeping with the sounds of the tires, we trudge down the road in disbelief, not wanting to face this new chapter of life without Ryan.

Meaningless days follow sorrowful nights as grief brands its scar on our souls. Time slips away unnoticed, and I exist in a shell of what was. One bleak morning, after dropping Chelsea at preschool, I pull my car into the garage and, with the engine still running, close the overhead door. I sit frozen and wait for a decision to come. Finally, after what seems like forever, I turn off the ignition, go into my house, and wait for 12:30 to come so I can pick up my daughter from school.

Finding the will to survive had not been my first thought. I just wanted to breathe, to open my eyes without the flood of tears, and to figure out how I could possibly live my life without Ryan. I hear about The Compassionate Friends, a support group for grieving families, and I am eager to meet other parents who I know will understand the depths of my loss. From my first meeting on, I mark my calendar for the first Tuesday night of each month and begin to attend these meetings faithfully. I feel robbed of more years with Ryan, until meeting the mom of a child who had died as a toddler makes me so grateful for the five years I had had with my son.

Still withered by anguish, at the suggestion of my support group, I start scribbling my sorrow in notebooks while assembling the courage to go on. Pondering my survival against Ryan's death, I search for answers as I write. I soon discover that healing is a process, not an event. It takes years of consistent journaling and regular attendance at meetings before I begin to find a way out of my grief.

After several months of delivery, I notice that the arrival of the monthly newsletter from The Compassionate Friends is somewhat sporadic and wonder why, until I see that my label is addressed by hand. At the very next meeting—and still feeling a little bit shy—I wait until all the other members have gone to approach the chapter leader, Eileen. After exchanging a few niceties, I tentatively ask if the labels are always addressed by hand. When she answers yes, I eagerly offer to print all the labels from here forward, and Eileen gladly accepts.

For the first time since Ryan's death, it dawns on me that I'm thinking of someone else instead of focusing almost solely on my own grief.

Over the next several years, as my healing begins getting traction, the need for regular attendance at Compassionate Friends lessens but my need to give back remains strong. I continue to print the labels for many more years, and to journal, as I move forward on the path of recovery.

Finally, a little more than a decade after Ryan's passing, amidst the bright hues of spring, I am ready to forage my escape from the dark at long last. Picking at threads of the past, I am heartened by the memory of a particular tale of kindness that invites me in.

On the night of Ryan's last birthday, December 7, 1992, following cake and ice cream festivities, we retreat to a local tree farm to select our Christmas tree. As we eagerly crunch through the snow to pick out our family tree, Ryan excitedly blurts to the attendant that it's his fifth birthday, and then ducks behind me for cover.

Surprised by my shy son's pronouncement, I turn towards Ryan and smile. Beaming, he giggles proudly while the enthusiastic attendant claps as she sings "Happy Birthday." Later, as we emerge from the sea of evergreens, she hands him a five-dollar bill. That small act of kindness becomes my salvation and the impetus for what would come next.

In that moment of joyful reflection, everything finally makes sense. Sharing various acts of kindness with strangers will celebrate our son's zest for life and allow Ryan's spirit to live on in beautiful and meaningful ways. With the grace of time, I had awakened to live life again. I find gratitude dwelling beneath the scars and unpack a reason to smile.

Deciding where to begin is easy. Cleveland Metro Hospital had given our family such compassionate, extraordinary care, and I am delighted to pay it forward in Ryan's honor. Organizing a toy drive for Christmas on Ryan's birthday affords me a new sense of purpose and brings happiness in the way only giving can. With the help of a bevy of flyers announcing the December event, hundreds of new toys are collected for donation to the hospitalized children.

Joy warms our hearts as a fleet full of family and friends heads for the hospital. On this slushy, cold, wintry day, my best friend Lisa adorns us in red Santa hats. It would have been Ryan's sixteenth birthday, and for the first time in years I am beaming.

Once inside, we cheerfully cart the many boxes of toys up to the pediatric floor. As we unpack the toys from the boxes, one of the staff excitedly says they will last for a number of years. Next, we visit the PICU, leaving them a large basket of fruit. I explain our reasons for giving, prompting several nurses to share their own fond remembrances of Ryan. I float my way back to the car and realize, for the first time, that I have given myself permission to be happy without any guilt or remorse.

As surges of grief wax and wane, new acts of kindness emerge. On the giving tree at my local grocery, I find myself drawn to the wishes of five-year-old boys and rush out to buy them their gifts. In the line at the drive-thru at Starbucks, I pay for the car behind me and do the same for the cars at McDonald's. When traveling, other anonymous gifts follow at tollbooths along the way. Each small act of kindness whispers softly for me to go on.

Having been an introvert all my life, at first I was only comfortable doing these acts of kindness anonymously. I felt like a fairy godmother who sprinkles confetti and vanishes before it can hit the ground. But as my practice of paying it forward flourishes, I feel moved to share this powerful lesson in giving and step farther into the light. The more openly I give in Ryan's honor, the more others around me find their own meaningful ways of doing the same—and always on my sweet son's birthday.

Ryan's uncle Gordon stands outside of Goodwill and offers twenty-dollar bills to shoppers entering the store. One of the recipients took his twenty, added another twenty to it, and gave forty dollars to the Catholic Works of Mercy in Ryan's honor.

Over time I hear of other Pay It Forwards as well. One woman orders the "Happy Meals" at McDonald's but has the cashier surprise someone else with her fries and drinks. Each winter, warm coats, hats, and gloves are given to those in need, and when warm weather arrives, out come the tricycles and bikes. Pay It Forwards also show up in ways as simple as doing something kind for someone with or without them knowing it. And all these acts are done lovingly in memory of our little Ryan.

On Ryan's thirtieth birthday, I was surprised to learn through a Facebook post that the daughter of a dear friend had visited our local bakery on a secret mission. Katie asked if they had any birthday cakes ready for pickup later that day. When they showed her the various confections, Katie directed her three-year-old Dylan to choose the one he wanted to pay for as a gift in memory of Ryan.

It is December 7, 2016, Ryan's birthday, and I wake excited about my plans for the day. A quick trip to Dunkin' Donuts and I'm off to Elmcroft Nursing Home with all the goodies. At Starbucks, I present a hundred dollars for two gift cards: fifty to pay for coffees in the store, and fifty for the drive-thru line outside. When the patrons try to pay, they're handed a Pay It Forward card adorned with Ryan's picture as the inspiration for the gift they had received.

Feeling fulfilled and quite happy with my day, I drive to the nearby Target for one more deed. My instincts lead me to a boy about Ryan's age. After explaining my yearly birthday custom to his mom, she gives her permission and I hand a ten-dollar gift card to her son.

Walking towards my car, I pass a woman pushing her young daughter in a cart. After a moment's hesitation, I feel compelled to turn back in their direction. "Excuse me," I say a bit timidly. "Today is my son's birthday. He passed away when he was five, and I would like to give your daughter this Target gift card as a pay it forward on his special day." I barely finish talking when tears begin rolling down her face.

"I *must* hug you," she blurts, and then begins sharing her story with me.

Meme, too, had suffered unthinkable loss. Two children. Both babies. And they died just a few years apart. Instantly grief connects us. It was the price we had paid for love. As our stories unravel between us, I am sure God had led me to them. On that crisp December day, while standing shivering in Target's parking lot, two relative strangers form a bond that will last a lifetime.

A little more than a year after Ryan's death, God blessed Joel and me with another son, Zachary, who we named in honor of Zak, Ryan's favorite character in *Fern Gully*. Unbeknownst to us at the time, we later discovered that "Ryan" means "little king," and "Zachary" means "God remembers." How fitting that is for our sons!

Since 1994, picking out our Christmas tree on Ryan's birthday would become our family tradition—a tradition that remains to this day. Now Chelsea, Zach, Joel, and I are joined by our son-in-law Anthony and our baby granddaughter Norah on our annual outings.

Once the tree is safely strapped to the car, we head to dinner together, where we happily reminisce about our day. As the plates are cleared, Chelsea and I assess the other patrons to choose the perfect family whose tab will be added to our check.

In the twenty-five years since we lost Ryan, giving still provides us with hope. Each random act of kindness intercedes in the magical way that God and grief so beautifully connect love and pain.

Our Pay It Forwards are now celebrated throughout the year, as well as on Ryan's birthday. What began as an effort to save myself now enriches my life beyond measure.

With his spirit of pure love and kindness, our precious Ryan lives on.

\* \* \*

**Tina Zarlenga.** While searching for a reason to go on after losing her five-year-old son Ryan, Tina discovered that giving back would actually save her. Through an ongoing campaign to Pay It Forward for Ryan, Tina uncovers great joy. She shares stories of inspiration and hope, as well as her journey through grief, with emotional essays of life on her website Unraveling My Heart the Write Way (www.unraveling myheartthewriteway.com). Published essays can also be found in *Bella Grace Magazine*, The Compassionate Friends, as well as many online communities. Tina lives in Medina, Ohio, with her husband, Joel, just a few short miles from their two surviving children, Chelsea and Zach. When she's not busy running, writing, or reading in her favorite book-store, Tina will no doubt be reveling in the joys of life with her little granddaughter, Norah.

# III

# ACCIDENT

Grief feels like being in suspended animation—like being caught in a web with nowhere to land.

—Sharon Gabriel Rossy

# I'll Be Seeing You

### By *Michelle Barbuto*

John

$\mathscr{M}$y name is Michelle, and I'm the second born of four children. I grew up in a small steel mill town in western Pennsylvania. The town was really nothing special, other than families became rooted here more often than not. Families knew each other or knew someone who knew *that* person. It was an intimate place; you couldn't step out of line without your parents finding out about it rather quickly.

I participated in gymnastics, track, and cheerleading, and I was on the dance team in high school. Since I was little, I dreamed of being a nurse or ballerina when I grew up, and finally made my decision when my grandmother passed away on my twelfth birthday. I knew then that I had to be a nurse and work with geriatric patients so I could be with the elderly as they transitioned from this life to the next. I'm fairly certain, though, that I was unaware at that time that children pass away, too. One never wants to think the unthinkable.

In 1989, I was set up on a blind date with a man that made life seem exciting. We had many things in common, including—oddly enough—the same dream of having six children. He was a hard worker, and we were thrilled that our families approved of our relationship. We were married a few months later, on June 23, 1990.

Between 1990 and 2001, I gave birth to six children—four boys and two girls. I was blessed to be able to leave my nursing career in order to stay at home and raise the children. During those years, I attended every sporting event, class play, and church service in which my kids were involved. I made countless trips to the doctor, pharmacy, and grocery store (usually with all six of them in tow). My life was (and is) centered on my children.

I had a deeply rooted faith and trust in God, and over the years, the Catholic Church became my second home. I helped with vacation Bible school, CCD, and adult formation, and was also a Eucharistic minister. My church family gave me peace and joy, and I loved having my children with me to help prepare the various games, crafts, and teachings that I presented.

Although I loved being a mom, our marriage was strained and difficult, and in 2008 my husband and I parted ways. Afterwards, I was depressed on a near-daily basis—I felt empty and very lonely inside. Life was scary, and I was unsure what the future held for my family. I had six kids, ages seven through eighteen; no job; and no idea what to do to keep us intact. I had always loved fitness and, in addition to being a nurse, I was also a personal trainer. But that never was full-time and I couldn't figure out how to earn all the income we needed in order to keep us afloat.

Although I was an LPN (licensed practical nurse), by this time I hadn't worked outside the home for eighteen years. Because LPN jobs were scarce, I gathered the strength to return to college to complete my RN (registered nurse) degree. Thank goodness I had kept my nursing license current, so the only requirement for acceptance into the program was to take and pass a test—which I did.

Going back to school at my age was frightening, but I succeeded. In May 2011, I graduated with my associate's degree in nursing and successfully passed the Pennsylvania state nursing boards on June 23, 2011 (a date I rededicated to something good). The next day I was hired by a medical rehab facility and started working there full-time in July.

This was to be the first time I'd be pulled away from my children for any considerable length of time. Thank goodness they were all old enough to pretty much fend for themselves. But overnight I went from never missing a meet, game, or tournament to missing most of them. I hated not being with my children, but needed to keep a roof over our heads and provide them with some sense of stability and a firm foundation.

This sudden life change left me feeling confused and overwhelmed, but I couldn't let my children know how I felt. I never wanted to be a single mom, but now I was one, and I had no choice but to keep moving forward in my life. I just kept putting one foot in front of the other, and along the way, I learned to be strong in the face of obstacles and the challenges life brings.

As the months and years began to pass, I found a sense of security and pride in the accomplishment of working full-time in a job that I loved that provided for the children, despite opposition from some friends and family. I saw along the way that God gave me signs that I was on the right path in life. I continued to work full-time in my nursing career while doing personal training on the side. Fortunately, I was able to marry my two passions of being healthy and inspiring wellness in others. I smiled more now and noticed that I felt more complete.

The children were all growing up, and my son John was due to graduate from high school, so I went with him to look at colleges and technical schools to get clear on what his career path would be. I vividly remember one particularly beautiful morning that we'd spent touring his school of choice and enjoying breakfast and great conversation together afterwards.

I loved having this one-on-one time with my wonderful son. John always smiled, always looked for the good in life and found it. My heart swelled with joy when he was around, and this trip made me realize that I needed to find ways to spend more one-on-one time together.

John was born on a warm April day in 1996, the fourth of my six children. He was handsome, happy, and always the first one to lend a hand to help others in whatever ways that he could. He was also my daredevil; there was always a glimmering sparkle in his eyes. John was always the first to try anything—and the first to be hurt, too. A standing joke in our family was that John could break a bone playing chess. I always thought I needed to wrap him in bubble wrap to protect him.

He loved sports, too, although his thin stature more often than not held him back.

John also had a great passion for riding his motorcycle. He took the required safety course in preparation for getting his license, and I was proud of how responsible he always was. As he grew into a strong young man, John was filled with hopes and dreams, and watching him walk his talk made my heart sing.

In the middle of May 2014, John asked if I would give him a few dollars so he could take his girlfriend out to dinner and see a movie. Since he always helped me, even without being asked, I gladly gave him more than he had requested.

When he returned home, John texted me about the movie, *Heaven Is for Real*, and told me, "You have to see it, Mom!" In retrospect, what a powerful last film that was for him to see, and want me to see it, too. Looking back, I know it was the first sign of things to come.

Earlier in May, my son showed up at my door with a dozen purple roses for Mother's Day. He hid them behind his back as he entered my office, and with a sheepish grin he announced, "Happy Mother's Day, my beautiful mother!" I choked back tears as I stood to hug him and tell him how much I loved him.

By Memorial Day weekend, the roses had withered, and as I went to throw them into the garbage, I had the strongest sensation to save and press one of the flowers. *That's silly*, I thought. *They're already dead. John always buys me flowers. I can save the next one.* And I threw them away. Looking back, I see this as the second sign of John's upcoming passing, but I certainly didn't see it that way at the time.

May 26, 2014, was a beautiful, warm and sunny Memorial Day. I was scheduled to work a daylight shift but traded another nurse and worked her evening shift instead. In the early morning, I woke up and went shopping to pick up a few last-minute groceries.

By the time I returned home, John had already left to spend the day with some friends. The rest of us had an early afternoon cookout, then I left for work, so I didn't see John that day at all.

At 7:30 p.m., I had just returned from break when my phone rang. I remember so clearly the words from my oldest son, Vincent: "Mom, can you leave work now? John was in an accident and he's not breathing." I also clearly remember the feeling; it was suddenly cold, empty, and hollow. Everything was echoing, and I went numb.

My life and world changed in an instant some moments later when John's father called with words no parent ever wants to hear: "I'm here, Michelle. I'm sorry. He didn't make it."

*How can someone so young and so full of life be gone all of a sudden like that? Isn't dying for the elderly and sick? How can life be so unfair?* Yes, I had all of these questions and more. My work friends surrounded me, but their words made no sense in my ears. I seemed to be frozen in time while I sat there, stunned. Then suddenly, I heard my son, from behind me, clearly say, *I'm so sorry, Mom. I love you so much.*

I looked for him all around, but I could not see him, and I knew then that it was all true. My heart shattered into pieces as I sat with my friends, sobbing. In a flash, the only life I ever knew was gone. I felt like I wanted to scream, but no sound would come out. I wanted to hit something badly, but I knew even that wouldn't make me feel better. Mostly, I felt like dying, and I was sure I was dying inside.

The day following John's accident, our church family reached out to have a candlelight memorial Mass for him, followed by a gathering with food, in order to give the children an outlet for their grief. When they told me of their desire, I agreed to it. There was a warm, soothing rain in the air that day. We went to church and arrived just before Mass was to begin.

As we entered, I couldn't believe what I was seeing—only one pew was empty, and it had been saved for our family. People were standing along the walls and around the entire perimeter of the church. The Mass was so beautiful, and as the youth choir from John's high school sang, I could tell they were singing straight from their broken hearts.

The news and media were all around, as they had been since John had passed. John's friends had brought his Jeep to the church before the prayer vigil, and the media captured an amazing photo of the Jeep parked in front of the church, with a huge vivid rainbow lighting up the sky in the background. That was my divine signal that John had made it safely home.

Our community, family, and friends were around us all week, with literally hundreds of people at my house daily. They saw to it that we never ran out of food or drinks, and the community really surprised me with all the gifts of love they so graciously gave. I hadn't realized what an impact my son had on people, but now it was undeniably evident to me—and although I was completely heartbroken, I felt proud of my beautiful son.

I found out some time later that on that Memorial Day, John had slept in and missed going with his longtime girlfriend, Taylor, to a family picnic, so he opted instead to spend the day with his childhood friends, at the creek near our house. After first spending some time with his little brother Michael, John hopped on his motorcycle and rode to the creek, while his friends all followed in their cars. On the return home John lost control of his motorcycle. Trying to jump off, his chest hit the handlebar, breaking a rib that severed his aorta. He was gone in an instant.

I often think back and wonder, *What if John hadn't slept in that day?* or *What if I hadn't traded shifts?* I know it doesn't really matter, and that this thinking won't do me any good. Still, sometimes I can't help but wonder.

As a personal trainer, I know what the body needs to feel good, but this grief was a whole new monster that I wasn't quite sure how to handle. I had dabbled in running in the past, but not to the extent I was about to endeavor.

One of my good friends, Marc, really helped save me that summer—showing up almost every day, insisting that I go running with him. Most days I didn't even want to get out of bed. Although I only saw darkness and felt empty inside, I went.

Some days we ran two miles, some days eight. Most days I cried, screamed, and begged for my son to come back. As I ran, however, I began to notice the birds, wildlife, and flowers. I smelled the air and looked up at the sky, seeking the meaning to life, and I thought about how fragile and delicate life truly is, and how people are here and then gone in what seems like an instant.

These days and these runs brought purpose to my life again, and in retrospect, they brought me *life* again. I knew that on days I didn't run, I would cry all day long. Conversely, on days that I did run, while still heartbroken, I found myself more aware of the kindness, peace, and love that is in this world. So, it became my mission to run every day, to take the breaths that John could no longer take, and I made a conscious choice to live for my son.

My friend Kathy is a massage therapist and Reiki practitioner. She called one day and asked me to come see her. When I got there, she gave me a much-needed massage and it was the first bit of relaxation I'd had in quite some time. As I was gradually able to relax with her, my sealed heart began slowly to open.

After Kathy finished massaging me and giving me Reiki, she left the room. When I got dressed and went to see her in her office, she sat silently at first for a minute. *Did John come through to her?* I wondered. I don't trust easily, and I am skeptical most of the time—you have to have proof to make me believe that something is actually real.

When Kathy said, "He was always the one to cuddle with you," it took away my breath and I slumped down in the chair because I knew, without a doubt, he'd come through. When John passed, I said to his lifeless body, "I won't believe anyone is hearing you unless they use the word 'cuddle' when they talk." My favorite nickname for John had been "Cuddlebutt," chosen for the many days of his youth that he'd spent cuddling with me. He was such a Cuddlebutt that he'd often snuggle up in my lap while I ate breakfast just so he could be near me.

Kathy said that John kept saying, *I'm sorry*, and when I asked her why he was sorry, that it was an accident and not his fault, she replied, "He's so sorry for making you cry. He sees you crying a lot." Then I remembered that when John was a baby, if I even pretended to cry, his eyes would well up and large tears would roll down his adorable cheeks. I knew then that our bond was quite special and that he hated to see me cry.

About two weeks after John passed, my friend Leighanne went to see an Angel Reader team regarding her own life. Angel Readings are purported to be sessions where the psychic or medium is used to deliver a message from angels, archangels, or departed loved ones. However, when Leighanne sat down for her session, the readers said that the spirit of a young man who had recently died in a motorcycle accident had followed Leighanne into their office—and proceeded to channel my son! Unsure if I could handle what was told to her, Leighanne chose not to reveal this to me until a few months later, when she gave me the audio recording.

Listening to it, I learned that my son had orchestrated her being called there that day since they had a last-minute cancellation, and also arranged for her to have free time so she could go. John told the reader of his passing, and although no one there knew the specifics, they were certain it would all make perfect sense to me—and it did.

The Angel Reader asked, "Who is Shawn Michael?" My son's name is John Michael. John kept repeating to the Angel Reader, *This [accident] just happened.* He wanted her to tell me that he wasn't alone, and—astonishingly—John revealed who he was with by name: *Louise* (my grandmother), *Frank* (his great-grandfather), *Tom* (his father's best friend), *Pap* (my grandfather), and his *dad's dad*. John kept saying, *I'm so sorry*, just like he did at my work the day he passed away.

He went on to say that he'd gone the wrong way—*I should have gone the other way*—and confirmed that he lost control of his motorcycle. He told how his grandfather *pulled me up* and that the angels allowed him to walk back and forth through a big tunnel of light.

He said things had been prearranged in his life, what was to be and what not to be; that his father and I set his scheduled and God-appointed time. He said that even though I didn't have time to prepare for his funeral, I did a *great job*. He also said, *That's my mom* (something he always used to say to me, or about me to others). *That's my mom.*

There are a few monumental times for a grieving parent: birthdays, Angelversaries, and changing of the seasons. The first change of season from summer to fall was really tough. It was a reminder not only that there is an ending to things, but also that life goes on. I wanted to shout from the rooftops, "Why is everyone going on when my son *can't?*" The grief of a mother's love. My heart shattered into a million pieces every time I would think about it.

This is what we face every day, but I hold on to God's promise of reuniting us one day when the time is right. The leaves on the ground remind me of life and death, how we are all here "for a season" and that seasons go by so quickly.

Don't waste your season doing the wrong things or sitting back and waiting for life to make you happy. Life is what we make of it. Enjoy today and hold yesterday in your heart, because we never know what tomorrow will bring.

After John passed I was given a gift of a daily devotional reader that has proven invaluable to me. I read it every morning, in the quiet hours when I can pray, think, and feel. Emotions come in strong at times and often with no advance notice. I just feel them and allow myself to be with them.

I remember the good times that I was gifted with my son John, and they are treasures. I've learned to look at the beauty in life. I came to a deep understanding of appreciating every day for what it is—the beauty along with the darkness. This road of life is filled with many bumps, twists, and turns. We need to ride it all out, stay positive, and find our passion. I no longer date things or pay attention to time frames. Things either happened *before* John passed or *after*. I couldn't tell you what year, because my brain no longer processes things that way.

A few weeks before John passed, he and I started a project to stain the kitchen cabinets here at the house that was not yet completed by the time of the accident. I had dabbled with it through the years, but just never had the heart to finish the project without him.

One day in 2018, I woke up early, gathered the supplies, and completed staining the cabinets, with love, to honor my son. It was for him that I finished the project. As soon as I pulled up the last bit of tape, the song "I'll Be Seeing You" came on the radio. I knew this was no coincidence, that it was a sign from my son. I sank down in the chair and wept. John was watching me and was proud of me for finishing what the two of us had begun together. He wanted me to know we will see each other again.

The signs are always there; keep your heart and your eyes open. You will know when it's a sign meant for you.

I didn't want to be a grieving parent, a member of this exclusive club, and I would do anything to change this path I've been forced to walk on. But here I am, through no choice of my own, trying to find my way—dealing with emotions that seem to come out of nowhere, closing my eyes to feel his hug, his kiss, or hear him speak.

I have no more tomorrows with John; I only have memories. I get the feeling now that closure is something I will never achieve, but finding a way to walk with grace and honor my son's memory is what's always in the forefront of my mind.

My children and I honor John each year with a Memorial Day picnic where we gather and spend time remembering. This day is usually highlighted with a balloon release or a lantern release, sending our love up to heaven, hoping John sees them and smiles down on us. We also make a video clip each year compiled of pictures or videos the kids have. We take turns. It's our way to honor John's memory and each express how we saw him when he was alive.

If I had my way, no other parent would ever walk this painful path filled with grief. Most days I don't know where to go or what to do next. I live in the moment . . . but I guess the key words there are *I live*. I live to honor my son, I live to love my children, I live to show others love, and I live to be happy and laugh, as my John so often did. I live . . . until

I see my son again. And when I do, he will get the biggest hug and kiss ever from his mom, who loves him with all of her heart.

That's my Cuddlebutt. I miss you and love you forever.

\* \* \*

**Michelle Barbuto** is a mother, nurse, and health/wellness advocate. She says, "I am your neighbor, your sister, your daughter, your friend. I am a survivor, a grieving mom, a believer. I live each day to the fullest to honor my son's memory until we are reunited. Not all days are easy, but with God, all days are possible."

## • 11 •

# Living the Dream

## By Tim deZarn

*Travis*

$\mathscr{T}$ravis Lucas deZarn was born October 17, 1989. Right in the middle of his Cesarean delivery, my wife Gail shouted, "I think I just felt an earthquake!" Sure enough, the deadly San Francisco earthquake, with a magnitude of 6.9, had just hit. And so, Travis came in with a bang. He popped out of the womb emanating light, just like his mom, and I loved him with all my heart from the start.

In the first couple weeks of Travis's life, I told Gail, "I'm so lucky to have you. I could never do this by myself." Uncharacteristically, she snapped back, "Don't *ever* say that again! If you had to raise this baby by yourself, you could."

That December, when Travis was two months old, we decided to travel back to Ohio, to show off our precious son to our families. Gail wanted some extra time with her mom because she felt it might be their last Christmas together, so she and Travis flew in ahead of me and I followed a few days later. After spending Christmas with Gail's parents in Cleveland, we drove to Cincinnati to visit mine. We stayed there a few days, before heading back to Cleveland to catch our flight home.

On the way, Gail asked, "Hey, Tim, remember when that counselor asked what we'd do if we had to leave each other for a job or some other reason, that we'd have to do it with full love in order to get through it? Like in order to let each other go, we'd have to be *that* much in love?"

"Yeah, I remember," I said.

Gail looked at me, with her beautiful, penetrating blue eyes, and said, "I think we're there, aren't we?"

"Yes, I love you that much."

Four days later, Gail was dead. She'd gotten sick with what the doctor first thought was the flu, but it was viral hemorrhagic pneumonia that killed her within forty-eight hours.

Over the months that followed, I often thought about suicide and taking my son along with me, but I knew in my heart *that* decision wasn't mine to make. One night, while I was rocking Travis in my arms, I was singing a song to Gail that I had written for her after she died. When I looked down at Travis and his bright blue eyes locked on mine, I realized the depth of our love. I shouted to my sister Teresa, who was helping us settle in at the time, "You know that deep love moms talk about?" Through my tears of joy, I cried, "I have it. I do! I *feel* it!" At that moment, I knew I was ready to take care of Travis on my own. And I did. Those were wonderful times, bonding with each other and sharing in every moment.

That spring, "Laurie," an old friend of ours, came back into my life and we began dating long distance. Spending time with Laurie brought me back to a conversation Gail and I had when she was pregnant with Travis. *If anything happens to me, at least Laurie will be there for you.*

I guess I took this literally, because Laurie moved in the following fall. Two years later, Laurie and I had a horrible breakup, and I didn't want her to see Travis anymore. But I consulted a child psychologist to make sure I was doing the right thing. We talked about whether or not a child remembers relationships formed at Travis's age, and I'll never forget his response: "We don't know for sure, but if this woman loves him, can a child ever have too much love?"

Shortly after that, I woke up out of a dead sleep, paralyzed. A presence was clamped around me, not letting me release from its grasp.

Gail's voice whispered, *Lie still. Lie still.*

"Gail?" I asked, wanting to make sure it was her.

*Yes,* she said, *lie still. I don't have much time. You can't use Travis against Laurie. You can't do that. I'm sorry, I have to go now. I love you.*

And she was gone. I leapt up out of bed and slapped myself on the face. *It was real.* It was clear I had to allow Laurie to see Travis.

I knew I was the marrying type, but after Laurie, I decided there wouldn't be anyone else for a while. Travis was all I needed, and we were inseparable. He was my buddy, my world, my everything. Adventures abounded. We played in the park, the pool—I even took him to people's houses, where he was always the life of the party. At the zoo, Travis loved to ride on my shoulders so he could see all the animals he loved. He'd hold my head tightly, laugh and giggle real loud. And just as I'd take him down off my shoulders, he'd squeeze me tight, hold my cheeks in his little hands, look me in the eyes, and say, "I love you, Daddy. I love you so much!"

Ours was a love that was beyond anything I'd ever felt before. It was a depth of love I never knew possible. As Travis grew, I taught him everything I could. But as it turned out, Travis was the real teacher all along.

During those early years, we would sometimes fly home to visit family. On one such trip, when Travis was about three or four, he was staring out the plane window at the puffy white clouds and blue sky. I said, "Trav, what are you thinking about?"

He looked at me, then looked out the window again, and said, "I'm just thinking about how much I love everybody in this whole wide universe." I realized in that moment that my beautiful baby was growing into a truly remarkable little boy. I knew he was changing me and that he'd affect other people profoundly. Travis would spread his light and his love to everyone.

A couple years later, I went with a friend to see a stage production of *The Taming of the Shrew.* Every time Bianca walked on stage, the entire audience leaned forward to pay closer attention. The actress who played her was scintillating.

Afterwards, I asked my friend where the woman was who played Bianca, and a stunning, petite blond standing next to me said, "That was me."

I smirked, "Yeah, right." On stage, Bianca was tall with long brown hair and a true Shakespearean cleavage, and there was no way I believed this was her.

But she said again, "It *was* me!"

"Okay. Well, you're fantastic!"

Afterwards, during dinner at a nearby deli, I was showing my friend a recent picture of Travis when the same actress, Janine Venable, asked inquisitively, "Did you say *Travis*? Can I see that picture?" I handed the photo to her. "Oh my gosh!" she said. "I know this boy. I've watched him grow up for the last four years through his pictures on one of my best friend's refrigerator. She was one of your wife's friends and babysat Travis often."

Everyone was stunned by this supposed coincidence. Aside from her being beautiful, talented, smart, and funny, this definitely seemed meant to be. I felt this was kismet and knew I had to get her number. I didn't think I had much of a chance, though, so I asked if she could help with my résumé, as she'd mentioned during dinner she was good at that sort of thing. Lucky for me, she agreed.

Janine polished my résumé as promised, and I took her to lunch for the help. For the next few weeks, we did a good job keeping it casual, but I knew I wanted to see her more and more. One night, I asked Janine if she wanted to grab a bite together. When it came time to pay the bill, I asked, "So, is this a date? Because if it is, I'm paying for it. If not, we can split the tab."

Janine smiled and said, "It's a date."

And so, the courting began, and Janine quickly became an important part of our lives.

One afternoon, Janine and I took Travis to see a children's play and afterwards the three of us went to lunch. Travis was sitting next to me in a booth; Janine was across the table.

Travis looked up at me, smiling. "So Dad, when are you gonna ask her to marry you?"

I immediately excused myself to the bathroom, knowing full well I was in love with Janine, but scared to death to dive headfirst into this incredible, wonderful water, afraid that I might just drown. But dive we did.

Our love grew, and we enjoyed every single minute together. The two of us. The three of us. It didn't make any difference. We were quickly becoming one.

Nine months after that lunch, I proposed to Janine, and a year later, on October 12, 1996, we had an elegant wedding and recited our vows with a tuxedo-clad, seven-year-old Travis standing with us. We became a family that day, and Janine, Travis's mother.

Janine was so dedicated to being Travis's mother, *becoming* Travis's mother, that she insisted on not having a child of our own until this part of our family came together. And it really did. Full of all the trials and tribulations that come with parenting and a new marriage, the strength of the love we shared made our bond grow even stronger as time went by. We were a family, in the truest sense of the word.

We traveled some, mostly to visit family. I coached Travis's teams while Janine was his biggest cheerleader—in every respect. She volunteered at his school and helped with his homework. She loved Travis and guided him in ways that only a mother could. Three years into our marriage, we knew the time was finally right for Travis to have a sibling.

Janine got pregnant fairly quickly, and the three of us awaited the arrival of this new baby with happy anticipation. We were overwhelmed with joy when on May 23, 2000, our beautiful daughter Emma was born. That special love I felt for Travis was multiplied with the birth of my baby girl. Travis was ten, and he bonded with his sister instantly. He loved Emma with his whole heart and soul. Janine and Emma went to all of Travis's Little League games. And ever the doting big brother, Travis went to Emma's preschool to help out and meet all her friends.

In high school, Travis played lacrosse after he and two buddies started a team in their freshman year. Their first two years were rough, but by their senior year, they were in the top ten in Southern California. Travis loved the game and became well known for it. Following in his parents' footsteps, he also liked to dance and sing and act, and did it all with great enthusiasm and passion.

When Gail died, my hopes of having a family like this died with her. But now, since Janine, so many wonderful things were happening, I could hardly believe it. We were a family, the four of us. We loved each other so much and we were happy. We also had a dog and two cats, and for the next seven years, life was the one I'd always dreamed of.

In early August of 2007, Travis came to me and said, "Dad, there's something wrong. I stopped dreaming. I don't have dreams at night anymore, or anything. I'm really afraid, Dad. I think I might die."

I explained to him that there are periods in people's lives where sometimes they don't dream, and that he shouldn't worry about it too much.

A couple weeks later, he approached me again. "Hey, Dad, I figured out why I'm not dreaming anymore."

"Yeah, why?"

"Because I'm *living the dream*," Travis said.

There it was again, his indomitable spirit, which reminded me that I was living the dream, too. This gave me some peace of mind, but I was still worried.

Later in September, Travis came to me again and said, "Dad, I'm really afraid I'm going to die. I'm really afraid."

Immediately, I thought of Gail, but I didn't share that with him nor with anyone, afraid that if I did, it could happen. Instead I said, "Oh, that's not going to happen, son. It's rare that teenagers die."

Then he reminded me that three friends of his had died during high school—from a car wreck, a rare heart malfunction, and suicide, respectively. Even though this was scaring me, I tried just to brush it off.

"You'd better get real, Dad. Teenagers die!" Clearly, he was upset.

Later that month, just as Travis was settling in at Cal State Long Beach, his maternal grandfather died, so he and I flew back for the funeral. This was the first time Travis had been to Cleveland as a young adult, and he got to meet a lot of cousins he hadn't known. He enjoyed his time with them immensely and vice versa.

At the gravesite of both his grandparents, Gail's grave was there, too. Travis had never seen his mom's burial site, and it affected him deeply. He fell to his knees, touching the headstone, and started to sob. I placed my hand firmly on his back to let him know I was there, and also to let him experience what I knew was one of the most heart-wrenching times of his life.

Then Travis pointed to the words on Gail's headstone and said, "If I die, Dad, I want this on my headstone."

"You're not going to die," I said, in a vain attempt to reassure myself more than him. But I never forgot what he said.

After that, Travis and I separated from the rest of the mourners and walked down to the shores of Lake Erie, nearby. We skipped rocks and talked about how vast the lake looked and about many other things I can no longer recall.

What I can remember, though, is the urgency in Travis's voice when he suddenly demanded we leave. "We need to get out of here *now*! There's too much death here. I'm really afraid I'm going to die!"

"You're not going to die," I said, "and our flight leaves tomorrow morning."

Travis was adamant. "No, Dad. *Now!*"

So, we returned to the house and packed up, said our good-byes, and went to the airport, but all the planes were grounded due to inclement weather, so we went back to his cousins' house and spent the night.

We flew home the next morning, and Travis drove back to college. Shortly thereafter, he called my sister, with whom he'd always been close, and said, "Hey, Aunt Teresa, I think I'm going to like college. I'm doing okay now." When Teresa telephoned and told me what Travis had said, I finally stopped worrying about him.

Our family celebrated Travis's eighteenth birthday together on October 17. We hadn't thought he'd be driving up from Long Beach, but he called last minute to say he was looking forward to his favorite birthday dinner of sloppy joes, potato chips, and coleslaw, with pumpkin pie.

About a week later, Travis's car was acting up, so we swapped cars—my Honda Acura for his old Volvo. Then, on November 2, Travis came up for a date with his girlfriend, Hannah, and to see Emma's soccer game the following day. After the game we were walking across the fields to switch cars when Travis said, "Hey, Dad, you think I could keep your car for tonight? I'm seeing Hannah and I don't want to drive my old car." I had an inkling not to give him my car, but Travis gave me his signature smile and I couldn't say no.

We continued walking together across the field, just as we had done for years, talking about this and that. He was going off to hang with his friends and take Hannah out, so we hugged, like always, and I jokingly made him kiss me good-bye.

Later that night, at around midnight, I started worrying because I hadn't heard from Travis since we'd walked off the field that morning. Whether he was going back to campus, staying at a friend's, or coming home to sleep, Travis always, *always* called.

I tried calling him, calling his friends, and reached no one. By 1:30 a.m., I was in a panic. I woke Janine and said, "Something's wrong. Something's happened. Travis hasn't called. Something's wrong!"

Janine assured me that everything was probably fine, which was usually true, and I was trying my best to believe her. I couldn't sleep, though, so I paced, talked to myself, and prayed and cried outside.

Later, I woke my wife again. I was sure that Travis's obsessive prediction of death had come true, but I prayed that if something had happened, at least he was still alive.

The knock on our front door came around 3:00 a.m. I looked out our window and screamed, "Janine! Janine! Come here!" I opened the door and yelled to the policemen standing on our front porch, "Is my son dead?! Is my son *dead*?!" They kept asking me questions. And all I could do was ask over and over if my son was dead.

Finally somebody answered, "Your son has been in a car accident." I yelled again, "Is he dead?!" Finally, the one cop answered. "Your son did not survive."

I collapsed to the floor and crawled on my hands and knees through the house, outside, to the back—screaming, crying, uttering sounds I never knew were inside me. I ran into the shed and broke everything I could. Then I ran down the driveway, where I purposefully hurled my body into the wooden fence, knocking it down, desperately trying to feel some kind of pain other than this horrific, excruciating pain I had never felt before in my life.

Word of Travis's accident spread quickly, and the Monday after his death, I was bolstered by the support of my friends from a twelve-step recovery program of which I'm a member. I was in a meeting by noon that day, and this continued for the next month. They kept showing up, insisting I go with them to meetings. So I went. Every single day. Even after twenty-three years of sobriety, I needed to be around people like me, who thought like me, so I wouldn't do some-thing I shouldn't.

I soon learned that as Travis was leaving Hannah's house around 11:30, he had warned the family, "If you go back out, be careful. It's really foggy outside tonight." So, he knew the driving conditions and he knew the streets. But at one of the steepest and curviest parts of the road, Travis was hit by a woman almost head-on and died instantly.

Suddenly, our house was packed with friends and strangers alike. One couple came to see us that I had only met one time before—Jess and Tia. Travis was close with them and their four daughters. They were kind enough to bring us material on grief recovery, which I put aside to read later. They asked if there was anything they could do. When I said no, Tia asked, "Are you sure? Anything, anything at all?"

I wasn't sure I could find a big enough place for Travis's memorial, so they offered their gorgeous home in the Palisades with a big, beautiful backyard that overlooks the ocean. We were so very grateful.

Jess and Tia not only hosted the over five hundred friends and relatives who came to Travis's memorial, but they insisted that we not pay for anything. They even flew over a dozen family members to California, who otherwise would never have been able to make it. They brought our family to us, to Travis, and we will never forget their extraordinary kindness and generosity.

If a memorial could ever be perfect, Travis's was. It was joyous and painful, full of laughter and tears. People shared wonderful things I never knew about my son, and I also heard of a few shenanigans that reminded me of myself when I was his age. Apparently, he loved breaking into people's empty pools to skateboard, and once he even got in trouble with the police. Travis took off running, with his two friends, and got away. Travis was no angel and caused his fair share of trouble—I guess like most other teenagers do.

At the end of the memorial, doves were released. They flew out over the ocean, and as they flew back around east, one dove stopped and landed in a tree, right in the backyard where we all were gathered. As it happened, Jess told me that Travis liked to sit under that tree and gaze out at the ocean, just below where the dove was now quietly perched.

The dove remained there for a good while. Then, as people were starting to leave, we watched it fly away from the tree, out toward the ocean. But it didn't turn around like the others had. Instead, it kept flying and flying, toward the horizon, until we could no longer see it. It vanished up into the horizon.

In the days, weeks, and months following Travis's memorial, the pain was so horrible, and I felt so useless. I suffered paralyzing post-traumatic stress disorder and had an overwhelming fear of abandonment. It was during the first six months that I seriously contemplated killing myself, and I even put myself in some dangerous situations. But giving up was *not* in my blood. Even more important, I knew I had a seven-year-old daughter and a wife who loved me—although I felt I wasn't much good to Emma as a father, nor to Janine as a husband—and I loved them both with all my heart, so I stayed.

I've recently gotten to know Travis's high school writing teacher. This past year, he spoke at Travis's twenty-ninth birthday celebration. He said, "Over the years, I've taught thousands of kids, but there's only a handful I remember distinctly—and Travis I will never, ever forget. He was a hardworking student, and when he came into the room, albeit a little late, he brought so much light and laughter. As far as I was concerned, Travis could pretty much do whatever he wanted. He truly enriched my life."

Travis always wanted to wear the number 22 on his lacrosse jersey (not sure why), and one of his teachers gave me a letter to be read at his memorial, which says, in part,

> Your lacrosse number has many significances. I think it's only right that the number 22 symbolizes charisma and a force of nature. Your charisma and charm allowed you to be a true force of nature. Both on and off the field. It was great seeing your teammates and friends pass your jersey around the other day. They were so proud of your battle wounds on the field, as this showed your passion and utter respect for your teammates. This is also symbolic in your jersey number, 22, as 22 represents universal love. . . . Travis, we thank you for the creativity and warmth you brought with your charm and charisma, your reassurance, encouragement and laughs you brought with your smile and above all, for the light of 500 suns that radiated within your heart.

Travis was the only player at Palisades High to ever wear 22. After he died, the school permanently retired the number.

After Travis died, 22s started showing up everywhere. A friend picked up an order of food for a crew of people at the house and was given a numbered placard as he waited, 22. From that point on, 22 was everywhere—and I mean *everywhere*—and in the oddest of places, too.

Once, I was in Canada shooting a movie, and on a day off, I went on a run in a nearby park. As I came to a finish, I arrived at a large empty lot where I stopped to stretch for a few moments and, as I often did, began talking out loud to Travis. "Come on, Travis, give me a sign that you're with me. Come on!"

As I started across the lot, there were no delineated spaces anywhere. But, as I walked toward the far end of it, there was *one* space with *one* number—22. No numbers anywhere else. Just this one, 22.

Sometime shortly after we lost Travis, I was walking down a street in Santa Monica when I noticed this huge outdoor staircase and thought they must be "the stairs" I'd heard so many people speak of around town.

I climbed them, and it was tough. So, I made the decision right then and there that this would be my new place for exercise, my *church*. My first goal was to climb the steps twenty-two times, of course. It took me a while, but I did it. Then, on my fifty-sixth birthday, I decided to match my age, and climb them fifty-six times. Travis's birthday was approaching on October 17, so I decided to hold a fund-raiser for a scholarship in his name. I added what would have been his age, nineteen, to mine and called on a lot of people to join me in raising money.

On the day of Travis's birthday, I managed to complete all seventy-five trips on the stairs, and I had challenged others to complete as many as they could during the time it would take me to climb mine. We raised a good amount of seed money for the Travis deZarn Scholarship, which is still awarded each year to the most inspirational senior player on the Palisades High lacrosse team.

During the early years after Travis's death, Janine and I found great help in our grief recovery group at griefHaven, an organization that helps parents who have had a child die. Through them, we learned that people grieve in different ways. Janine tended to grieve privately, and told me later she had to, because she felt she had to be the one to keep our family together—and she certainly did.

I talked about Travis dying with everybody I met. I even wore T-shirts with a picture of Travis, along with his birth and death dates, and this was both difficult and freeing. Dozens of people saw my T-shirt and shared with me how their child had died, or how their relative or friend's child had died. My shirt gave them permission to tell me their stories, and me to tell mine, so it was healing for everyone.

Travis wasn't the best, the biggest, or the fastest on the lacrosse field, but whenever he got knocked down, he never stayed on the ground long—and he'd always bounce back up, grinning from ear to ear. So, that's what I did on those stairs, and that, along with griefHaven, got me to the other side of the horrible sorrow. Climbing those stairs helped save me because it affirmed, for me, that I was choosing to live life again.

During times of my deepest grief, an older man named Kenny would sometimes approach me at the end of our twelve-step meetings.

I'd have just finished crying and yelling about Travis, and he'd tap me in the middle of my chest, near my heart, and whisper, "Unexpected inner resource, kid. Unexpected inner resource." Then he'd gently touch my cheek, smile, and walk away.

I'll never forget that guy. He was right about the unexpected inner resource. I haven't drank, and I haven't purposefully hurt anyone. I've been a dad to my daughter Emma and a husband to my wife Janine.

Because I have endured multiple deaths, the fear of abandonment still comes up on occasion, like when someone is late to meet me or fails to show up at all, and I jump to the worst-possible-case scenario in my mind. But I'm grateful it's not nearly as bad as it used to be.

In 2017, Janine and I starred in *Surrender*, a play that explores a couple's search for meaning and the power of their love for each other after the death of their child. As tough as it was emotionally to go where our roles demanded, doing so brought us to a deeper level of healing and strengthened our marriage even more.

Years ago, when Gail and I were still in New York, someone said something demeaning to her that brought her to tears. I was bent on revenge, and when I took off with the intention of getting it, Gail tried to stop me. I asked, "What would *your God* have me do?"

"I don't know what 'my God' would have you do," she yelled back, "but I do know what *love* would do. Why don't you think about that?!"

Love has me staying here in this world with my beautiful family, Janine and Emma, trying each day to do what *love* would have me do. I fail often at these pursuits, but—just as Travis taught me—when you get knocked down, you've got to bounce back up with a smile and enjoy the rest of the game.

I still see that wide-eyed Cheshire-cat grin of my son's as he laughs at me, and with me. I feel his undying spirit around me, alive in my heart—forever. I am grateful for every second of the eighteen years Travis and I had together, and I'd do it all over again, even if it ended the same way.

So, I keep *living the dream.*

\* \* \*

**Tim deZarn** is a multi-award-winning actor of stage and screen. He has appeared in over 130 TV and film productions, as well as dozens of stage plays. He graduated from the University of Cincinnati with a degree in business and education, and after teaching high school and coaching football, he dabbled in real estate, insurance, and the law, before devoting himself completely to acting. Tim loves working out, and when he's not busy with his family or involved in community service, he can often be found on those stairs in Santa Monica that he credits with helping him through his grief recovery. Tim lives with his wife, Janine, and their eighteen-year-old daughter, Emma, in Culver City, California, which has been their home for the past twenty-one years.

# Embracing Love and Survival

## By *Tamara Gabriel*

*Tamara and Janna*

The year was 1997. I was thirty-three, my son Ryan was eleven, and my daughter Janna was nine. I'm a twin, and oddly enough, both of my children were born on our birthday. I've always loved life and strived to live it to the fullest. I tried to be a good person and live by the values I had been taught in my church, but I sometimes fell short of the mark. I always had a love of God, though, and perfect or not, I knew I deserved to be happy.

After suffering through more than my fair share of abuse, I left my husband in March of 1997, because I didn't want my kids to think ours was what a marriage should look like. It didn't take long for me to adjust to being a single mom, and for the first time I felt happy living my life the way I wanted to. My family, however, disapproved and we had only sporadic contact. My dad is an Eastern Orthodox priest, and my parents did not understand all that I had been through or why I had to take my children and leave. They were worried about what people would say (the divorce) and were harshly critical and judgmental.

I had recently graduated from massage therapy school and was beginning to live my life with a sense of peace, serenity, and calm. My son, however, was quite difficult—he had been diagnosed in preschool with emotional problems, as well as an attachment disorder. Although quite brilliant, as he got older, Ryan had his own set of emotional challenges that included a diagnosis of conduct disorder.

Ryan had great difficulties getting along with his high-energy sister, Janna, who had been diagnosed with attention deficit hyperactivity disorder (ADHD) at age seven. Even though they had trouble getting along, Janna was always very loving towards her brother. Sometimes, I looked at her and thought, *She's the only thing I've done right in my life.*

Not understanding the situation, my family believed I was the problem and that my kids were perfect angels, but they weren't on the other end of the phone when the school called to tell me the various challenges my kids were dealing with. Many people, including Ryan, were angry with me for leaving my husband, even though I knew it was ultimately better for the kids and me.

My mom had offered to take Ryan over the Fourth of July holiday weekend, and I welcomed the break. Ryan deserved to have some special time with his grandparents, and I was looking forward to having alone time with Janna.

We were invited to spend the day at a friend's, and on the way stopped at a restaurant to grab a quick bite to eat. Janna had been craving pancakes and sausage, so I treated her to the hearty, delicious breakfast she had been hoping for. We ran some quick errands, then headed down the road towards my friend's house.

Although the sun was shining, a small rain shower had fallen on the newly paved roads, causing them to be slick. We were on a one-lane highway, speed limit of fifty-five, on the back roads in Upstate New York. Janna was enjoying some of her favorite candies, and she and I laughed as she told me jokes—she was so darn funny.

Feeling so full of happiness, I looked at my daughter and smiled. "When was the last time I told you I love you?"

"Last year," she said. "Just kidding, Mom." And those are the last words that I remember.

The next thing I knew, an EMT named Pete was knocking on my window, telling me we'd been in an accident. I'd met Pete years ago and had a great deal of admiration for his work as a paramedic, and had often joked, "If I ever get in an accident, I want you to be there." So, when I saw him standing outside my window, I started yelling, "Hey, Pete! It's me! I've had an accident and you're here!"

I looked over and saw my daughter slumped over and thought that we'd pulled over to take a nap. But somehow, I was on the other side of the road, and I felt very confused and disoriented. I looked down and saw Janna's clothes on the floorboard and lost it, especially when I was told that they were taking her by helicopter to the trauma hospital.

I was transported by life squad to the local hospital, but Janna needed the Jaws of Life to be removed from the wreckage. Not understanding what happened, I was in quite a panic. About a week or so later I read in the paper that my car had hydroplaned and slammed into another car coming in the opposite direction, and I had lost consciousness upon impact. Though later I turned to booze in an attempt to drown my grief and shut out this terrible trauma, that day I had not been drinking at all.

When I arrived at the hospital, I called my friend Christa to be with me and told her to call Janna's dad and ask him to go to the trauma hospital to be with her. She suffered head trauma and a broken pelvis. I had a concussion, broken nose, and some internal bleeding. I didn't care about my injuries, though. I only wanted to see my baby girl. While in the ER, I phoned the trauma hospital that Janna had been airlifted to and learned from the head nurse that she was in serious, but stable, condition. After hanging up, I was given some medicine to calm me and make me sleep.

The next morning, I left against medical advice to see my daughter at the other hospital. By the time I arrived at the Pediatric Intensive Care Unit, some of my family members were there and my husband's family was there, too. But no one expressed any compassion for me, and the welcome from everyone was pretty much superficial. There was a chill towards me from both sides of the family, but all I cared about was my daughter. She was on life support, and I was told from the start that there wasn't much hope that she'd survive.

Thankfully, I have always believed in God and the power of prayer, and while in school for massage, I had started my own spiritual journey, reading books by Louise Hay, Wayne Dyer, Marianne Williamson, and others. I believe we are all here to learn lessons, and I thought mine was to take care of and love my children no matter what.

After six long, torturous days a friend, who is a psychic, came to visit and told me that Janna was gone. I rushed to the hospital, lay by her bedside, and told my precious daughter good-bye, and when her dad came in, I asked that he do the same. I went outside and proceeded to wail on the front lawn of the hospital, rolling around, not caring about anything except releasing the excruciating pain that was inside me.

Janna left this earth the next morning. I had gotten a phone call from the hospital that they were giving her CPR and that she may be gone by the time I got back there. And she was.

I was weak, beat up, and feeling helpless, and all I wanted to do was to lie down and die with her. I vowed to never forgive myself for killing the one person I knew who had always loved me. When I tried making sense of what happened, I was sure I was being punished for leaving my marriage.

I had been seeing a therapist since I left my husband and increased my sessions to twice a week after Janna died, to help me cope with my loss and also the post-traumatic stress disorder (PTSD) from the car accident. I started seeing the therapist more often—and drinking more and more to deal with my horrible life. I wasn't used to crying so much and feeling so bad all the time.

Not only had I lost Janna, but I no longer had a family that cared about me. In their eyes, I brought shame to the family. Still mad at me for leaving my husband, they may have thought that I deserved this. I hated myself and thought, *Why should I stay alive when people hate me so much?* I was trying to drink myself to death and woke up every morning pissed off that I was still living.

Each day I'd put on nice clothes because Janna always liked when I looked pretty, only to end up on my couch, doing nothing all day. I wasn't eating and was constantly nauseous from all the trauma.

Ryan became so difficult that we had to go into counseling because he was very abusive towards me. The therapist warned, "If he keeps living with you, he will learn to continue to abuse women." I ended up letting my ex-husband take him.

Now all alone, I was left to deal with multiple autoimmune diseases, no car, no money, divorce, death, and trying to survive. I felt like

Job from the Bible story, who had lost everything, and I hoped that if I could keep my faith, my life would eventually be restored tenfold.

I had always believed in love and had recently read an article by Elisabeth Kübler-Ross that stated that the only reason we are here is to learn unconditional love, forgiveness, and compassion. Those words touched my soul, and I knew that God was working in my life by sending me messages, or maybe they were from Janna.

I cried out, screaming in my apartment, that if God helped me get through this, I would help as many people as I could so that my daughter's death would not be in vain. This was right around the time of my and my twin's birthday, and also my children's. No one from my family called me, and I felt really alone, like nobody even cared if I lived or died. I sat feeling hurt and sorry for myself for a while, but then, in the back of my head I heard my mom's words from years earlier: *The best revenge is the revenge of having a good life.*

My friend Christa, who had gotten sober a few months earlier, told me I should try going to an Alcoholics Anonymous meeting. She had watched me drink every day since the accident, and I had expressed several times wanting to die. Christa came to check on me often, even though I had been drinking daily, crying to myself on my couch. She took me to a meeting, and after I shared, women came up to me, gave me their numbers, and told me I never had to drink again, no matter what. I got in the car and threw their numbers out the window screaming, "YES, I DO!"

Eight months after Janna's death, Christa insisted I go with her to another meeting. When I did, the members there said to *let us love you until you can love yourself.* I thought, *That will never happen because my own family deserted me and I'm a horrible person who killed my child.* But I kept going to meetings, and I'm happy to say that on March 7, 1998, I took the last drink I ever had.

Louise Hay is one of the authors I had started reading, and she wrote about healing yourself using affirmations. I had begun using them to help me—I would tell myself, *I deserve to be happy* and *I deserve love.* I learned in my recovery that I could be willing to forgive myself, and Elisabeth Kübler-Ross's words became my foundation with which I could rebuild my life. I would heal myself with love, compassion, and forgiveness, not just for me but for all those around me who had turned their backs to me in my times of deepest need.

Throughout my healing I also attended some support groups for parents who lost a child, thinking for some reason I didn't belong there.

I went to therapy twice a week. I read many books on healing and books about life after death by George Anderson and others. My healing journey to rise above my pain and survive to help others became my mission.

When I was just five months sober, I started bringing recovery meetings into my local jail once a week, to take the focus off my own grief by helping others. I would feel better every time I left and was also able to connect with other women, letting them love me and get to know me for who I am. Being around other people was vitally important in ridding me of the shame and guilt that I had about my life and the way I had lived it. I thought to myself, *If I isolate myself, then what everyone said about me is right and I am a piece of crap!*

Shortly after my loss when people turned away from me, I wrote a poem about the importance of hugs:

### If You See Me

If you see me, do not run . . .
I know that talk is not much fun.
I know your hearts are sure to tug,
But all I need is just a hug.

The days are good, the days are bad,
Sometimes I'm happy, sometimes I'm sad.
But just to know that you are there
Is all I need to know you care.

You will see me all over town,
Life goes on all around . . .
I don't know if you know,
I don't know where to go.

I know you're scared and so am I,
So don't be afraid to see me cry.
I see the care in all your eyes,
I feel your sadness in distant good-byes . . .

I know you're glad not to be in my shoes,
It's sure not easy to have my blues.
I am a mom alive and well,
I have a son who's doing swell.

So if you see me, do not run,
I know for sure talk is not fun.
I know your hearts are sure to tug,
But please for Janna, just give me a hug.

Tamara Gabriel, 1997

I was trying to take the fear of grief out of the closet and teach people that they don't have to say anything, but instead can simply give me a hug. After my poem was posted in the local paper, many people approached me saying they'd read it, and then just gave me a hug.

The trauma, guilt, and separation from my family were intense, but I kept putting one foot in front of the other. It was an awful time. I was even hospitalized for a brief period. But I wasn't sick—it was just intense grief that I experienced.

I worked at a substance abuse treatment center in Upstate New York in 2002, and met the psychiatrist and thought, *He's a wonderful man.* I only worked there for a short time because it was so difficult watching some of these young women choose drugs over getting their kids back that I felt compelled to resign. Not long after, though, I returned to the rehab facility with a woman I was helping and was reintroduced to the psychiatrist while I was there. He recommended some homeopathic practitioners to help me with my PTSD symptoms.

I made myself a list of affirmations regarding what I wanted in terms of a healthy partner and realized I needed an equal partner and someone who would be able to handle me. Shortly after that, my therapist remarked that she had noticed how much better I was doing on the homeopathic medication.

I called to thank that wonderful doctor and invite him for dinner— and we've been together ever since! The irony is that everyone (Ryan, my ex-husband, and both families) all said I was the crazy one, and I'm the one who married the psychiatrist! I was learning to accept love and love myself, in ways I'd never imagined, and could finally believe that my daughter's death had a purpose.

After meeting Rich, I was so filled with shame that I was afraid to tell him my story, thinking he would run away. Instead, he told me I am his hero—that I am amazing and strong and should be dead. He said that the fact that I'm still alive after not only losing my child but also being the cause of the accident, plus alienation from my family, is nothing short of a miracle. With his background as a psychiatrist, he marveled at my resilience, saying that the chance of survival is slim to none for a person who had endured the challenges I did.

For some reason, after Janna's death I was drawn to the colors green and purple, not realizing why at first. One day, I had a strong vision of two arms coming together, with one arm green and the other purple. Having studied Reiki, a form of energy healing, I had learned what the colors represent. Green stands for compassion and the heart chakra, and purple for the crown chakra, spirituality and community.

I drew the arms into a symbol I called Healing Hugs and, using that name, started a nonprofit community in 2013 that helps parents who have lost a loved one with funeral-related services or other expenses. It started with a Facebook page that has now grown to over two million followers.

The page posts inspirational healing messages for those who have lost a loved one. I receive messages all the time saying how helpful Healing Hugs is. Soon, I hope to have more programs available for support groups and raise additional funds to help even more people.

I have organized Zumbathons (Zumba marathons) since 2016 and raised about $6,000. The money is used to help parents with funeral expenses, and sometimes groceries, rent, or whatever financial need they present to me.

Through the years I was aware my son used marijuana and didn't know until he was about nineteen that it had progressed to hard drugs. The thought of losing another child terrified me. I used God, prayer, and my affirmations to help me. I got him into treatment and, at age twenty-two, he finally turned a corner. At that time, he came back into my life, and we now have a solid relationship. He has apologized about how he loved hurting me, punishing me, and making me cry. Upset with his past behavior, he said that the thought of treating me badly makes him nauseous. Ryan lives with his girlfriend, has a good job, and is enjoying a much healthier life. Sadly, his dad was not so fortunate and drank himself to death several years ago.

When he died, Ryan and I returned to New York for the funeral. When my ex-husband's mom asked if he could be buried on top of our daughter, I said yes. Compassion and forgiveness were there, and my former mother-in-law even apologized for how she had treated me when Janna died.

My aunt Sharon, who lost her son several years ago—also in a terrible accident—apologized for how horribly the family had treated me, and said she never realized how awful it was until she walked in my shoes. Around that time my parents also came back around and apologized, and I'm grateful we've been able to heal that relationship too. Surprisingly, when my mom apologized for being so awful to me, I told her how grateful I was—it taught me to be strong and independent, and without that challenge I wouldn't be where I am today! I live in Tucson now and so do my parents, and it's wonderful to be in close contact again after so many years of their absence.

Having support, using the tools I've learned in recovery, I seek always to focus on love rather than fear. Marianne Williamson's book *Return to Love* has really helped me put the pieces of my life back together, and even allowed me to finally have a loving relationship. I made a firm decision to get this life right and to heal with love, and survive, so I don't have to learn these lessons all over again.

One of my favorite quotes is from Wayne Dyer: *When you change the way you look at things, the things you look at change.*[1] This philosophy has helped me see things differently in my life today when it comes to other people and situations. I have learned how short life is and how fast it can change. I am back to living my life to the fullest and filling it with as much love as possible. I still volunteer—at the local jail after nineteen years of recovery from alcoholism, and with Donate Life of Arizona, which promotes organ donation. I was able to donate heart valves and corneas from my daughter and I, too, am a recipient of a cadaver bone in my neck due to an injury I suffered in the fatal accident.

I have been in and out of hospitals for various health issues and even suffered a life-threatening illness in 2016, due to hardware that was placed in my neck during spinal surgery. I contracted a bone infection, as well as an abscess on my spine and my brain. But I wasn't afraid and thought, affirmatively, *God's not done with me yet.*

To keep my daughter's memory alive, I'll help almost anyone who asks. When I think back to those days of wanting to die, lying in my cockroach-infested apartment with no hope, and no love, and compare it to my awesome life today surrounded by loved ones and an amazing husband in our gorgeous surroundings, I know that I am taken care of by Janna and God. Every step I take in the good life I have today allows me to forgive myself for believing that I killed my child. It's also a powerful reminder to keep moving forward in forgiveness of myself and others.

A couple of weeks after the fatal crash, I felt compelled to reach out to the twenty-six-year-old driver who had also been involved in the accident. I wanted to tell him I didn't blame him for the collision, that I understood it was just an accident on his part, and that I wasn't coming after him in any way. He cried and was very thankful. I didn't know the full impact of my reaching out to him until his mother called me the next day, in tears. She was very grateful and told me that for the first time since the accident happened, her son was finally able to drive once again.

Two things make me especially grateful that I survived. First, if I had killed myself, Janna's memory would have died with me; and second, I would have never known the person I was intended to be or the beautiful life that God had in store for me. I try to help other women see that if I can do it, they can too.

Sometimes, it seems that my husband is my reward for all the pain and suffering I have endured, and all the hard work that followed. I have kept my faith and my life has been replaced tenfold, and it gets better with each passing day. In many ways, I've never really had it so good.

## NOTE

1. Wayne Dyer, *The Power of Intention* (Carlsbad, CA: Hay House, 2004), 183.

\* \* \*

**Tamara Gabriel** is a licensed massage therapist, spiritual mentor, and runs a women's spiritual empowerment group called WOW (Women's Original Wisdom). She is the founder/creator of the nonprofit organization Healing Hugs (www.healinghugs.net), with over two million followers on Facebook, that raises money for funeral and other expenses for parents who have lost a child. Throughout her twenty-one years of recovery, Tamara has volunteered at twelve-step recovery meetings at her local county jail. In addition, she volunteers for Donate Life of Arizona helping people register to become an organ donor to save lives. Happily married to Dr. Richard Barnes, the couple has been running their office in Tucson for the past eight years.

# Know There Is More

## By Ernie Jackson

*Quinton*

*L*osing a child is every parent's worst nightmare.

But what if I told you the transition of our son, Quinton "Q" Stone Jackson, opened up our perception of that idea to a whole new world? My wife, Kristine, and I can talk about the tough stuff, the pain, the grief and how much we miss our son, but we don't. Our focus, instead, is on something else entirely.

As a man who had always been consumed with providing for my family and finding meaning for my life via professional success, our son's exploits after he crossed over rocked my world in such a way that, simply put, I will not and cannot ever go back. Quinton showed us, in no uncertain terms, there is no death and that we are all eternal. As a nonreligious man, this was the most divine epiphany and one I would never have imagined.

Quinton was born into our lives December 15, 1999, joining his older sister Cheyanne who was five and a half at the time. A remarkably happy baby, Quinton and his sister got along great from the start, and they always were very close. For much of Quinton's young life, whenever I wasn't working, he and I jumped at the chance to be together. He was always either in my arms or sitting right next to me. As he grew, our family seemed to divide into two camps—usually, the boys and the girls. Kristine and Cheyanne were like-minded and so were Quinton and I. Very often, in fact, even though he was just a kid, Quinton and I acted like partners. It seems we were always hanging out together, working out, tossing a football, or just lying around and cuddling. Q was my little pal.

Looking back—although I loved my family and spending time with them, I was very consumed with my work. Before the car accident that took Quinton's life, I was basically living a lie, deceiving myself about what was most important in life. My priorities were completely off. Because work and how others viewed me gave me self-worth, I usually overworked and came home from the office on empty. I had no reserves left for my family.

But everything changed as a result of the accident—the way I viewed myself, my relationship with my family, and even my inability to express painful feelings shifted.

As the date of the tragedy grew closer, some odd things began to happen. First, I was *very consciously* looking for a message—something, anything, to give my life purpose. Next, *I felt a change coming.* For a man who was adept at not feeling, for me to even sense a change coming made no sense to me whatsoever. All the same, in the weeks prior to the fatal accident, I acted on that perception by removing my personal possessions from my office a little bit at a time. At the time, it made absolutely no sense given that I not only needed my job, but I had absolutely no plans or intentions to find another one.

The third thing was the kicker. We changed our vacation plans *to avoid death.*

Let me explain.

For years, we enjoyed our annual family vacation in Puerto Peñasco, Mexico, nicknamed Rocky Point. In 2009, the swine flu had greatly impacted Mexico and there had also been a drug cartel killing in Rocky Point. While I wasn't deterred (because I needed my vacation and always loved being there), our extended family was aghast that we would even consider going there again that year, and they begged us to reconsider.

Kristine and I discussed what to do. She and our daughter Cheyanne and my mother-in-law Nellie all feared that we might end up dead if we went to Rocky Point. Feeling disappointed, because for years I've always looked forward to our annual family trip to Rocky Point, I agreed to change our vacation plans *to avoid death*. Instead of returning to Rocky Point, we decided to rent a houseboat on Lake Powell—a picturesque reservoir on the Colorado River—and enjoy our week of togetherness there.

The unusual happenings—or, as I came to call them, ahas—continued. Although our vacation plans came together nicely, there was an undercurrent that wasn't the usual vacation excitement. We all had the strangest sense of foreboding as we drove to Lake Powell from our home in Conifer, Colorado.

After our arrival, Quinton was perceivably different—he was more quiet than usual, and we often noticed him staring off in the distance in silence. He was also uncharacteristically cautious and insisted on our going slowly when he rode with us on the Jet Ski.

The beauty and majesty of the land formations around Lake Powell had me captivated. I saw faces everywhere in the rocks. And, toward the end of our trip, I had a vision. Because of Quinton, I have learned to differentiate between dreams and visions. My later research confirmed what I had immediately come to understand that day—dreams are blurry and quickly forgotten, while visions (and visits) are lifelike and not forgotten.

During the morning of the day before we were set to drive home, I had the most crystal-clear vision of Quinton dying. To this day, I can recount the specifics of my vision as if it just happened. It so rocked me that I awoke and excitedly told Quinton and Kristine all about it.

To that, Q said, "Dad, it won't happen like that. I would just swim away." But more than what he said, it was the way he said it that struck me. He sounded far older and wiser than his nine and one-half years.

Then, the next day, the unthinkable happened—our little boy left us (or, in popular vernacular, he died).

Oh, such a sad tale, right? Well, not so fast. While I am sorry that the stage must be set, it must be so you can feel what I felt that day; so you can sense the awe and amazement that I felt during the summer of 2009. The details of the accident are unimportant other than to say that I had pulled our vehicle onto the side of the road when another car barreled into us.

When uninjured Cheyanne stepped out, she saw her entire immediate family sprawled in the dust and bleeding. I sustained a head injury and broken bone. Kristine, however, had severe injuries, needing Flight for Life to transport her to the intensive care unit at the nearest hospital. (If you wish to learn more, I go into great detail in my first book, *Quinton's Messages*.) I will say that the accident made absolutely no sense—at all. And in a sense, the accident was the beginning.

Thirty hours after Quinton transitioned (died), while I was alone in my room, I felt my left hand being held. I was very conscious of it. I knew my hand was being held and I knew that I was alone in my room, but I was oblivious at that time as to what was possible. In that moment of awareness and ignorance, the best explanation I could come up with was, *Wow, this must be the manifestation of all the prayers.* This was thirty hours after Quinton's passing and the prayers were just getting started, but I never again felt that sensation.

Because I was unknowledgeable, it took weeks for me to realize that my son had been holding my hand. Once that became clear, I told everybody. One person eventually challenged me and asked how I knew, and I responded, "Because Quinton always had the softest hands and all of us loved walking hand in hand with him when we could." But at the time this happened, this knowledge had yet to pierce my conscious awareness.

When the chaplain came to visit us in the hospital, offering comfort and prayers, I wept uncontrollably, for the first and maybe only time in my life. Looking back, I realize how important it is to allow ourselves to have our tears as we grieve—the weeping helps us purge our emotions. I still tend to keep my emotions locked up behind a strong facade most days, but I've come to welcome tears whenever they do show up.

Five days after the accident, reality was setting in and I stayed blindly busy to keep it from registering too deeply. I needed to keep busy, to keep doing, to keep myself from feeling the intense pain I was in. As is common with many men, I put on a stone face and tried to hide my feelings, especially from myself. As a deliberate distraction, I became deeply involved in the business of getting us home, watching over as best I could those who were helping and supporting us, and communicating status updates to our community.

The fifth day following the accident, Kristine was still in the hospital and I found myself curled up in a corner—my proverbial dark place—having dark thoughts. As I was wondering if my son was alone in the darkness, something spectacular happened. At that precise moment, Chris, a dear friend of ours, bolted into the hospital room where most of us were congregated.

Excited and out of breath, she exclaimed, "Please get everybody here—I can only tell this once!"

After friends and family were gathered, Chris explained that a medicine man in full gear came up to her in the lobby of the hotel where she was staying. As he stood before her, he clasped her hands and said, "A little boy sent me to find you. He wants you to know that he is fine."

I gasped, as did everyone else in the room. This moment forever pierced my consciousness with the divine knowledge that Quinton is not really dead!

My next thought was, *Why didn't I know?*

From there, I vowed to study and learn so I could begin to understand what was really going on and where Quinton was that enabled him to send people messages.

It turns out that Quinton's visits were just beginning.

That summer, we noticed hummingbirds in nature acting in an odd and unusual manner. They were doing things that they had never done before. To set the stage for this strange behavior, this poem spontaneously came to my friend, John McDonough, when he heard what happened:

In an instant,
*in the beat of a hummingbird's wing,*
Faster than the blink of an eye . . .
. . . nothing will ever be the same.
There is only before and after
that moment in time.
Before is a gift that no one can steal;
After is a choice, a story yet to be written.
To not create a beautiful tomorrow
would be like throwing away
all of the yesterdays.
Today, I cannot see that future;
the dark clouds that surround
yet comfort me
block out that sky,
that rainbow after the storm,
beaconing me toward tomorrow.

John sent this in an e-mail to me three days after the accident. He told me that he sometimes gets messages in moments of tragedy, and he assured me that he didn't write this alone. We had John's inspiring poem printed on prayer cards and distributed them at Q's memorial service.

Now I see hummingbirds as important messengers. For instance, many of our friends donated a nine-foot-tall spruce tree in Quinton's memory, to be planted in our yard. Many attended the tree-planting ceremony and watched in amazement as a hummingbird hovered right above the top of the tree, staying for the entire dedication, just hanging out.

On another day, a hummingbird greeted Kristine as soon as she stepped out of the house, and flitted directly in front of her face for several seconds (really close—within twelve inches).

On another occasion, a hummingbird tried to get inside our home by flying into a window. We picked up the unconscious bird and gently stroked it until it regained consciousness. Once conscious, the precious little bird flew into a nearby tree and sat there for what seemed like a very long time, just watching us.

On each of those occasions, we knew that these were definitely signs from Quinton—that somehow he was influencing all those hummingbirds.

Still just getting started . . . Toward the end of July, after showering in what had been the kids' bathroom, I looked in the mirror and saw Quinton's reflection as he walked across his bedroom. This sight stopped me in my tracks; I was filled with wonder and awe!

Within a week or two of that, while walking down a hall in our house, just as I passed Quinton's room, I heard him call out, "Dad!"

Again, I was totally awestruck.

These incidents were all driving home the realization that pierced my consciousness soon after Q transitioned—the divine realization and knowledge that he was not dead. Instead, he was there with us always. I was able to embrace the divine knowledge that *there is more*; the divine knowledge that there is no death after all.

And the beat continued. . . . Four months after our dear son crossed the threshold to the other side, he came to me in the most amazing visit. It was more than a dream, which is fuzzy and quickly fades. A Dream Visit is really quite different. My experience and that of others is it is *vivid* and *lifelike*. There is another difference: Given the *clarity* of the experience, it is *remembered*.

My alarm had gone off because I had planned on going to the gym (working out helped me in my grieving process), but on this particular morning, after turning off the alarm I went back to sleep. *Immediately I found myself on the east side of our home. At my feet were the shadow of deck rails above me and the shadow of a hooded figure. I instantly knew it was Quinton. I stepped out onto the grass and prepared to look up and behind me; I expected Quinton to dissolve before I could see him. Instead, when I looked up I saw him, vividly. He was wearing a hooded robe and I saw his face. He had a buzz cut* [in life he alternated between growing his hair out and having it buzzed]. *And then I saw his expression. Quinton looked surprised that I could see him and then he began looking a little anxious. Me, on the other hand, I was beginning to freak out because I was excited. I shouted Quinton's name three times and each time I said his name I moved closer to consciousness. As I yelled out to him for the third time, he tore off his robe and jumped off the deck, into my outstretched arms. When I opened my eyes as I lay in my bed, I felt Quinton's peaceful and loving energy within me.*

Quinton came to Kristine too, but it took a while. Because of the pain she was in after the accident, and painkillers, she didn't perceive Quinton for two years. The first time she did, he visited her in her dreams. One night she had forgotten to take out her earrings. While she slept, they began to pinch her earlobes; it was then that Quinton came to her. He looked at her and said, "Mom, you don't have to hurt anymore." Instantly she awoke only to find her earrings had been removed from her ears and neatly placed on her pillow.

Quinton didn't only visit us, he also came to my sister, his classmates, and even one of his teachers. How is all of this even possible and what does it mean? I have learned (through what seems like hundreds of conversations with others and dozens of books I have read) that this means there is no death, period. People from all walks of life and religious backgrounds have experiences much like these. In short, this is the norm.

What is the message? The message is, "There is more!"

From here, I invite you to begin your own research and discover what that means to you.

\* \* \*

**Ernie Jackson** has written two books about Quinton: *Quinton's Messages* and *Quinton's Legacy.* He and his wife Kristine have been married twenty-seven years, and they have three beautiful grandchildren from their surviving daughter, Cheyanne.

• *14* •

# Seven Lessons Learned from a Personal Journey of Grief

## By Sharon Gabriel Rossy

*Gabriel*

$\mathscr{B}$y 1997, I had gone through what most would consider the "normal" experience of loss—two grandmothers, my aunts, an uncle, my father-in-law, and my dad had all died in the normal cycle of life. But in 1997, witnessing my niece Tamara bury her nine-year-old daughter Janna served as my first real lesson in grief and survivor guilt. Janna had been on life support for a week after she and her mom had been in a terrible car accident, until she finally drew her last breath.

With very little help from me or others, Tamara was dealing with the loss of her daughter, the breakup of her marriage, and coping with her eleven-year-old son Ryan and his behavioral issues all at the very same time. On many levels, much of what she was going through was not clear to me nor did it necessarily make sense to me or the rest of our family.

Although Tamara's grief was palpable, she didn't necessarily "behave" in ways that we thought "fit" with this tragedy or our "standard" of how one should grieve. She sought out her friends and seemed to reject being with us. As her family, we were not only confused, but at times we were pretty judgmental.

My niece was caught between her grief, her family, and her husband's family, with everyone watching every move she made. Sadly—and unbeknownst to us at the time—our horribly judgmental behavior lasted a long while. When Tamara needed our unconditional love and support most, we were incapable of giving it. As a result, my niece became estranged from her family and remained so for several years.

**First lesson learned:** No one can ever know what a bereaved person is experiencing.

One person's experience of grief may be very different from another's. No one can judge what is right or wrong in how that grief is displayed. There were terrible realities and gut-wrenching decisions to be made. To look upon a beautiful nine-year-old princess—with barely a bruise on her body, who for all purposes looked like she was sleeping—knowing the reality that she was not going to survive was unfathomable. Yet we all had preconceived ideas of how grief and mourning should take place. It took a long time before I truly understood what my niece had been going through.

So, how do we survive grief? There is no preparation for grief—I truly believe that the death of a child is never reconciled; there is no "closure." It is out of the order of nature. We are not supposed to bury our children. The human psyche is geared toward life—death leaves too many unanswered questions and oftentimes torments us with the unknown. Grief has many faces and many levels. It forces us to face the randomness of life, which is often more than we can do.

We become identified by our loss—regardless of how death occurred. It seeps into our bones and becomes a part of who we are. I remember saying over and over, I can't believe this is my life.

My own personal tragedy struck suddenly, catastrophically, and without warning. Gabriel, the eldest of our four boys, died August 1, 2006, at the age of twenty-seven—having just left our house probably ten to fifteen minutes earlier. The weather was dicey; a severe thunderstorm had blown into Montreal. But Gabe—always the hero—had decided to pick up his girlfriend Laura who was working late downtown. Off he went, never to return. Gabriel was crushed to death when a diseased tree collapsed onto his car on his way downtown.

Laura called looking for Gabe because he was late and not answering his phone. His bedroom was in our basement, so I ran down to his room to look for him, or to see if he had somehow forgotten his phone. The silence was deafening—the room felt completely devoid of Gabriel. My eyes became fixed on his favorite jeans, folded neatly across the top of a chair. For a moment, time stood still. Then my maternal instinct kicked into full gear. As I stood in his doorway staring blankly ahead, a chill shot through me and a single thought burned in my mind. *He's not coming home.*

Nicholas, our youngest, was out that night with some friends. Justin and Luke, who were home, rushed off to look for Gabe, each in a different direction. Laura called again, hysterical and incoherent. Her sister Deanna had picked her up from work, and shortly after they set out to look for Gabe, the girls arrived at the scene of the accident. Two more calls, from Justin and Luke, and a visit from the police confirmed the worst. What I had already felt in my heart was true; my beloved son Gabriel was dead.

It was surreal. I kept wondering when the nightmare would end, when I'd wake up and realize it was all just a really bad dream. This could *not* be happening to my family. *Why? How?* Suddenly, there were hordes of people in my house: police, relatives, and friends. I kept thinking, over and over, *They shouldn't be here. I need them to all go away.* I was in a corner of the room watching myself, but not really comprehending what was happening.

My three other sons were all that kept me from collapsing completely. They looked to my husband Richard and me for strength. As much as I wanted to scream and wail, somehow the shock of it all kept me contained, at least to a certain extent. My brother Kenny, an Eastern Orthodox priest and the father of my niece Tamara, took charge, calling various family members and helping with funeral arrangements.

Richard and I were told to bring pictures of Gabe for display on top of his coffin and kindly encouraged to have a closed casket. Though two of my brothers advised strongly against it, I was adamant that our family see Gabe privately because there was absolutely no way I was going to bury my son without seeing him, touching him, and kissing him one last time.

Gabriel was a powerful force in our family. He seemed to pop out of the womb that way. With his bright, clear-blue eyes and ferocious energy, he seemed ready to take on the world. From the start, he was always so active. As a baby, Gabriel was also difficult and colicky. Sometimes, the only time I could get him to sleep during the day was to put him in his carriage and take him for long walks—even when it was freezing outside. My little guy was taking his first steps at nine months and flipping himself out of the crib by the time he was fourteen months old.

In fact, one memorable night Gabriel hoisted himself up out of his crib to the ground and opened his bedroom door so many times that out of sheer desperation at four in the morning, Richard finally removed the doorknob so we could get some much-needed sleep.

I loved rocking Gabe to sleep, a process that sometimes could take forever. When he was about eighteen months, I tried to wean him from that daily practice. But Gabe would just lie in his crib and cry out, "Rock me, Mommy! Rock me!" It broke my heart, especially when Richard took the rocking chair out of his room because he believed enough was enough.

As the eldest of four, Gabriel often felt he had to take charge. In April 2006, a few months before he died, Richard and I went on vacation to France and left Gabe in charge at home. A few days after arriving in Paris, I got an e-mail from him saying, "You need to get home now. Nobody is listening or keeping the house clean!" When we arrived home, Justin, our second son, told me, "Never go away again and leave him in charge. I don't think I can live under his regime."

At the same time, Gabriel was an incredibly sensitive soul with a larger-than-life personality. He loved to argue about everything and could hold a room under his spell forever. Gabe was a gifted storyteller and loved to tell tales about all of us, often noting correctly that our family could be our own comedy show. He could make the opening of a beer can an enthralling experience and tell a story about it that would last for three hours. Gabe was famous for making the simplest of things an event of epic proportions.

Gabriel was a philosopher. Because he was so sensitive—and probably because he was my first—I often felt the need to protect him when he struggled with school or his life in general. He wasn't naturally competitive, and at the beginning of each school year, he would be teary and emotional, even timid. But as he grew into himself, he possessed a tremendous energy he was always trying to harness. We often spoke of that with each other, which made our already close connection all the more special to me.

Gabe also shouldered the incredible burden of being the eldest and the expectations that placed on him. He and his dad struggled with that because Gabe didn't fit quite into the mold that his dad envisioned for him. Richard expected him to follow a "normal" trajectory for his life and studies, but Gabe was more of a free spirit and had a hard time figuring out exactly where he belonged in the world.

When Gabriel died, the house became suddenly quiet. It was disconcerting. Even Hugo, our English Labrador retriever, would sit at the top of the basement steps and whine. It seemed he was always looking for Gabe to reappear. Apparently, unbeknownst to my husband and me, a whole other life went on with our sons and their friends at night in our basement, and Hugo would hang out in Gabe's room during the festivities.

His girlfriend Laura gave us a gift—a message Gabe had left on her cell phone only a few days before he died. Luke, our third son, managed to transfer it to our computers. I still listen to it, and it makes me smile and laugh and cry because it is so typical Gabe, with his energy and enthusiasm for life, giving her a pep talk on what a wonderful and successful person she was in her job. What follows is a very condensed version of his effusive three-minute message:

> This is Gabriel. This is a conversation I'm having with your machine. . . . I'm talking purposely to your machine, so you will hear this in the morning. Have a very good day and I want you to be smiley. If you're tired, so be a little bit tired. . . . You'll be fine. . . . You're so fine that you could afford to not be okay for a year and still be ahead of everyone. . . . I think you're an amazing person. You're a beautiful person inside and out—notice I said inside first. . . . You're doing everything that anyone could possibly want when they're forty. . . . You're set, you're perfect, just go with the flow . . . like in a Vince Vaughnish kind of way. . . . Live like that! . . . I'm getting a fifteen-second warning because I'm using up your entire mailbox. I hope it was worth it. Have a good day. Give me a call when you can. [*Gives a kiss.*]

Twelve years later, Laura, now married, still feels a powerful connection to Gabe and to us. We love that she still feels a part of our family and probably always will. Recently, while on vacation with her husband, a Red Hot Chili Peppers song came on the radio that she knew had been a favorite of Gabe's. Laura told me there was absolute silence in the car for forty-five minutes. Then finally, Laura and her husband had a long conversation about Gabe, which she said was as disturbing as it was exhilarating.

The sheer number of friends that came to the funeral and to our house is a testament to the special soul Gabriel was. People I'd never met told me that my son was a beautiful soul who couldn't stand to see anyone hurt. They shared stories of how Gabe had changed their lives. We had so much to learn about Gabe and *from* Gabe, and sadly the latter would no longer be possible. It was unimaginable that I would never hear Gabriel's uproarious, infectious laugh or his incessant rapping about anything and everything under the sun.

Our whole family went to grief therapy one time, and then I continued on my own for about two years. I also joined a support group my therapist ran for bereaved mothers, which was good. It was a safe space for me to express my feelings, frustrations, and fears. I had been angry for a number of reasons and couldn't necessarily express them out loud in a healthy way, so therapy really helped work through a lot of that.

When you lose a child—no matter their age, whether it be an expected or sudden death—the world as you know it changes. What were once simple, normal acts that we performed daily in natural ways are no longer normal. Our world has forever changed in fundamental ways that cannot be explained in words.

Even grocery shopping became an emotional experience for me. I would burst into tears in the middle of an aisle of canned goods—not because soup or green beans or corn reminded me of Gabe, but because the simple, mundane act of buying food represented another lifetime ago, when my life was still "normal."

**Second lesson learned:** The death of a child opens up a dimension of life for which we are never prepared.

How do we move forward, or live with a "new normal" (a phrase used in grief work)? Personally, I think of it as a new reality because normal no longer exists. We once shared a life with someone who is no longer here, and that cannot be ignored or dismissed.

A while after Gabe was gone, I began to notice that people were staying away from me. For many months, I thought they were being "respectful" and giving me space. But I eventually realized that, more often than not, other people can't really handle our grief. It frightens them. They don't know what to say or how to handle our sadness. I hate to admit this, but I'm painfully aware that members of our own families and even close friends are as capable of shutting us out as anyone else.

I remember telling one friend that what happened to me wasn't contagious. She looked shocked for a moment, and then burst into tears. As soon as she was able to speak, she apologized because what I said to her had hit home. Somehow, illogically speaking, she'd been afraid because *if it happened to Sharon, it could happen to me, too.*

**Third lesson learned:** The importance of connecting with people who either had a similar loss or at least have the capacity to "get it."

I started to weed out those in my life who were toxic or petty. It became increasingly difficult to be around people who were caught up in trivialities and what I considered to be minor, fixable dilemmas of ordinary life. Basically, I cut my losses.

Those around us, including ourselves, want us to be better. Life goes on with or without us—and people need to see us "get better" because somehow it is an affirmation of living. Others make attempts at trying to "help" us by saying some of the most ridiculous comments birthed out of their own discomfort with our grief.

I heard endless statements like "Thank goodness you still have the other boys" or "You have a great wedding to look forward to" because Justin had been planning a wedding.

My response to that is: "No one is more aware of what I have than I am. How do those things replace what is no longer here?"

We all handle grief differently. A year after our son died, Richard hiked up a huge mountain in Argentina as part of his way of dealing with our loss and connecting deeply with Gabe. I also believe he needed to feel alive.

**Fourth lesson learned:** Grief is a lonely journey.

Yes, you can grieve with others in your family but in the end, it's a very personal journey that each person must experience in his or her own unique way. We need to give ourselves space to grieve. Most have difficulty understanding that this loss is unlike any other. As a parent, I struggled not to burden my boys with my grief. When Justin became engaged eight months after Gabe died, it was incredibly difficult for me, as I'm sure it was for him, too. Justin's life was moving forward and Gabriel, the big brother whom he adored, was never going to have that experience.

When I was a child, my paternal grandmother lived with us. She would cry often for her deceased son, my uncle, who had died years before from suicide. At the time, I could not understand it—I was young when he died, and it was hard for me to understand how much and how long she had grieved him. It was something I never got—until I lost my own son—because the reality of losing a child is unlike any other loss. **This was my fifth lesson learned.**

I believe there are some universal elements to grieving, and there are other elements unique to each individual and his or her family history. No matter how similar the circumstances, we can never know *exactly* how another person is feeling. I have learned that for those who grieve, their story is the hardest; their experience is the most difficult and most horrific. We can say we know what they're going through, but we cannot ever know what anyone else is truly feeling. We barely know what we're going through ourselves.

In my support group for moms, our grief binds us in profound ways, yet each of us has our own story, our own perspective, and our own ways of coping. The irony of it all is that our grief is shaped by our past, and our future is shaped by our grief.

Someone once said that grieving is a lot like peeling an onion. As you peel through each layer, you strip away the emotions and the tears flow and flow.

A friend told me after Gabe died that he didn't know which was worse—losing his own son at the age of nine to a brain tumor, which took about one and a half years, or losing someone suddenly, without warning. He said, "At least we got to say good-bye, but you're still never prepared." Interestingly, the face of grief ultimately becomes similar for all of us, regardless of the circumstances.

As a mom, here are some of the hard truths I've learned during my own tough journey through grief:

- No matter how you replay the scenario, the outcome is always the same.
- You torment yourself over the "what ifs."
- You struggle with the guilt and regrets.
- The range of emotions is overwhelming—you don't know quite what to do with yourself.
- You are not in control of your life—it's an illusion. You are powerless to change the situation.

- The powerlessness reflects the uncertainty of what lies ahead—there is no formula for this.
- Like it or not, the reality of life takes over—only it has another face.
- More than anything, I worried about Gabriel being alone.
- The void is immeasurable and unfathomable.
- There will be multiple losses—some will be obvious, others more subtle.
- Grief feels like being in suspended animation—like being caught in a web with nowhere to land.
- Family takes on a whole new meaning. I became hypervigilant—especially if there was any discord.
- The first year you're in shock. The second year, the reality sinks in that this person is never coming back.
- People felt the need to spout all kinds of euphemisms and theories about God, suffering, and destiny, which almost pushed me over the edge. At that point, I decided I earned the right to say whatever I wanted in rebuttal.
- And finally, all I could think was: *I can't believe this is my life.*

And then *what? How do we go on from here?* **The sixth and probably hardest lesson learned:** Give ourselves permission to live.

Grief keeps our loved one alive for us, so it's hard to let the grief go. We fear if we're no longer paralyzed by our grief, that somehow we're forgetting them altogether. Someone who lost their twenty-four-year-old son suddenly from meningitis asked me three questions that really go to the heart of grieving:

1. Will I ever be happy again?
2. Will I ever laugh again?

To these two questions, I answered, "Yes, but it will be with a clause attached. It's never going to be quite the same."

3. How did you get through it?

I told her, "One second at a time." I promised her that at some point down the road, she'll look back and think, *I can't believe I'm still alive.*

**Seventh lesson learned:** Keep moving forward.

We are not powerless in how we cope. We can keep our loved ones alive not just in our hearts, but by talking about them. By not being afraid to say their names. By not letting them become the elephant in the room. When you lose someone you love, you earn some rights to say how you feel and to do what feels right for you. Don't be afraid to say you're having a rough day. If others can't handle it, that's their problem, not yours.

The relationship never ends—it changes. People like to talk about the "first year" being the hardest. I say, yes and no, because there will be a lifetime of firsts that this loved one will miss.

It seems an oxymoron to think that the death of a loved one can result in anything remotely hopeful. Yet somehow, three years after Gabe's passing, I managed to return to school to finish my master's—because I knew it was something my son would have wanted.

Many people reached out to me because of the tragedy I had been through. That pushed me to start a support group for grieving mothers and train to become a psychotherapist specializing in grief work. My clients know that I get it because of all I have lost. In my work with grieving parents, I emphasize that it's a second-by-second, minute-by-minute journey.

Grief isn't a disease that has a cure or that one overcomes. We learn to deal with it at some point, but our lives have been permanently changed—like losing a limb: You adapt, but the loss is the loss. When we feel the pressure to "get better," it only makes things worse. The process cannot be pushed. We live in a culture that wants to deny death, not accept it. Yes, our grief is frightening to others—but that cannot and should not be our burden.

Two of our sons are married now, and one has three children—which probably saved me from myself. When my first grandchild was born, a beautiful little girl, my heart stood still, not sure if it was ready to open itself up again. But Alessia and her siblings, Cristiano (whose middle name is Gabriel) and Aria, are truly the blessings I never knew I was missing. All of our grandchildren know Gabriel, even though they've never met him. His pictures are everywhere, and we talk openly about him a lot. They love hearing stories about Uncle Gabe. But every photo taken of our expanding family still hurts because someone so special is missing.

A year after Gabe died, we created the Gabriel Rossy Memorial Fund to raise money for underprivileged youth programs in Montreal.

Our first undertaking was an enormous intergenerational event with over five hundred people in attendance. It was a lovefest of sorts and felt like a family affair. When family and friends had first said they wanted to do something in Gabe's memory, our initial reaction was, "We can't do this. This is too hard." But we held three major fund-raisers between 2007 and 2010, all of which were immensely successful. I don't necessarily recommend this approach, though, because frankly it is emotionally draining and at times I would think, *I can't believe I'm even doing this.*

People have said, "It must be therapeutic. It's got to help you with your grief." I think to myself, *Are you kidding me? How can anything help with my grief?* In reality, I think there was a more selfish motive—we wanted to keep our amazing son's name alive. So, yes, good has come from this tragedy, but it certainly is not the path I would have chosen.

As an aside, we all get reality checks when we least expect them, sometimes out of the mouths of babes. Our youngest son, Nicholas, who was twenty at the time, came to me after our second event and asked bluntly how many of these fund-raisers we were planning on having. He said, and I quote, "You know, Mom, we're never gonna forget Gabe. We love him and we think about him all the time, every day. But he wasn't exactly a philanthropist. And I doubt he would do this for us."

That brings me back to the first lesson learned—everyone needs to express their grief in their own way.

Take each day one step at a time. There are no time frames or right or wrong ways to grieve. The most important thing we can do, as I said before, is to give ourselves permission to live. It won't be easy. Maintain your sense of humor—you'd be surprised how that can carry you through some rough moments. One day you'll look back in amazement and realize that somehow you've managed to survive.

\* \* \*

**Sharon Gabriel Rossy** has a master's degree in education psychology and counseling from McGill University in Montreal, Canada, and holds the title of psychotherapist from the Order of Psychologists in Quebec. She now works primarily in the field of grief and bereavement and conducts monthly support groups for bereaved mothers. Sharon lives in Montreal and loves spending time with her husband Richard; their surviving sons Justin, Luke, and Nicholas; and three grandchildren. She also loves growing tomatoes.

# IV

# SUICIDE

Remarkably, as far down as I go into the deep pit of mourning, that's how high I've been able to ascend into newfound heights of joy.

—Meryl Hershey Beck

# "I Crossed Myself Over in a Stupid Way"

## A Mother's Story of Recovery

### By Meryl Hershey Beck

*Meryl and Jon*

*"I, Jonathan Hershey Beck, de-cided the time has come for me to die. I am doing this because there is nothing left for me. . . . I do not want a new job. I do not want to move to a new city. I do not want new friends. I am ready to move on beyond this human form to whatever exists after. . . . I am not killing myself because I am depressed, sad, or lonely, or any-thing else along those lines. I am do-ing so because I feel it is time to move on. I have been debating this for some time now. . . ."*

At the age of thirty-five, my son chose to end his life here on Earth. I had no idea he would take this step and, as he later said, "cross myself over in a stupid way."

### A FEW MONTHS BEFORE . . .

The year was 2011, and I was a happily divorced woman, living in Tucson, Arizona. Although I am a licensed professional clinical counselor, instead of seeing individual clients I spent my time teaching energy therapies and doing Reconnective Healing sessions. In addition, I invested hours each day working on the final edits of my first book (*Stop Eating Your Heart Out: The 21-Day Program to Free Yourself from Emotional Eating*), to be released in the spring of 2012. My adult daughter, Alison (Ali), also lived in Tucson with her husband and children, and my adult son, Jonathan (Jon, Jonny), lived in Florida.

Life was good, and I had no complaints. Except I sometimes worried about Jon. He often came to visit us in Tucson and loved being with his sister and nieces, who adored him. But I saw pain beneath his smile, and a constriction in his energy, with shoulders as solid as cement. Although loved by family and friends, Jon longed for a romantic relationship, which never came to be.

A few years earlier, he'd met a woman I'll call Lola, and they became instant friends. Jon hoped for a love relationship with her but settled for friendship because that's all Lola wanted from him. They saw each other every few months. . . . Jonny, living in Orlando, would fly Lola and her young son out from Phoenix, and the three of them would spend weekends traipsing around Universal Studios and Disney World. Jon exuded joy in the photos he sent—spending time with someone he cared about in his most favorite places.

When he visited me in Tucson, Jon would also drive up to Phoenix and spend time with Lola and her son. Although he never verbalized it to me, I could tell that he hoped that if he tried hard enough and did all the right things, it would one day blossom into more than a friendship.

Jon had a job doing computer-assisted drafting (CAD) and seemed to get along well with his colleagues. When budget cuts were made, however, he lost his job. Although he sought a new one, nothing materialized.

He was thousands of miles away from me, living alone, no job prospects, and no close friends in the area. His only enjoyments seemed to be video games, opening days of new movies at the theater, and theme parks. I suggested he move back to Tucson and live with me, but he wanted to stay in his adored Orlando, theme park heaven on earth. I joked that he thought moving back with his mommy was a fate worse than death for him!

My heart ached for my son—he seemed very alone and his occasional smile seemed to be plastered on rather than real. I made lots of suggestions: "Why don't you join a club? The JCC? Take a class? Do online dating?" But none of my ideas hit the mark for Jonny.

Other than the pain I felt for what I perceived as Jon's silent suffering, I'd lived a charmed life without any major losses or grief. Sure, I had grandparents who had passed away, and even aunts and uncles, but no major, deep grief.

Then in the summer of 2011, my dear friend Julie lost her battle with cancer and, for the first time, I felt truly bereaved. My Pollyannaish life had disappeared in an instant and I experienced the profound pain of loss. Even though I felt the grief and it hurt, I soon returned to my regular life, and focused on finishing the final revision of *Stop Eating Your Heart Out.*

### Jon's D-Day

**October 12, 2011.** My deadline for completing the book. I sat at my computer all day and immersed myself in writing, revising, and editing. When I received a text message from Jon that said, "I just wanted to tell you I love you," I replied, "Thank you. I love you too," and got back to my writing.

The last chapter of the book begins with a quote from Richard Bach: "What the caterpillar calls the end of the world, the master calls a butterfly." That chapter included other butterfly references, too, such as "Like the butterfly spending the first part of its life in a chrysalis, I too spent my early years in hiding, keeping myself separate from others. Joining a 12 Step support group was the beginning of my metamorphosis." And in the last line of the book, I address the reader: "Just like the butterfly, you are in the process of transformation. And, as you emerge from the darkness of emotional overeating, you too will soar."

Although I knew butterflies represent transformation, I had no idea how important butterfly sightings would become for me, nor why. . . .

**October 15, 2011.** While on my daily walk with the dogs in the arroyo behind my house, a motionless butterfly appeared on the path in front of me. I mean right in front of me, and I almost stepped on it. I gently lifted it and placed it off to the side where no one would trample it. Much to my surprise and delight, a few seconds later it flew away.

For many years I have believed in an afterlife and that people who have "crossed over" can send us messages. Seeing the butterfly, I knew it was some kind of communication from someone who had passed on, and I thought my friend Julie had contacted me. Feeling grateful and happy, I smiled to myself knowing the butterfly was a message from the other side. They often say there are "signs" after a loved one passes, and this surely seemed like one to me.

**October 17, 2011.** I received a call from my distressed daughter: "Have you heard from Jonny?"

"No," I quickly replied, without it fazing me. Knowing Jon, I suspected he went to Las Vegas or the Bahamas for the weekend (something he had done in the past) and didn't tell me because I would have voiced my disapproval about his extravagant spending.

"I'm worried," she continued. "His best friend Dave hasn't heard from him either. Both Dave and I got an *I love you* text from him on the twelfth. When I got it, I immediately called Jonny and asked if that was a suicide message and he assured me it wasn't and even made plans for what we'll do together when he visits us next month. It's not like him to not call Dave or me. I'm going to ask Dad to have the police check his apartment."

Ali's worry jarred me into a state of worry, too.

A few hours later the phone rang, and my ears nearly exploded with the piercing sound of Jon's dad, my ex-husband, screaming over and over, "He's dead! He's dead!" My knees buckled and I collapsed into a chair. Hanging up the phone, I screamed, ranted, and shouted, "No, no, no! We would have helped you, Jonny . . . I'm so mad at you!"

The police had opened up Jon's apartment and discovered the body of my sweet, heart-centered thirty-five-year-old son. I thought of the butterfly. Yes, it had been a sign, but it wasn't from Julie, as I'd thought. It was from Jon. The butterfly came to me three days after Jon had killed himself. It was the first of many messages from my son.

At first, I was in shock. And then the agony, pain, despair, and anguish flooded me. Just like in the movies, I shrieked. I wailed. I howled, and I sobbed. I felt like I couldn't breathe. My friends rushed over to comfort me, surrounding me with love and energy, and helped me breathe.

Although I don't particularly believe in hell, I panicked, wondering if I could be wrong and Jon would end up in hell. Assuring me that God is a loving God and there is no such thing as hell, my friends' words gave me some comfort.

Many years earlier, as I watched the TV show *Medium*, I began to believe that some people could really communicate with the souls of the departed. Several of my friends (Robin, Dana, Carol, Barbara, Morgan) have that skill, too—they have an uncanny ability to connect with the spirits of people who have crossed over. They said they could get messages from my son, and relayed the following information in the early days after his passing. . . .

Morgan told me that she saw Jon put his arms around me and Alison and whisper in our ears. Since we were busy reminiscing, we didn't hear him. Sitting quietly a few minutes later, though, I distinctly heard, *Mom, I am okay now.*

Later, the message came through that he needed me to forgive him and I released the anger, knowing he did what he thought he needed to do at the time.

My wonderful, loving friend Robin was out of town, but I was on the phone with her constantly. She told me she wanted to feel sad but couldn't because he was right there with her. She gave me many messages from him, which were very consoling. One of the first things his spirit said to her was, *The human didn't know how to deal with the feelings.* He also said he was concerned with how all of us were doing, that he was okay, and—in typical Jonny fashion—he expressed his concern was for us. He assured Robin that he had beings with him, surrounding him, and all was well.

I believe that Jonathan's spirit had chosen a life that was much more challenging than he could handle. It wasn't anyone's fault—he just needed to reorganize and start again. Along those lines . . . The day after we learned of Jon's suicide, my daughter told me that her four-year-old daughter, Talia, asked her why she was crying, and Ali told her that it was because she missed her brother. Talia explained to her mom, "First he will be an angel, then he will be a baby again, and then grow up." Out of the mouths of babes.

Other messages came through, too. . . .

*Jon said he was glad no one found his body right away because it gave him some time to get acclimated.* Whew! This relieved the huge guilt I had been feeling because it took five days to discover he had died.

I heard that Lola had gotten married a few days before Jon had chosen to end his own life. Brokenhearted I'm sure, Jon shot himself straight in the heart. *He said he was so sorry for what he had done. He realized right away it was a stupid act, and he asked for our forgiveness and to not be angry with him.*

*He told us again and again that he's fine, he's great, and he's in a wonderful place.* Yay! We were all so happy to hear this.

*He repeated that it was dumb to kill himself and no one should ever do it. His actual words were, "I crossed myself over in a stupid way."*

A few weeks later I contacted a professional medium, George Lugo, and Jon came through right away. George started by saying, "I have a young man here who keeps insisting I tell you he lost weight." Ha! A few years earlier Jon had quit smoking and put on some weight. I suggested he follow the food plan (aka diet) that his sister and I were using, and he declined. It's funny that the first words from him were that he had lost weight. It convinced me it was really Jon.

*He said it wasn't painful to die and his grandparents were there to meet him when he crossed over.* During the call, Jon (known for his caviar taste in purchasing quality items and taking really good care of them) said, *"I can't believe I ruined a good couch."* Yes, he shot himself on his gorgeous couch and it had been totally ruined. This sounded like a typical Jon-type comment.

As a licensed counselor, I have been trained to look for signs of potential suicides, and, as frequently happens, I missed them with my own son. In some cultures, however, ending one's life is a choice, although our culture here in America doesn't support that choice at all and instead condemns it.

For instance, I heard that Tibetan monks and other advanced souls choose to die when the time feels right for them, and they choose the full moon to exit the body—it gives them more energy to make the transition. Jon did not have the ability to will his body to die and needed to use a gun in order to leave. Interestingly, just like the high spiritual beings, he chose October 12, which was the full moon.

My wonderful friend Jan sent me to a website that said:

Choosing death is wholly at the soul's discretion . . .
   You-the-soul establishes several exit points for a lifetime for two eventualities:

1. You feel complete with your life mission and goals, so you return Home.
2. You see no possibility of your life mission being met under the current circumstances, so you call it quits.

I believe that Jon fits into that second category—he chose a life path that was much too difficult and challenging for him, and he needed to call it quits when he did.

My good friend Barbara, a psychologist, wrote in an e-mail:

> I hope and pray that you are accepting this as his chosen path. As much as we think we knew a better way for him, we don't truly know his path. His path is his own. It is for him alone to direct as he sees fit. He will learn and grow from this experience. I know that his angels were there to collect his soul as he crossed over and they were there to help guide him in his spiritual lesson. Now it is our path to heal though the grief.

Others, too, have written or told me that Jon is okay and that they see his spirit surrounded by light beings. My darling Maureen said, "I see Jon's spirit in the glad company of angels who are enchanted by his sweet nature."

At the memorial service, I gave the eulogy and ended with the following words:

> I understand Jonathan. I understand his reasons. I am no longer angry. A part of me is at peace with the decision he made. I do feel horrendous sadness, as if a piece of my heart was ripped out and is now missing.
>
> Although he didn't feel like he had much impact in his lifetime, Jon's death has already transformed others. It is allowing some folks to radically take stock of their lives and make different choices.
>
> I love you Jonathan and, although it fills me with sadness, I support the decision you made.

## THE AFTERMATH

After hearing the news, the shock and numbness moved into excruciating pain—a piece of my heart had been violently torn out. Although in the past, I (a recovering compulsive overeater) turned to food for comfort, this time I had no appetite. Day after day, I only managed to choke down a little plain yogurt with raw honey.

For the next several days, weeks, and even months, you'd find me sitting on the backyard swing overlooking my large koi pond. Hours would go by and I'd be hanging out there, doing nothing but swinging.

Six months after the suicide, I noticed something new had appeared in the pond—a pair of mallard ducks. Each day I looked forward to watching them and said to myself, "This is the first time I feel happy." I believe Jon sent them because he knew how much they'd delight me. And right after the ducks appeared, a young peregrine falcon showed up on the fence encircling the pond. The falcon (and what seem to be his mate and offspring) still shows up often, especially during family celebrations. Thank you, Jonny!


## LIFE GOES ON


What I've learned in these past years since the unspeakable happened is that life does go on. I continue to put one foot in front of the other and just keep going. Grief still shows up and surprises me at times, and I'll feel, again, like I am suffocating and gasping for breath.

Yes, I still visit the place of profound grief and despair. But I don't live there, and I don't dwell there too long. Remarkably, as far down as I go into the deep pit of mourning, that's how high I've been able to ascend into newfound heights of joy. What a roller coaster ride it's been. Who knew that going down deep into the intense pain could be a springboard up into ecstatic bliss?

Sometimes losing a child totally destroys the parent. Even worse is a suicide. Unfortunately, some parents who have lost children (especially to suicide) end up taking their own lives.[1] In fact, I happened to meet two unrelated people who told me they wished this book had been written years earlier because after their siblings suicided, their distraught moms killed themselves too.

I understand those moms. I know their indescribable pain and agony. I also know it's possible to not just *survive* such a tragedy; it's also possible to thrive.


## MY ACTION STEPS


*Support System*

After receiving the worst news of my life, I immediately called my close friends and family. Those in Tucson rushed over to hold me and comfort me. The out-of-towners held me energetically and kept me blanketed in the love and light they continued to send. I have a wonderful, loving biological family, and they, too, were shattered. I also have a devoted, supportive "spiritual family"—these are close, heart-centered, like-minded, spiritually connected friends.

These spiritual family members know how to send energy (see "Sending Energy Exercise" in the tools and techniques section at the back of the book). It's a technique that uses imagination and intention (basically, they picture me and imagine sending good thoughts, prayers, light, and love my way). Right after Jon transitioned, I started asking my "family" for energy, a practice that remains to this day. I also called out for support on Facebook (it's truly been a godsend), as well as phone calls and texts. Whenever I feel myself drowning in grief, I reach out and ask them to send energy, and thankfully they hear and respond. I can actually feel the heavy emotions abate as I rise up out of the quagmire of deep grief and step into the world of the living again.

*My Own Spiritual Practices*

Many years ago, I was an active member of a twelve-step recovery group (food was my drug of choice) and attended meetings on a regular basis. Afraid to believe in the punishing God that I thought existed, I tried to convince myself I was an agnostic. Listening to various speakers at meetings, however, I came to believe in an unconditionally loving God—a Higher Power who loves me no matter what. This Higher Power became an important part of my daily life, whom I rely on during challenging times and thank for all the gifts I've received.

Since Jon's death, this connection to Source has intensified and I feel completely cared for and supported. I seek to be in conscious contact with Source daily and continue to keep myself filled with light. Each morning, I meditate and then do light work: I picture filling my heart with love, light, joy, and God. Next, I imagine bringing in love and light from the Universe and sending it into my body and then deep into the earth to ground it. Then I bring earth energy up through my body and send it out into the universe.

*Energy Practices*

In addition to doing light work and asking others to help fill me, I use energy psychology techniques. Several years ago, I created SourceTapping, which is an upgraded version of EFT (Emotional Freedom Techniques)—the most well known of the energy psychology techniques. As I recite specific words from a script, I release painful feelings while tapping on acupressure points on my face, hand, and upper torso. Tapping is like needle-less acupuncture and helps us let go of emotional pain and bring in feelings of comfort and peace in its place. You can download the SourceTapping script for free at my website, www.SourceTapping.com.

After Jon died, I used tapping daily to keep my energy moving, and I continue to use it often (for myself and others) to diminish pain and heal whatever remnants of grief remain.

I noticed, in those early days and weeks, I could not even look at the chair where I had been sitting when I received the news, and I couldn't talk about that moment with anyone, either. It was a trauma, and for months I exhibited post-traumatic stress symptoms. Although I tried to see a local trauma therapist, we were never able to set up a session. So, I took matters into my own hands. Literally. I thought perhaps I could clear the trauma myself by tapping, and it worked.

Every morning on my "inner work walks" (doing inner work as I walked the dogs), I thought of each section of the call I received and did the tapping. Within a few days, the memory remained . . . but without the stabbing pain of the feelings. Now I am able to sit in the chair, tell you who called, repeat what was said, etc. Although I wish I had never received that horrendous call, I have released the trauma around it.

*Feeling the Feelings*

There is no right way to grieve, and I allow myself to have all my feelings. Even seven years later, grief still pops up at unexpected moments and catches me by surprise. I welcome it, witness it, and let it move through me like a breeze. On those occasions when the waves hit hard and I feel like I am drowning in grief, I remember to call on my spiritual warrior friends to send light, love, and energy. It works; I always feel so much better afterwards.

*Forgiveness Work*

Upon learning of Jon's suicide, I was, understandably, angry and distressed. Jon has asked for our forgiveness, and I feel fortunate that I've been able to forgive him. It's said that *resentments rot the container they're in*, and I have chosen and continue to choose to let go of resentments and forgive.

Because it includes a forgiveness component, SourceTapping has helped me forgive. In addition, I often use Ho'oponopono (a Hawaiian forgiveness technique): Thinking of the person and my upset feelings, I repeat, in any order, "I love you, I'm sorry, please forgive me, thank you."

Sometimes, in order to forgive, I try to understand the feelings and needs that lie beneath the action. Jon did what he felt he needed to do, and he had no idea how his actions would impact us, the people who love him so much.

Yes, I forgive him. I forgive him with all of my heart.


## CONNECTING WITH JON'S SPIRIT


The October 15 butterfly was the first message I recognized from the other side. I continue to get what I consider other messages and signs:

- Jon was technologically savvy and seems to be reaching out to us through cell phones and radios. I flew from Tucson to Cleveland for the memorial service. As we taxied for takeoff, my phone rang. I showed my seatmate my phone, which was, in fact, turned off—yet Jon (I believe) finagled it so a call would come through! During the memorial service, too, Jon stayed in touch by causing phones to ring all over the place.
- A few weeks after Jon's death, my six-year-old granddaughter accompanied me on a few errands. She sat in her booster seat in the back and I had the radio off, so I could hear the little chatterbox talking. At the bank, I sat waiting to have a document notarized and asked if my bored granddaughter could have a piece of paper. She spent a few minutes busily drawing a picture. When she showed it to me, I told her I liked her beautiful flower and asked what was in the middle of it, and she replied, "That's Uncle Jonny's face."

  After leaving the bank, I secured my granddaughter in her booster seat and started the car. The radio popped on with Nat

King Cole singing an old song, "The Very Thought of You." As I listened to the lyrics, my eyes bugged out when I heard him singing, "I see your face in every flower."

Wow! I knew Jon was good with technology. I had no doubt he had sent us this message as I sat holding my granddaughter's drawing of a flower with Uncle Jonny's face in the middle.

- Very late one night as I slept, the smoke detector (located on a high cathedral ceiling in my bedroom) went off. I didn't have a broom or a long stick handy to dislodge it, so I asked my son for help. "Jon, please turn that thing off until morning." Sure enough, it stopped blaring. And then it started again—at 7:00 a.m.

- A few months after Jon's passing, I thought I heard his voice during a meditation. Immediately I started questioning this and thought I must be making it all up. So, I said to the voice, "Jon, if this is really you, then heat up the [ceramic] pendant I'm wearing." The voice replied, "Ma, there are some things I haven't learned how to do yet!" The words and the tone of the voice sounded just like my son and made a believer out of me.

- I continue to get messages directly from Jon, and sometimes he sends them through other people. For instance, I booked a massage with someone who didn't know my history. As she began the treatment, I heard a *kerplunk* and asked her about the noise. She replied, "The spinning ball on top of my desktop waterfall just fell off. How strange." I told her my son had recently died and she said, "He's here—he's a huge presence. He said to tell you he's happy and feeling great, and he loves you." I believed her and had a knowingness that he was with me.

I am grateful for the continued communication I have with Jon. It seems I connect with him more now than when he was on the earth plane. I talk to him daily, and I also ask for his help and guidance. Many times, when thinking of him, I turn on the radio and smile as I hear the lyrics "I see your face in every flower." Sometimes I can physically feel his presence and the huge amount of love he is emanating.

Through the years, Ali and I have talked to George and other mediums and continue to get messages from Jon. He says he is great, and he is helping other young people adapt when they cross over.

In a recent meditation, I told Jon how much I miss him and want to see him. I saw an outline of a head and heard the words, *Mom, I am just light now . . . and I am all around you.*

Although I love and miss my son and often wish he were still here, my life is full. Even though I sometimes sink into deep grief momentarily, the time spent there is getting shorter and shorter. And, since I've experienced the lowest of lows, I also have been able to experience the highest of highs in deep and blissful joy.

I feel Jon's presence when I tune in. He is my guardian angel now, and has told me over and over, *I have your back.*

I feel his love, and I am at peace.

## NOTE

1. Ping Qin, "The Impact of Parental Status on the Risk of Completed Suicide," *Arch Gen Psychiatry* 60 (August 2003): 797–802.

\* \* \*

**Meryl Hershey Beck**, MA, MEd, is a retired licensed counselor, author of *Stop Eating Your Heart Out*, and creator of SourceTapping. Meryl still communicates with Jon, during meditation or through a medium. They have an easy relationship now and are actually more connected than ever even though he's no longer in physical form. As a master teacher, she conducts international workshops and trainings on such topics as grief and loss and is a frequent presenter at international conferences. Even though she suffered major loss, Meryl is still known by many as "The Ambassador of Joy." Learn more at her websites, www.StopEatingYourHeartOut.com, www.SourceTapping.com, and www.LossSurviveThrive.com.

## · *16* ·

# A Gift from the Stars

### *By Janice Crowder-Torrez*

*Anthony*

*M*ost of my adult life I've spent working in health care, first as an RN and then as a certified nurse midwife. The stress of working in multiple environments where bottom lines were more important than health care delivery was troubling. The numbers of patients needing health care services increased, while available services dwindled. Working long hours with longer commute times made me an easy target for burnout.

Arriving home late to care for family was often met with easy convenience foods, short showers, and falling into bed, only to wake up the next day for the same routine. Days off consisted of running errands for groceries, laundry, and medical appointments. Because the health care business is a 24/7 operation, working weekends and holidays was commonplace, even expected. Finding family time or vacation time was next to impossible as schools adopted year-round scheduling with families juggling kids on different tracks.

Our family of four (my husband, son, daughter, and me) was lucky to arrange several four-day getaways twice a year. Camping in the High Sierras or a quick trip to San Francisco became our preferred vacations. Occasionally we had to forgo our four-day getaway due to last-minute scheduling changes or an unexpected health crisis. Always on autopilot, my body continued to go through the motions, while my brain often struggled to make sense of it all.

Relocating to Tucson, Arizona, in 2011 was a last-ditch effort to escape the rat race lifestyle I had created for myself in California. Moving to the open desert provided a tranquil, healing, and much-needed lifestyle change.

Our elder child, Anthony, had been living on his own in an apartment near the Claremont Colleges (California), enjoying the headspace many graduate students share. But after facing several health crises, and without getting the results he desired, he called us for help several months after I had moved to Tucson. Anthony had been plagued since birth with insomnia, allergies, joint pain, and bruising. The fact that physicians were unable to correctly diagnose the root cause of his symptoms led him to experience many treatments, which often did little to help, and in some cases caused further harm.

At the age of thirty, Anthony finally saw both an integrative medicine physician and a geneticist in Tucson who confirmed his suspicions. In addition to a severe mold allergy or toxicity known as CIRS (chronic inflammatory response syndrome), he suffered from Ehler-Danlos syndrome (EDS), a collagen disorder often described as hypermobility syndrome. Many in the medical community do not seem to understand there are varying degrees of EDS—in 2017, thirteen subtypes of EDS were identified. While current research seems to point to many contributing factors, there appears to be a genetic component, a link to the pollution found in our air, food, water, and soil, as well as a connection to childhood traumas such as accidents, falls, surgeries, bullying, abuse, etc. Anthony was quite relieved to discover this was not "all in his head," as many physicians had led him to believe.

Anthony moved to Tucson in October 2011 and continued to enjoy hiking and exploring the desert until his pain became too unmanageable. Although we did not sense it, I now think he knew somehow his days were limited. Almost two years to the day of his arrival in Tucson, my beloved Anthony chose to exit. In spite of his health history, my firstborn's death came as an unexpected shock. The county sheriff arrived at our front door on a Friday evening, October 4, 2013, to announce his untimely death.

My son's passing was both numbing and paralyzing. Time became irrelevant, and grief, overwhelming. As many will attest to, the loss of one's child does not follow any natural order. Neighbors delivered meals, offered a listening ear, and sent their condolences. I am forever grateful for their kindness.

Several years later, I heard or read the following phrase, and I continue to carry it with me always: In cases of unexpected or traumatic death, "When the soul is being called, the body must leave quickly" (author unknown).

Have to admit . . . I would never have arrived at the place I am now without my son's exit. Although sometimes difficult to explain, I am grateful for this experience. Has it been a tough journey? Very. And will it continue to be? Maybe. But I think once I have completed my purpose, I too will be ready to move to the *Next Place*. But not yet—my soul is still growing.

When I experienced the loss of my child—or, as I now prefer to say, when my child passed—my world as I knew it stopped. My grief journey was not only about the loss of my son's physical body, but a dramatic shift occurred in my belief system, as well as every story I had believed to be true, including my position in the universe. I started to wonder, *Who am I?* and *Why am I here?* and I began to question every single part of my life. What is, and what was. What did I like about my current journey or my past, my child, my family? What was the true meaning of life?

Some background. Looking back, my life has always been less than normal. But it was *my* normal. Certain experiences as a child were unusual, but I was not given permission to share, being part of the *be seen and not heard* generation. Looking back, I think my human spirit wanted and needed some kind of validation of my existence or the experiences I had. There were also many traumas in my life as a child, teen, and adult. But now the details don't seem so important, although acknowledging they happened is.

To make it brief, I buried a lot of my history.

Having a child is an amazing experience. I believe it awakens something inside of us. And I realized early on my son was a gift.

Anthony's curiosity at a young age was met with more questions and startling discoveries about the universe as seen through his eyes. Many referred to him as extraordinary. At the ages of two and three, he often pointed toward stars in the sky and cheerfully said, "I'm from there!" Although we often made jokes about this, he was pretty adamant.

Anthony also had a very advanced vocabulary, so much so that his dad and I often had to consult a dictionary to understand the words he used in everyday conversation. Many adults would look at him, pause, then look at us and ask, "Where is this kid *from?*" We repeatedly shared our own puzzled expressions while pointing to the sky or the stars and said, "He says he's from there!"

An early fascination with religious texts shaped Anthony's thoughts about nonviolence, love, and kindness. His grandfather (a USAF pilot, mathematician, and engineer) shared his thoughts about the expansiveness of the universe, while his grandmother (a creative, intuitive woman) shared her imagination and love of nature. It was no surprise, then, that my son and I often spoke of alternate or parallel universes. Both of us were convinced something far greater than our energy-filled earthly life experiences existed.

Anthony graduated from CSUSB (California State University, San Bernardino) with his Department Chair's Award for "Most Outstanding Graduating Senior." His love of science and the arts became his foundation, plus his passion for glassblowing. But it was his genuine kindness toward others that is remembered by most. His willingness to anticipate the needs of others before being asked was a rare and appreciated gift.

When he was in elementary school, we often kidded Anthony about his being *the boy in the bubble.* Numerous medical appointments to different specialists became the norm. Soon it was no longer something to laugh about. It was difficult. Working many shifts with overtime became necessary to cover high insurance rates and over-the-top medical bills. Our life became different, but I was used to having a different kind of life, so I continued to work and ignore my feelings. Working in health care, I knew how important it was to be kind and show compassion to my patients or clients. Somewhere along the way, however, I discovered my work ethic had become a distraction from life. Burnout was frequently a problem; finding any kind of balance was rare.

So . . . my son, of all people, became my *guide.* Sometimes it felt like our conversations were as if I was talking to a perfect stranger. He was so deep, so philosophical, and so unique. Anthony would often speak in such a way that I truly believed I was speaking to someone not of this world. It seemed odd. But there was something about his knowledge and insight that told me he was different from the rest. I guess he, too, knew he was different because I often heard him mutter under his breath, "Why can't I just be normal?"

As my *guide*, when I sustained an injury, he quickly offered suggestions, such as both restorative and gentle yoga, then meditation to calm my mind. Taking me to several classes, he explained why it was so critical that I continue on this path.

After my son passed, we discovered just how many people he had helped—people from all walks of life. Some he had met online and some lived in different states, and many were struggling. When we started calling the contacts on his cell phone to notify them of his passing, many were in disbelief and convinced we were playing a cruel or sick joke on them. Many spoke of their deep conversations with Anthony on life and death, but it was his extreme kindness, his humor, his unrelenting desire to understand how everything in the universe worked, and his love of music that everyone remembered.

Music seemed to be my son's constant companion. Often seen wearing headphones when he was alone or working on a project, Anthony would turn and smile while listening to his many different selections of music and quickly inform me, "I'm healing my brain."

After the initial shock of his passing, which lasted weeks, our family began our grief journey. We met with several grief support groups that did not end up working for us—many people were still bitter and angry years after their loved ones had passed, and I was determined to honor my son's beautiful spirit by sharing all the joy he brought to my life.

We decided to *mourn* Anthony's passing during Tucson's "All Souls Procession" and carried larger-than-life pictures of him through the three-mile downtown walk. Being part of this celebration of loved ones lost provided hope and tremendous healing.

Several weeks later we celebrated my son's life with a memorial service. His kindness toward others in their hour of need, his love of life, and his sense of humor were all recognized and will always be a part of his legacy. In addition, he is revered for his vast wealth of knowledge— he knew so much about everything, and yet he was so humble about all of it. His collection of friends and healers in the community, including some from out of state, emulated his love of truth, creativity, and music.

My continued search for answers to my son's untimely death, wondering what could have been done to prevent this family tragedy, led me once again to question our health care system, including the many shortcomings of our mental health care system. Attending a class offered by NAMI (National Alliance on Mental Illness) helped explain how our mental health care system does and doesn't work. But I often wonder why the mental health community does not believe in or understand the strong connection between physical health and mental health. It is my opinion that *incorrectly diagnosed or undiagnosed physical illness creates symptoms of mental illness.*

Every family feels shock when another member dies so suddenly. We were no different. Although my son suffered a lot of health problems, his untimely death was still unexpected and traumatic. Most troubling was not having the opportunity to tell him how much I loved him or being able to say good-bye.

The month after Anthony's passing, I was guided to a phone session with a well-known certified medium, Suzanne Wilson, who suggested I might find the grief support group Helping Parents Heal (HPH) a good fit. I decided it was worth the two-hour drive to Phoenix to check it out.

At the beginning of 2014, several months after Anthony's passing, I drove to Phoenix for my first HPH meeting. Arriving early, I was invited into a conversation with a group of women seated comfortably in the lobby. Sharing their deep wisdom about our *life's plan* brought me comfort. They quickly referred me to Robert Schwartz's *Your Soul's Gift.* Opening the book, I immediately turned to chapter 11, on suicide. After rereading this chapter several times, I knew I had found some of the answers I was looking for. Both Herb and Anne Puryear warmly introduced themselves, giving me a tour of the center, while offering healing words. (Soon after, I began reading Anne's book *Stephen Lives!*)

Fortunate to meet Elizabeth Boisson, one of the two cofounders of Helping Parents Heal, I was immediately taken in by her incredible presence. This beautiful soul radiates a love that is difficult to explain in words except to say it's as if her heart, soul, and spirit energy are one.

Helping Parents Heal is a nonprofit organization dedicated to assisting bereaved parents. According to their website, www.helping parentsheal.org,

HPH's mission is to help parents whose children have passed on, giving them support and resources to aid in the healing process. We go a step beyond other groups by allowing the open discussion of spiritual experiences and afterlife evidence but in a non-dogmatic way. We welcome everyone regardless of religious (or nonreligious) background and allow for a very open type of dialog. We receive all and do not judge people or their children on the basis of life choices.

HPH's philosophy spoke to both my son's and my values, and the HPH meeting offered clarity and hope. We shared stories and validations. I started to understand how all of us create our own grief journeys, and left feeling very hopeful and at peace. It quickly became evident how personal our grief journeys are given our different histories and personal circumstances. I slept well that night and was excited to share the HPH meeting with my family. I knew then my husband's and daughter's grief journeys had to be their own; so, my (own) grief journey began.

Still searching for answers, my ever-growing reading list included works by many spiritual teachers and leaders. Surprisingly, I found many of the suggested reads to also be in my son's private collection of books.

HPH offered many resources. For instance, Sheri Perl Migdol's (The Prayer Registry) words helped alleviate my strong feelings of guilt, which are often associated with the loss of a loved one to suicide. Mark Pitstick's newsletter on Soulproof.com offered answers as to why our loved ones "die" and removed some of the stigma associated with my son's decision to leave. (Not condoning suicide, but the stigma often associated with suicide adds to the tremendous burden of grief often felt by those of us left behind.)

My continued reading allowed me to grieve privately while offering hope. Written by many different authors, the books expanded my awareness much in the same manner as my son's conversations. I realized how much I was going to miss my son's physical presence.

In addition to attending HPH in Phoenix, I sought resources closer to home. Near the one-year anniversary of Anthony's passing, I contacted Audra White of MISS Foundation in Tucson. (MISS Foundation is a volunteer-based, nonprofit organization that provides C.A.R.E.—counseling, advocacy, research, and education—services to families experiencing the death of a child.) In her meetings Audra illustrated how sharing our stories with other grieving parents helps create a sense of power, promoting healing.

My journey did not stop there. I quickly discovered with all of the responsibilities of tying up the loose ends associated with the tragic loss of a loved one, many of my friend and work-related relationships were dissolving. In time, my initial sadness was replaced with an increased awareness of the kindness of strangers. Someone held a door open for me at the local post office. Another offered a smile. I started meeting people in the most unusual and random places—on walks, in the market, at the bookstore. I found myself drawn to others who also shared loss and, in the process, began to recognize a purity of spirit, an authenticity that often occurs with soul growth.

However, my grief journey, which I now describe as a roller-coaster ride, took a plunge into deeper sadness. I kept replaying the tape, "What could I have done differently? How could I have prevented this tragedy?"

I knew I had to sell my son's car. Unable to bear the thought of not seeing Anthony's smiling face saying a big hello as he drove his car up our driveway, I arranged a visit with Jerry, an auto broker who had assisted our family with the purchase of several vehicles.

Explaining my situation, I decided to sell my car and keep my son's vehicle instead. Jerry turned to me out of the blue and very kindly said, "I'll bet you'll feel better if you take a walk every morning." Surprised to hear his suggestion, I wondered if he really understood what I had been through. On some level, did he understand this unbearable pain? However, I took his suggestion and I began to walk. And . . . I started to feel better.

My journey now began with me asking questions. *How many angels were now appearing in my day-to-day existence?*

Fairly quickly, I concluded that awareness was key. Instead of allowing old tapes to constantly replay in my head, I chose to retrain my heart and soul to feel, which required a lot of positive self-talk and meditation skill. In addition, creating a *sacred space* in our home to honor my son's soul and spirit became another important part of my healing. Photos, heart-shaped rocks, tiny Buddhas, Anthony's glass-blown art, feathers, smiley face trinkets, anything reminding me of my son's presence took up residence in this *sacred space*. Listening to his favorite music reminds me of his frequent comment, "Music helps heal my brain, Mom." His words are forever etched in my memory.

Eventually, each one of us finds our way to building a belief system which resonates with us. I learned grief has no timeline. Just as there is no right or wrong way to grieve. Our path or journey to healing is our path alone. Sometimes along the way, we become more open, aware, and accepting that we are part of something much greater, and our soul and spirit begin to grow. We learn to open our hearts again and discover that our physical presence here is truly limited.

Although attending HPH monthly meetings in Phoenix was comforting, in time I wanted something closer and, with Elizabeth's blessing, I became an affiliate leader of Tucson's HPH. After a slow start and location change, the attendance at Tucson's HPH meetings began to increase. These meetings have been honored with the presence of certified mediums, authors, and energy healers. Many parents experiencing loss now find healing at these meetings.

Because of other demands on my time, almost two years later I stepped down as an affiliate leader, treasuring the days spent with HPH. In addition to being a lifeline for others, holding that position helped with my healing, too.

Listening to my heart and soul, I soon discovered more time was needed for quiet reflection. Having ignored much of my past, it was now time for me to do some down-deep internal work of my own. My grief journey was now leading me toward my soul's growth.

But I also found my journey to be a mere drop in the bucket compared to the many challenges my son faced every day with bravery and courage. The physical pain he endured with EDS was rarely addressed by the allopathic community and often ignored. Treatment options were and still are limited. Pain medications covered by medical insurance offer little relief, while other healing modalities such as acupuncture and massage are not covered.

My son often said having an *invisible disability* was cruel and unusual punishment. He often wondered how he could afford to live. In spite of his education, work history, and many gifts, he was unable to find work in Tucson. Many jobs barely covered living expenses, and health care was not an affordable option. Unfortunately, he and countless others share this sad reality and far too often fall through the cracks.

A brief word about visions, dream visits, and validations. I firmly believe our loved ones continue to reach out to us and let us know our energy connections are still present. (While typing the last paragraph,

I glanced toward the arches of our front door and out of the corner of my eye saw my son walking down our hallway toward the kitchen, where we always spoke. It was midday, and the sun was shining brightly. I captured a quick glimpse of my son's six-foot-two-inch frame walking past the front door. I got up to follow, but he was no longer there.)

I now believe our soul energy is greater than what we have been led to believe. Keeping an open heart and a trusting self and honoring self-love, self-care, and self-forgiveness have become important life lessons for me.

Thank you, Anthony, for being an incredible teacher. You helped me understand the importance of an open heart, trust in self, and forgiveness. I am overwhelmed with gratitude for you and the gift of your beautiful presence. I cherish every moment of every day we spent together, and I love you with all of my heart till the end of time.

\* \* \*

**Janice Crowder-Torrez, MS (RN, CNM—ret.)** spent most of her professional career in California before relocating to Tucson, Arizona, with her family. She is currently busy writing a book about her son's life and the many challenges he faced in the course of his thirty-one years. Janice also spends much of her time exploring and practicing various healing energies including Focused Awareness Meditation, Holographic Memory Resolution, SourceTapping, and the healing power of music. Janice lives with her husband, Bob, and their two dachshunds, Roscoe and Dharma.

## • *17* •

# My Life Reconstructed

### *By Kelley Ireland*

*I* was thirty-four years old when my eighteen-year-old son Leslie shot himself in the head and died. He was my only child. A relationship with a girl he loved had ended and Leslie was devastated. My son was handsome, funny and smart, popular with friends and with girls. He was a happy, outgoing child and always adjusted well to changing situations.

I didn't notice anything really glaring in his behavior that would indicate he was considering ending his life, but only because I didn't have the tools or knowledge that would have brought something to my awareness. In retrospect, there were signs that were present that I had attributed to teenage angst and really nothing more. There were no radical changes in his behavior, his moods, or in the way he interacted with his family or friends. And I'm not alone in that assessment. Not one person came forward after the fact saying, "Yes, I knew he was considering this."

Leslie grew up around guns. His father was a hunter and outdoorsman. I never wanted guns in our home, but as in any marriage, concessions are made. So, guns were secured, locked in a cabinet, and the ammunition was stored elsewhere. But as things go, we tend to discount how smart and able our children are. Our son accessed a small .22-caliber pistol, and it was the weapon he used on himself.

When Leslie died, everything in my life took on a surreal quality. I busied myself with planning his funeral, intent on forcing people to see that he'd been a joyful, fun-loving boy who had lived a happy life. I was determined that he not be defined by his suicide, and I did all I could to prevent that from happening. At his funeral, people thought I was heavily sedated; I suppose because I was robotic, going through the motions of polite greetings, thanking people, and holding tightly on to my emotions. I simply could not allow people to see what I was feeling because I had not yet even accessed that well of grief myself. In reality, I was not sedated, but was merely in the fog of shock.

As I reflect back, I realize the layer of shock was so thick that I don't remember certain things about that time. It was some time after the funeral before the fog lifted, and once it did, the horror of the reality that lay before me was revealed. When it was, I began to obsess about my sanity and feared I was losing it.

Everything in my life changed forever the moment my son died. I could no longer connect to life, even in the simplest of ways. The sun was too bright, the trees too green. It was all too blinding, too much. I felt like I was living in a Salvador Dalí painting where the mundane was grossly distorted.

After the local paper posted Leslie's obituary, I received several calls from complete strangers telling me that they also had experienced the loss of their young sons to suicide. I met with one lady who, shortly after our meeting, had a mental/emotional breakdown and ended up in a mental health institution. I recall visiting her there, terrified I would "catch" what she had and end up there, too. I could almost feel it happening to me and was scared to death.

What felt like an endless videotape of Leslie's death scene played in my mind all day, during my waking hours. It started from the moment I received the call about my son's death, to the drive to his place after his roommate had found him, to the police arrival and departure, to our returning back home afterward, where my husband and I collapsed onto the floor and stayed there until the next morning. I later learned that getting onto the floor or ground is a primal reaction to trauma.

I became obsessed with thoughts of dying myself. Let me be clear, though: I was not suicidal at all. I just wanted to be dead. I kept hoping something—some accident or lightning strike—would kill me, so I would be finally relieved of the horrific emotional pain I was feeling. I did not want to live as I was, in constant, palpable pain. But each day I woke up alive and disappointed that I was. Alive, yet I existed in a world that seemed like nothing but personal darkness.

Eventually I returned to my daily life, but this endless tape played on unabated in the background of my various comings and goings. I became immersed in a black abyss of negativity and guilt, blaming myself for not seeing his plight, for not protecting my son as well as a good parent would.

The burden of Leslie's death was unrelenting. My immediate family was reeling from shock and grief, too. And though they were intensely supportive, they were struggling to get through each day, like I was. My husband feared for my safety as well as my sanity. He was also concerned for our marriage and did all he could to help me.

Our neighbor, Lucy, was a young, beautiful new mom. I would visit her and her new baby from time to time, and it always struck me how bubbly and positive she was. But it also bothered me that she was this way because I was anything but gregarious. Again, it was the "too everything" syndrome that was plaguing me, and this only added to my frustrations. Lucy was too much, her great life was too much, and it was all about to drive me crazy.

One day, I asked Lucy how she was always able to be so positive, and she said that she surrounds herself with great, uplifting people, which was very important to her. I remember leaving her home and grumbling to myself, *Oh sure, go out and get a dozen really great people and everything will all be great. Yeah. Right!* At the time, I was new to Tucson, so the only friends I had were coworker relationships, not *real* friends. I completely discounted what Lucy said and rationalized her behavior by telling myself that she felt as she did because nothing horrible had ever happened to her like it had to me. A big part of me felt I deserved my misery.

But I also knew I could not continue the way I had been living. I could not simply get up, go to work, come home, and go straight to bed every day, which was exactly what I had been doing. I had checked out of my life, my marriage, and to be honest, I was barely functioning.

Early on, within days of my son's death, I decided to find a therapist. I didn't realize that grief counselors even existed, but I found one near my home and went to see her. She was lovely and kind, but what I didn't know was that she was newly minted and did not have the experience to really know what the grief process was like, other than through her educational training.

This woman sent me home from our first visit with the assignment of creating my new life on paper, and I was to bring it back to her the following week. She was surprised when I returned a week later with a blank notebook. I could not even fathom a *new life* without my son and told her so. I only saw her a few more times before moving on to another counselor.

About ten years after Leslie died, that first grief counselor, who is a dear woman, wrote me a letter apologizing for her insistence that I focus on my new life without my son. She had recently experienced the death of her husband and was experiencing, for herself, her very first grief experience. She said she finally understood why I could not set aside my grief to focus on a golden future without my son. I will always treasure her apology because it meant so much to me to get such a heartfelt validation of my feelings so long after my loss had occurred.

I continued going to individual private therapy for years; intensely at first, and then sporadically, whenever I felt I needed more help. I also tried a couple support groups in the beginning—The Compassionate Friends and Suicide Survivors. Though Compassionate Friends is for parents who have suffered the death of a child, I didn't resonate much with this group. I also didn't feel a strong connection to Suicide Survivors even though I wanted to, because I felt I needed immersion in a supportive group of people I could relate to, that would help me begin to heal.

In the beginning of my grief process, it felt imperative for me to see others and how they had survived a week after the loss, a month, six months, a year, and so on. I couldn't even make it through fifteen minutes most days, let alone the rest of my life. I needed to see how these other survivors did it. *How did . . . how could they recover? Or could they?*

On my third try, I found a group that met weekly and was led by a grief counselor, who I credit with saving my life. This was a general grief support group for all death losses, and I attended for a year and a half. I learned that what all of us were feeling was normal. It was comforting to learn that other people talked to their dead loved one's photos, too. They also smelled their loved one's clothing and at times sprayed their pillows with the favorite perfume or cologne of the one who passed. And yes, they too sometimes felt strongly that their cherished one was still with them.

It was there that I learned that healing grief can only be accomplished by addressing it head-on and working through it; that it is the hardest emotional work we will ever do. I was assured that I would not always feel as I did right at that moment, and in time, life would return to a *different normal* and could actually be *good* and could even be worth living again.

I learned that loss is a normal occurrence in life, and we will all experience it in myriad ways as we go about living our lives. I also learned that in our Western culture, we don't teach people about the process of grieving—that it does not end at a certain time, that not all people will have the same experiences. I learned what being *stuck* in grief actually looked like. While I recognized that I had been stuck in my grief for quite a while, a little after my first year in the group I realized that was no longer the case.

After attending this group for as long as I did, I felt like I had been a real student of the grief process and I wanted to share the knowledge I had gained with other grievers. I would often speak to my mother about my grief group and she would tell me how glad she was I had found help, but that she wished there was something like it for people in small towns like hers, which was Globe, Arizona.

One day while I was vacuuming, I was inspired by a big idea. I have always joked that my *big ideas* always come to me when I'm cleaning house, but really, it turns out to be true. I asked my husband if he thought I could facilitate a grief support group in rural Arizona. I wanted to hold it in the town I had grown up in for people like my mother and others who had nowhere to turn to begin healing. Mental health care services were nearly nonexistent for them, and grief support was a foreign concept.

My husband felt certain I could do that and do it well. I took a drive over to Globe, about a two hours' drive from the city I live in, to start knocking on doors to see if someone would allow me to use a building where I could hold my grief group. I said out loud that if I was meant to do this, it would happen. If I was not, it would not.

For the meetings, I wanted a place that was not affiliated with a hospital or a church—a *neutral* place that people couldn't associate with their loved one's death. As I drove into town, the first place I stopped was the county courthouse. Nearly colliding with a county supervisor who was on his way out the door, I introduced myself and told him about my plan. Although we didn't have an appointment and he didn't know me from Adam, he immediately agreed to let me use a courtroom to conduct my group in, and even said he would have a janitor open the door for us on Sundays at the designated time! I took this as *the sign* I was meant to do this.

Calling the group "Good Grief," I did radio spots and wrote newspaper articles advertising it throughout the community. I explained the concept of grief as being a normal part of life that needed expression and work to get through and that in doing so the real healing could begin.

Eventually, Good Grief gained nonprofit status and I held the meetings twice monthly. At one point we moved our gathering place from the courtroom to the local chamber of commerce to accommodate the growing number of people who came. I was fortunate enough that therapists and even an author on grief and loss came and spoke to our group on occasion. I facilitated the group for several years until a job transfer caused my husband and me to make a move out of state, to Nevada.

Once settled in our new home in Reno, to aid in my own healing, I began attending events that I knew nurtured my mental and spiritual health—musical events, self-help seminars, drumming circles—and I saw healers of varying types. I did Reiki and yoga and pored over books on grief and loss. Some were excellent, and some were not.

In time, I went back to college and studied death and dying, grief counseling, and why people choose to die by suicide. I became a suicide crisis line volunteer and worked a night shift on weekends to try to better understand what drives people to take their own lives. Over the years, I attended many seminars by grief counselors and authors of books on grief.

At the time of my son's death, I had a very physical job as a US Postal Service letter carrier that tired me out each day, so I had no trouble sleeping soundly. This, in turn, helped with my depression and helped reduce the ruminations of my mind on my son's death. I focused intently on my health after learning how detrimental loss is to the immune system and how often people become seriously ill after a significant loss such as mine. I am not a religious person but consider myself to be spiritual, so I attempted to hone my spiritual chops by trying and using methods that worked, including many spiritual self-help books. What didn't work was cast aside. *Take what you like and leave the rest*, as I've often heard it expressed.

I always remembered Lucy, my cute young neighbor who had long ago moved away. I knew she had planted a seed in my mind about seeking people I wanted to attract and with whom I could cultivate good, healthy relationships. To my delight, I realized this was slowly beginning to happen.

My husband was a big advocate of the power of positive thinking, so I began to listen to tapes and embrace what I had formerly dismissed as his Pollyanna approach to life. I began to use affirmations, which were a popular part of New Age culture so prevalent at the time. Though I originally thought it was hogwash, and felt like a fraud when I said them, I forced myself to start repeating them. I later heard a term used by a popular TV psychologist: *Fake it 'til you make it.* That made me laugh because that's exactly what I was doing with the affirmations! At first, I didn't believe in them whatsoever, but after a time, like the very seed planted by Lucy, they took root in my heart and mind and I finally began to attract healthy and loving people into my life.

When I started Good Grief, I wrote and distributed affirmations to people for posting in various places around their home or office that they would frequently see, to remind themselves that they would not always feel as they did in the aftermath of their tragic loss.

I also started using affirmations to figure out how, even in the wake of my devastation, I could retrain my thoughts by choosing to reflect on all the good I still had in my life. I taped affirmations all over my house—on the fridge, on my bathroom mirror, in my car—and I also kept them handy in my pockets and even inside my purse. It didn't happen overnight, but in time I came to realize that not everything was lost to me, even if the most important person in my life was no longer with us.

Each day I could choose happiness, but it would not always be an easy choice. On days I felt particularly down or negative, tearful or sad, I learned to simply allow those feelings the space they needed to exist; that if acknowledged, they would soon pass, as everything always does. It is never a linear process from the point of loss to healing, and sometimes it's a one-step-forward-two-steps-back sort of dance, but we get there if we are willing to stay the course.

As time passed, another big idea dawned on me while I was caring for my elderly father. I noticed how my formerly active father's physical condition had declined over a fairly short period of time. I gave a lot of thought to how I might help other people do things that had become so important to my dad in his last years.

He wanted desperately to remain independent and live out his life at home. As a former workplace safety and injury prevention trainer, I sought out information about programs for fall prevention.

Not having a lot of luck with this idea, I decided to explore the possibility that the ancient practice of Tai Chi might be beneficial, though, oddly enough, I knew less than nothing about it. I thought it might be a good practice that was gentle, but effective, in helping with movement, range of motion, balance, and healthy longevity. I clearly recall attending a three-day Tai Chi seminar and leaving there on fire with the kind of passion one feels when they have fallen in love with Mr. or Ms. Right. I knew right then and there it was something I had to study and pass on to others.

Now into my sixty-third year, I've come to discover that if you want something bad enough and seek it with pure intention, you can make it happen—absolutely. I wanted to become certified to teach Tai Chi and Qigong, its sister practice (a warm-up), and the teacher I would need became clear. Knowing that this ancient internal art is learned at a very young age in China, I was compelled to go there and study. I felt a strong need to be learning in the place where it all began and immerse myself in the culture to further authenticate my teaching.

I have been teaching Tai Chi and Qigong classes for nearly ten years now, and I find it to be very fulfilling. My students range from cancer survivors to people with chronic musculoskeletal disorders like osteo- and rheumatoid arthritis, lupus, hearing loss, stroke recovery, and other chronic conditions that require movement for healing. This has made my life rich with purpose, happiness, and joy. Nothing else makes me beam as I do when someone tells me how much they benefit from training with me.

America's gun violence crisis is growing rapidly, and since my recent retirement, I have immersed myself in a gun violence prevention group, which, for me, is a meaningful and rewarding interaction. Too many people are dying every day in America by suicide and other forms of gun violence. It makes Leslie's death more palatable when I'm presenting "Be Smart" training to interested parties about the recognition of the signs of suicide in teens and arming them with strategies for prevention.

This is a free course provided by Moms Demand Action for Gun Sense in America for police departments, emergency responders, teachers, PTA/PTO personnel, doctors, and other community service professionals. The program is informational, with the intent of reducing opportunities children have to access and fire a gun. Through our interested participants, we are able to get our message to gun owners they come in contact with on how to properly store, lock up, and prevent unsafe access to guns.

I also participate in "Be Smart" tabling events with other gun violence activists at health fairs and festivals. Very grateful to participate in this cause, I often refer to myself as the Accidental Activist. If one person is positively affected by this and a suicide or homicide is prevented, it would not only be lifesaving for them, but also enrich my life beyond measure.

My son's death was twenty-nine years ago. There are still days I revisit my grief as if it was fresh, but it doesn't happen nearly as often as it used to and the feelings don't last as long. I'll hear a song on the radio, taste a food I knew he loved, and be right back at Day One. Sometimes that awful, endless recording plays again in my mind and I cry, feel lonely for my son, and rage the *Why? Why? Why?* at the Universe.

I often imagine Leslie with graying hair and see the children who look like him that will never come. I catch a glimpse of myself in a mirror and see his face in my own. People ask about my children or grandchildren and there are none to tell about. When I'm asked, "Why don't you have children?" I ponder whether or not to say something about my loss. Sometimes I say that I had a son die. Sometimes, to keep it simple, I just say I don't have any children. There are days I'm mad at Leslie, where I feel robbed, ruined, and victimized all over again. And there are days I feel incredibly guilty and tell myself I failed as a mother. Over the years, I've learned to allow those thoughts and feelings to come in. I acknowledge to myself that they're there, and I know that like clouds on a breezy day, they will soon pass if I just relax and let them move through me.

Interestingly, there is a Tai Chi movement called "Watching Clouds Pass." The narrative I use when my students perform this movement is: "We can never still our minds. Thoughts will come and go. Notice them and just allow them to come, and, like clouds, watch them pass quietly away."

I found dear Lucy through social media and thanked her for changing my life that day way back in her kitchen. She knows now what a profound difference that has made in my life, and I know that makes her feel glad.

I offer this story to you as hope. I want you to know, without doubt, that there's a rich, bountiful life to be lived even after you've lost someone you love so dearly. It takes work and a lot of time. After the death of your loved one, your life will look entirely different to you than your life "before" ever did. You will be a changed person afterward, perhaps in ways you never asked for or even dreamed possible. You may find you are more compassionate, more loving, and more accepting, and the grief will become an intricate part of the fabric that is your life. It will never go away or be forgotten, and you wouldn't want that anyway, if it could.

You *will* laugh again. You'll recover your old sense of humor in time and happiness will return. Every loss will transform differently for every person, but if you choose to, you absolutely get to be the boss and CEO of your outcome. You get to consciously craft a new life. And I'm here to tell you, if I can do it, anyone surely can.

There comes a time when we must make a conscious choice to be happy. It's a daily thing, that decision. At first, it feels forced. But in time it becomes another thread, woven into the tapestry of our lives. Bad things will continue to happen to us throughout life, and we will react to them in a number of various ways. But we can still choose to be grateful and happy no matter what, even in the wake of our most devastating losses.

I miss you so much, Little Boy, and I hold so many sweet memories of you in my heart. I'm grateful for every day we had together, and I look forward to being reunited with you again.

\* \* \*

**Kelley Ireland** is a sixty-three-year-old Arizona native who grew up in the small copper-mining town of Globe. She recently retired from a forty-year career with the federal government in risk management/occupational safety. Kelley is a gun violence prevention activist, a Tai Chi/Qigong teacher, and a fitness and nutrition enthusiast. Now divorced, she lives in Tucson with her English bulldog, Pyper, and her life partner, Azi.

# • 18 •

# Signs of a New Normal

## By Laurie Savoie

*Laurie and Garrett*

There it was again. The glow of *11:17* from my clock radio. "Hi, Garrett," I said, feeling my son's spirit presence. What a difference from November 17, 2010, when I experienced the horror of his suicide. Now the sight of those numbers inspires waves of love and connection between us. I know that Garrett is sending me hellos from heaven. And he does so frequently.

In fact, I joke that our relationship is better than ever. He communicates regularly through mediums and through my own mediumship abilities, guiding and encouraging me and others.

Of course I would love to talk to him in person, to hug him, and to watch him grow beyond his nineteen years as he experienced life on Earth with me, his father, and two sisters.

I wish I'd never had to race to his apartment that day eight years ago. There he was, my precious baby boy, with bare feet sticking out of his jeans, blood trickling from his nose, and a gun in his lap. Cartoons played in the background on TV. He left no note.

Now he tells me not to focus on his death. "It's not important to me. If you talk about it three hundred times, it seems like I died three hundred times. Well, Mom, I didn't, so don't dwell on it. Stop stressing about it."

He asks me to share that with other parents whose kids have died.

But the shock and despair of a child's death are so deep, you can't just deny it, squelch it, stuff it down. If you do, it's bound to erupt in less-than-healthy ways. Suicide is different from other kinds of deaths. Other people talk about the Accident, the Illness, or the Drug Overdose that took their child's life. How do you understand your child's choice to take his own life when it makes no sense to you? How do you talk about it when there is such shame around suicide? People still whisper the word. Sharing the moments around a suicide is part of the un-shaming process, and part of the healing.

The night before Garrett shot himself, an image of my deceased mother appeared in my dining room. "You'd better not be here for what I think you are here for," I said. It felt like my soul knew. I had just spoken to Garrett on the phone about his upcoming court appearance. In July he'd been arrested for possession of marijuana and drug paraphernalia. He was supposed to appear in court the following morning at 8:30.

When he didn't show up for court, my husband Tom and I panicked. For good reason.

"How are we going to tell the girls?" was my first question as Tom and I sat on a bench outside Garrett's apartment complex, utterly crushed, heartbroken, disbelieving. He had two sisters, Kailee, twenty, and Chantal, twelve.

His death shocked people from his apartment complex as well. They told Tom that Garrett was so nice, so polite. They got to see the true Garrett, the sweet, loving, and kind son, brother, friend, and neighbor. Not the mean, out-of-control man that drugs had made of him during the previous fifteen months. Although he was nineteen, he was mentally and emotionally more like a fifteen-year-old. I think drugs initially made him feel better about himself, more confident. He tried to act like a tough guy, bottling up all his emotions, but he was a sensitive kid.

We offered him rehabs, counseling sessions, and support groups, desperate for him to become himself again. We even asked his friends to shake him awake to his destructiveness. Nothing worked. We couldn't even help our own kid! Eventually Garrett dropped out of college, moved out on his own with his so-called best friend, and had little contact with us for six months—devastating for our close-knit family. Once when I stopped by to give him his health insurance card, he refused to talk to me. Very hurtful! Finally, we got fed up and changed the locks on our doors.

After his arrest, he reached out to us and Kailee, who was only seventeen months older than him. She was studying psychology at college in Canada. Fortunately he'd stayed close to her this entire time. She told us he was constantly conflicted, admitting to her that he'd felt awful about disappointing us. In his heart he was still that lovable little kid we knew him to be, but he was also aware of how far offtrack he'd gotten.

Now he was motivated to do what the court asked—get clean, get healthy, get a job.

Tragically, he never let any of us know how he really felt when the judge threatened him with two years of jail time. For a while after his death, I couldn't help but wonder: *Was the judge just trying to scare him? Should I have contacted her? Told her how sensitive Garrett was? Would that have made a difference?* He must have been terrified. He'd never before been in trouble with the law. Had he shown up at court that day, though, he would have realized there was hope for him. It was excruciating to know that, according to his lawyer, he would only have gotten probation.

For the first ten days after he left the planet, it felt like I'd left the planet, too. I couldn't eat or sleep. I remember watching Tom sleep. It was my husband who kept our family running. I looked to him to fix this, to make it right. It didn't even occur to me that this strong man might be just as fractured and numb as I was.

Our marriage changed. I have heard that 80 percent of marriages dissolve after the death of a child. For a long time I was unable to feel emotionally intimate with Tom. After all, it was thanks to our being in love that Garrett's life began. After his life ended, I didn't even know what Love meant. How can you love a child to the core of your soul and not have him with you on Earth to protect? I put up giant walls, not wanting to be hurt again.

Meanwhile I read every book I could get my hands on about the Afterlife. I sought out psychic mediums. I joined a Helping Parents Heal group. *How did we get here?* I wanted to know every detail.

*We can't change the past* was Tom's philosophy. He didn't want to explore Garrett's death. Although he missed Garrett tremendously, and misses him still, he prefers not to share his feelings or hear others' stories.

Our different approaches to pain didn't stop us from making a marriage-saving agreement early on, though. We vowed that when one of was going down on the carpet, the other would be strong. We would never both go down at the same time. In this way, we'd take turns holding each other and our family up.

While it took me years to be able to hug Kailee and Chantal again, for fear of losing them too, Tom stayed consistently open and affectionate with them, listening respectfully to whatever they needed to say.

I'm more guarded now, but I am healing, slowly getting back to being Me, although I will never be the Me from before.

A big part of my recovery is thanks to Garrett himself. He started sending signs from the Other Side right away, like *11:17* on clocks.

Then, a week and a half after his death, my aunt called from Canada with exciting news. In the midst of her phone call with her friend April, who also happened to be a medium, Garrett came through loud and clear with forty-five minutes of messages. April called me three days later and we spoke for three hours. She validated many things and gave us so much information that it changed the way our family grieved.

One night exactly two weeks after his death, my Bunco group came to the house bearing an Angel Tree, a candle, and pajamas for Chantal. For those unfamiliar, Bunco is a dice game. And the Angel Tree is as loving and magical as it sounds. It is an artificial Christmas tree that came with a note: "This angel tree is not only a tree, it is a friendly tree that is always watching over you...." Community members filled it with over two hundred ornaments in honor of Garrett.

My gift-bearing friends expected to be met by profound sadness. Instead I greeted them with the incredible information I'd received through a stranger in another country. Garrett said he was better than okay. He said he didn't have to do any special healing on the Other Side, something the medium had never seen before in a suicide. His words/her words were already helping me on my journey to wholeness. April called again that night while my friends were still over with the message that Garrett had actually arranged for the Bunco girls to bring the Angel Tree for his sister Kailee. April even told me Garrett wanted us to celebrate Christmas, something I never imagined we'd have the energy for. But we did.

In addition to the healing messages through April, I found a counselor who was spiritual. She opened me up to other expansive ways to view Garrett's death. For instance, she wondered what gifts I had received from Garrett's passing. Of course when she asked me that, I had to think long and hard! How does anyone look at their child's death as offering them gifts? Finally, I came up with answers:

- I didn't have to worry about Garrett anymore.
- I gained a new appreciation for what was really important and what was the small stuff.
- I began eliminating negativity from my life, including letting go of friends that weren't supportive.
- I became more gentle with myself.
- I started doing what was important to me, not what had to be done.
- I learned to accept help, like getting my house cleaned and accepting food, even many months after Garrett's death.
- I became even more spiritual.

Two and a half years after Garrett died, the Divine sent me a vision of a book that would eventually become *The Ripple Effect: Invisible Impact of Suicide*, a beautiful tapestry of words, emotions, poems, pictures, and songs that offer support to people like me, people left behind with so many raw feelings and unanswered questions.

With the support of my husband, daughters, and Garrett's friend Jessica, I gathered stories from family, friends, and other community members who had been in some way affected by Garrett's death. I didn't want to limit it, so I also included submissions from people affected by suicide in any way. I wanted this book to save the lives of those feeling hopeless enough to consider suicide—for them to know in their bones how beloved, worthy, and special they truly are and inspire them to make new, conscious choices.

Slowly, we are feeling like a normal, happy couple and family again. But it will never be the same.

Chantal survived her own depression and suicidal thoughts, triggered when she turned nineteen—Garrett's age when he killed himself. Fortunately she had been talking to a doctor and taking antidepressants. Tom encouraged her every way he could. He and Chantal became even closer than they'd always been, golfing, attending hockey games. She is back at college, studying hard and finding her way in the world.

When people ask me if I have guilt, I tell them no. I did not choose this, Garrett did.

In my heart I know I did the best I could at the time with what I knew. I know my son knew he was loved. Yes, I suffered many shouldas, wouldas, couldas. The Friday before Garrett ended his life, I visited him at work. When he said he would call me later that night, I told him I was busy with dinner plans. I'm not even sure he would have called me even if I'd been available. Yet . . . what if he had? For a long time, I couldn't stop replaying what I imagined was a missed opportunity to help him, until finally I was able to face that choice and move through it.

My grief and sadness have evolved into a passion to help others. I am very involved with Helping Parents Heal, a group of parents who understand. We talk about our losses, but we also laugh. We are joyous. People who don't know us cannot believe we are a grief group, let alone parents who have "lost" their child or children. It deepens my own well-being to know I have shown many at our Helping Parents Heal meetings that you can survive the suicide death of your child.

I have just completed an Advanced Mediumship class that I was invited into by Suzanne Wilson, The Carefree Medium. She says she has watched my natural gifts develop and get stronger these past few years.

The day of the Sandy Hook tragedy, Tom was a complete mess. I imagine he was reliving the horror of learning his son was no longer alive, and feeling empathy for all those parents learning about their children. I, on the other hand, was at complete peace the entire day. When Kailee came home from working her two jobs, she said, "Mom, Garrett has all of the kids. He is helping them into Heaven." Of course! That made perfect sense. Garrett had always loved kids, working with them as a camp counselor and in after-school sports programs.

Kailee and I have become a powerful team, aiding people in healing through Reiki, which we studied together. We both get messages from people's guides and loved ones on the Other Side. In heaven we're shown that our loved ones only know peace, love, and joy. They are happy and want us to be happy here too, which can feel like a tall order when you are at your rawest.

But we begin by being here for each other. Honoring our different styles and rhythms of grieving and healing. Encouraging each other to pay attention to the feather, butterfly, hummingbird, penny, words, or numbers we see again and again in the unlikeliest places. Our beloveds in spirit work playfully, but persistently, to reach us and reassure us that our relationships are ongoing and ever-evolving.

And so I say—you can do this! You are not alone. If you see a woman pausing excitedly in front of a microwave, clock radio, oven, or other time device beaming *11:17*, don't worry.

It's a good sign.

\* \* \*

**Laurie Savoie,** mother of three, turned her grief and sadness into a life-changing passion to help others and is spreading the message of Hope and Love in her book, *The Ripple Effect: Invisible Impact of Suicide.* Every penny made from book sales goes toward buying more books, which are donated to suicide prevention groups, schools, therapists, doctors, libraries, and families who have lost loved ones to suicide—in essence, anyone who has the desire to lift up someone's life. In addition, Laurie is actively involved in the Helping Parents Heal group, The Prayer Registry (a blog with prayers for children in heaven by Sheri Perl; www .theprayerregistry.wordpress.com), and HOPE ASAP (an online Facebook group started by Jennifer Dulski for people who have lost loved ones to addiction).

# *V*

# MENTAL ILLNESS LEADING TO DEATH

And my grief was as great for what he had gone through and what he had lost, as for his death.

—Lynda Crane

## · *19* ·

# Where There's Death, There's Hope

### By Laurie Mathes Arshonsky

*Austin*

$\mathcal{A}$s a young mom, I chose to raise my children to make their own decisions and be independent. While they were growing up, my life remained filled with friends. I volunteered at Hospice of Cincinnati doing Healing Touch (a heart-centered complementary energy therapy), and I painted in an art group each Tuesday called the Brushettes. In early 2005, I had also become a grandmother.

Then on April 7, 2005, eight days after the birth of my first grandchild, the unthinkable happened.

I was in a car with my friend Mary Kay, about to leave for Asheville, North Carolina, on an urgent trip to help my son, Austin, who was in his last six weeks of college before graduation and struggling with mental illness. There in the car, my cell phone rang. It was my son's father.

"Austin was found at the bottom of a bridge. He's dead."

My world crashed.

181

## MESSAGES AND JOURNALS

When Austin was little, I loved whispering two things into his ear, which I did frequently: "I always wanted a boy just like you" and "We will always have a relationship, no matter what."

From the very day of his death, I talked to Austin regularly in meditation and asked him to send me messages. From the beginning, I received plenty of them and continue to get them today, fourteen years since his transition. Because I remain true to what I first told Austin so long ago—that we would always have a relationship—I keep journals specifically dedicated to these messages from him, along with other related communications.

Here are a few of the messages I received from my son in the first month following his death:

**4/7/05:** "You can find me in the silence." "You have a choice: drama or personal growth."

**4/10/05:** "Do what you know to do." "I'm right here, I'm right here, I'm right here." "Be patient with yourself." "Take time for me every day." "I am so sorry. I love you so much." "Don't be sad too long. Get your joy back. Don't forget laughter!"

**4/12/05:** "Being peaceful is loving yourself."

**4/13/05:** "Don't look at how I died, look at how I lived."

These messages amazed me, so on **4/15/05** I asked: "Austin, am I making you up, or are you really with me?"

He answered that yes, I was making him up, but if I needed him, it was okay!

That's what I always loved about my boy. He accepted me for who I was. He loved to tease me, and he did it as often as possible. Of course, my mother cautioned me not to tell anyone he said that. She said, "Laurie, they'll think you're crazy!"


## SIGNS AND SYMBOLS

On several occasions since he left the physical plane, Austin has teased me.

One time, while I was driving, I saw an elderly couple in an old Mercedes-Benz convertible. The woman, seated on the passenger side, was wearing a scarf wrapped around her head. The top was down and the windows were all rolled up.

Sensing that Austin was with me, I laughed and said, "Austin, that's me in ten years!"

In my head, I heard him quickly reply, "Mom, that's you *now!*"

I laughed and cried, knowing that it was true.

Another time, I was doing healing work with a person who had been close to Austin, and I requested my son's help. As often happens when I do this work, my hands got really hot. I knew something powerful was happening and excitedly asked Austin, "What's going on?"

Again, he was quick with a teasing, but true, comment. "Mom, you're standing right next to the fireplace!"

Just recently, I gave someone a healing treatment with the help of my dear friend Dee, who is also a healer. When setting our intention beforehand, we asked for Austin's help. Afterwards, the client raved about how awesome he felt and what a great healing it was. Dee suggested that we close our eyes, thank Austin, and ask for a message.

As I did this, I could see Austin pretending to smoke a cigarette, something I knew he would *never* do. I was so confused. Then he pointed at me and I thought, *Ohhhh! He's saying to me, "You're smokin'!"*

At first, I thought I might be making it up, but I'm just not that clever—I didn't even get what he was showing me for a minute!

## NEW UNDERSTANDING

I also record my dreams as often as possible. After one dream, I awoke with a burning question in mind, *What is courage?*

One night about a year later, two years after Austin transitioned, I set my intention to receive a message from him while I slept. I was grateful the answer came that night and was clear: "Now you know what courage is. It is going on and helping people, even though you think that your life is over."

For me, that is what this experience was here to teach me. I see all the blessings I still have, and I am grateful. It was a profound moment. There is always a lot to live for. I am courageous.

Before Austin's early departure from physical life, I had trained to be a Healing Touch Practitioner. During the training, when I read a book called *Joy's Way*, by W. Brugh Joy, I set an intention to "transform my views on death." I wasn't even sure I knew what that meant, but I was certain it was important.

Three weeks before *the worst* happened, Austin and I were standing in the kitchen, talking. His affect was flat and he wasn't himself, which concerned me.

"Austin, I'm afraid I'm losing you," I said.

He calmly reassured me. "You know I do dangerous things, Mom, and I'm not going to live a long time. Do not be afraid. What you fear, you draw to yourself."

"Yes," I said, "but you won't do anything to hasten it, will you?"

"No, I love my family too much for that."

Later, as I thought back on that conversation, I knew my son had not purposely taken his life. For a while, I did fear it might have been suicide, but part of my journey has been about being willing to change my story and give it a positive slant. Over the years, my conclusions about Austin's death have been confirmed by a tarot card reader and a psychic, and now I wholeheartedly know that my son did not end his life. Mental illness killed him.

## HELPFUL PROCESS

Another great therapy I was fortunate to find came from a healer and social worker friend named Carolyn, who had studied The Work of Byron Katie.[1] My biggest issue at that time was my anger that Austin was dead. To this end, Carolyn asked me Katie's series of four questions:

1. "Is it true [that he's dead]?" *Yes.*
2. "Can you absolutely know it's true?" *No. He is alive in me.*
3. "How do you react when you believe that thought?" *I am bereft and feel like my heart is broken.*
4. "Who would you be without that thought?" *I would be happy.*

That simple process allowed me to see Austin's life and death very differently moving forward. I *could* choose to be happy. He lives in my heart. We are one. Carolyn also explained that we all die at exactly the right time. Not a minute too early or a minute too late. I trusted this friend, and having this piece of valuable information gave me incredible solace.

My son lived, and his life had an arc. He served his purpose and followed his bliss, which was helping others and being with God. He inspires still and has deeply impacted many, many lives over the years. Oddly enough, at the age of nineteen, Austin had set that goal for his future.

I discovered a touching example of this as I read the notes in a guest book after one of Austin's memorials. It was written by my son-in-law, Josh, about the last thing Austin had taught him:

> He said when you are angry, instead of fighting, hug the person you are angry with, and all anger and frustration will disappear. This is exactly the lesson of Austin's life: love everyone, do not hate. I will always remember Austin. I will tell stories of him to our son Shane. His uncle Austin's life was incredible, and he will be missed. We love you, Austin.

Seven months after my son died, I had a wonderful conversation with his college sweetheart, Rachel, and I was moved to write down what she told me:

> Austin lived an amazing life. He didn't waste a drop. He got out every ounce and more! He didn't waste a minute.

## PUSHING THE BOUNDARIES

I know that Austin is happy. I don't need to worry about him anymore; he's safe and whole. I can talk with him anytime I want to and take him with me whenever I travel.

Austin was very adventurous. He was all about pushing personal limits—his and everyone else's. When I'm away, out of town, I challenge myself to go beyond my comfort zone as much as I can, in memory of my precious Austin. In September 2016, I felt so close to my son in New Zealand when my husband, Steve, and I did a zipline course with six ziplines and two rope bridges. We were 1,200 feet above the ground and I was terrified. While screaming Austin's name loudly and yelling out various curse words, I faced all my fear head-on—knowing that Austin was there on my shoulder, laughing his ass off and cheering me on the whole way. I felt so close to my beautiful son. It was a peak experience, and I will cherish it always.

At the top of the Sydney Harbor Bridge and the Sun Gate at Machu Picchu, I enlisted some fellow climbers, and on the count of three we all shouted, "Austin, Austin, Austin!"

I'm sure he heard us! People are always so touched and happy to partake in our shout-outs to Austin.

In my purse I always carry a small stone with Austin's picture decoupaged on it by my most conscious friend Sophie. In February 2017, I had it out in Peru, at a Mother Earth Ceremony that reminded me so much of the Sacred Fire memorial we had for Austin shortly after he died that I became emotionally triggered. I knew I needed to share my tears with my tour group without apology, shame, regret, or discomfort. That's precisely what I did, and it helped immensely.

Do these sorts of things make people uncomfortable? If they do, their feelings belong to them and not me. Touchingly so, many have thanked me for helping them cry for their own loved ones who have passed. It is a gift to be able to teach others that there is more to life and death than we see with our physical eyes.

When people I don't know ask, I don't repeat the story of Austin's death. I don't want to and have no need. It's my son's story, and it belongs to him. I express myself and my feelings instead, through work in watercolor. I enjoy painting numerous pictures of Austin: doing yoga, in the garden, in portraits, and standing atop a mountain in the Himalayas. It is very therapeutic for me and is much like meditation: calming and healing.

For the last three years, I have been teaching "Beginning Watercolor" to cancer survivors and doing so fills me with joy. To quote one student whose life was changed by taking this class, "It lights up my life with happy!"

Mine, too.


INTUITIVE GUIDANCE


Psychics have been a part of my healing process since Austin's death, as they have confirmed my various messages and led me forward. More than once I've been told that Austin and I had a contract, and that he was only meant to stay on this plane for so long. I guess I somehow always knew that deep down.

On July 15, 2005, a psychic name Jean told me of Austin, "He is learning now. He plans to travel with you on this side and help you. A psychotic break gave him the nerve. He was out of his body immediately and didn't have pain."

On the morning of October 18, 2005, I awakened from an incredible dream and quickly wrote it down in my journal:

> I dreamed I flew up in the air in a four-wheeler and stopped at the edge of a cliff. I was afraid we'd go over the cliff. Then we did, and I closed my eyes. We landed so gently, I could hardly feel it. This was about trusting the unseen. I am sure it was like that for Austin when he leapt [off the bridge]. It was a leap of faith and he landed softly, painlessly, into the arms of angels who deftly carried him to the light.

This awareness was later confirmed by a tarot card reader, as well as another psychic.

One time I was "conversing" with Austin in a dream, and he told me to make an appointment with a particular psychic that I had once recommended to a friend. I did, and when she touched in with my son, she marveled to me that Austin was one of the most spiritual spirits she had ever channeled. As soon as she said that, Austin told the psychic to tell me to be sure to tell more people to go see her!

My kid was like that. If he liked something, he would tell everyone to go do it and insist on it.

## FAMILY, TALKING, AND SHARING

Talking to people about Austin gave me much comfort. My daughter Ashley and her husband Josh gave me a tremendous gift—which has been an integral part of my survival. The very first Sunday after Austin's death, they began coming with their infant son Shane to our home for dinner. Even though her own heart was broken, Ashley's sensitive soul allowed me my grief, and she was always an understanding and compassionate listener.

I looked forward to our family dinners every week, and I'm grateful they continued for more than ten years. In those early months, knowing I still had Ashley—and now a beautiful grandson—gave me a reason to live. Then three and six years later, respectively, Ashley and Josh blessed us with two more wonderful grandsons, Ari and Eli. My grandchildren fill me with so much joy, and hope has been restored to my heart.

Losing a child has caused me to be introspective. Looking back on the way I raised my children, I do have one big regret. Because Austin was a special needs kid, born with learning disabilities, I know I poured more time and attention into him than I did my daughter. Ashley seemed to come into the world with keen intelligence and extraordinary problem-solving skills. Amazingly, at the age of four, she easily solved a logistics problem for me that had been causing me great distress. Yet, if I'm completely honest, I know Ashley learned to be so self-sufficient partly because she had to, since I was always so consumed with caring for her brother, and I made no secret of that. I am fortunate because my Ashley is very kind, compassionate, and forgiving, and has a generous heart.

Not long after Austin's death, my brother Charles offered me words I found to be so wise and healing, I felt compelled to write them down right away:

> Austin is alive. He awoke to a larger dream. . . . Every consciousness of nature is Austin. His perceptions are so pure and kind. People can learn from him. . . . You don't have to keep him alive. He IS alive! At some level, he chose to be here for a short time. We all have the ability and the right to leave. He was what he was and who he was. Everything he could be is realized.

Shortly after Austin made his transition to higher planes, his friend Joy told me, "You are so lucky to have been Austin's mom for twenty-three years." What a lift that was, and what a gift. I often tell myself that when I find myself pining for Austin. I've learned it's the spin we put on things that makes us happy or miserable, and I choose to be happy.

Counseling was a great help to me throughout the first year. When I volunteered at Hospice, there was a counselor available to me who listened attentively and with great compassion to all my sadness. He assured me that I was a super mom and that I had done everything I possibly could have each day to keep my son healthy.

Austin had struggled with learning disabilities and attention deficit hyperactivity disorder (ADHD) as a child. On the day that I was to travel to Asheville to see him, the psychiatrist who had treated Austin when he was younger met with me on short notice to advise me of possible ways I could help him. I still remember the doctor's kindness. What a blessing my relationship was with that man.

Recently, I went to see the doctor again, and he pulled me out of a short slump by reminding me it was time to let Austin go. He always told me we get to choose when we die, and coincidentally (or not), he died about a week after our visit. I'm so glad I told him during our appointment how much he had helped me, and how much he meant to our family.

In college, Austin majored in outdoor leadership; he taught people to be stewards of the environment. It was fitting and comforting that we planted many trees in local parks around our home in Cincinnati in Austin's memory. On the second anniversary of his death, we held a tree rally and visited those trees, and then planted flowers and sang heartwarming songs. The two that stand out in my mind are "You Are My Sunshine" and "Spirit in the Sky."

A few months later, my husband Steve and I took his parents— who were visiting us from California—to see a few of the trees on our little tree circuit. While sitting in the backseat of our car, I felt a chill loop down my neck on the left side. This has occurred frequently over the years, and I interpret it always as Austin letting me know that he's there, breathing down my neck, so to speak.

This time, I heard him say, "Mom, this is absurd. Grandma and Grandpa are on vacation, and you're dragging them around to see your dead child's trees?!"

I was laughing and crying all at once and so was my mother-in-law, which is really the best therapy of all.

These chills that run frequently down my neck remind me of the bond and close relationship my beloved son and I had—and still have to this day.

One New Year's Eve, I felt them before a party we were about to have. I was so excited, I started shouting, "Happy New Year, Austin! Happy New Year!"

Clear as day I heard him say back, "I'm not deaf, Mom!"

## GRIEF SUPPORT

After the shock of the initial grief, which was filled with near-endless tears and too many sleepless nights, one of the first things I did was join a grief support group that met at a local Catholic church. I found it helpful to share my feelings with other people who were also grieving.

Then I went to a different support group elsewhere that was specifically for people who had lost children. It was not quite as helpful to me as the first, but I did meet a lovely couple there who, like me, also wanted to move forward and do positive things in remembrance of their twenty-two-year-old daughter Julie, who, synchronistically, had passed the same week as Austin. Before my son died, I had known at least ten other mothers who lost a child, so I would have lunch with them—and interview them—to learn how they survived after the death of their beloved daughter or son.

Six months after Austin died, I started hosting and leading my own grief support group, Strength in Mothers (a play on strength in numbers). It began with six other women, and we use a number of different tools that support our healing. These ladies knew other like-minded moms and invited them to join our group, until we grew to just over a dozen. We still meet every month in my living room, where we cry and laugh together, sharing stories of our kids and our victories. Members have told me that I am an inspiration to them. They are certainly an inspiration to me.

## CHOICES AND DECISIONS

Early in my grief, I was crying a lot and understandably so. When my husband Steve had finally had enough, he said, "Laurie, it's time to make another choice."

It was like getting hit over the head by a two-by-four, but I hopped on the clue bus, chose happiness, and stopped crying immediately. That was a big turning point in my healing.

Some kids die of a drug overdose. Austin, on the other hand, hated drugs of any kind, and often didn't follow medical directives. These included medications prescribed for him to keep his symptoms of mental illness at bay. It was a choice Austin made not to take them, and I get it. The side effects of some prescription meds can be challenging.

When Austin was ready to enter the world, my obstetrician mistakenly assumed he was my first child and therefore didn't hurry to get to the hospital. While I waited in labor and delivery for hours, Austin was in distress and unable to get enough oxygen to his brain. Consequently, certain pathways became blocked, causing dysgraphia (an inability to write coherently), ADHD, and sensory motor damage.

When my son was eighteen, I explained what had happened during his birth and told him how sorry I was that it had. I asked Austin if he thought we should sue the doctor before the statute of limitations ran out.

He responded in typical Austin fashion. "Why?" he said. "I'm not in a wheelchair and I can play lacrosse. I wouldn't be who I am if this hadn't happened."

Austin seemed to instinctively understand that this suffering gave him the great gift of compassion.

One pitfall I did not ever want to succumb to was blaming myself for what ultimately happened to my son. After his death, I could see clearly how everyone in his life felt, in hindsight, a responsibility to have "done more." But the truth is, there was nothing more any one of us could have done.

When we struggle, we suffer. And I decided, in the end, that there was enough suffering already without my blaming myself for Austin's death.

It's always confusing to know what to call the anniversary of the death of someone we love and how to mark it. Friends suggested several names to me, including Sunset and Angelversary. This dilemma was solved for me during a visit to Grace Kelly's tomb in Monaco.

I asked the tour guide why there were flowers decorating the tomb. "It's the birthday of the Princess's death," she replied.

That, to me, was the best term I'd heard yet. Austin used to loudly proclaim, "Have fun every day!" So, we now celebrate the birthday of his death and entry into a new phase on this continuum we call life. All is well!

My goal has always been to be myself—to remain the joyful, caring, compassionate, and funny person I was before my son died. Hard as it has been, I am the better for this experience of loving someone as deeply as I love my Austin—even though he is no longer with us in physical form. It's made me be the very best I could be. I have learned and grown so much, more than I ever knew possible. I am following my purpose in life, which is to make the world a better place through my love and my service to others.

This is one club no one wants to belong to, but I'm a strong leader here—and I choose to embrace it!

## NOTE

1. Byron Katie, *Loving What Is: Four Questions That Can Change Your Life* (New York: Three Rivers Press, 2002).

\* \* \*

**Laurie Mathes Arshonsky,** proud mother of Austin and Ashley, and stepmom to Susie, Cynthia, and Rob, is also YaYa to her five grandsons, ages three to thirteen. She is a watercolor artist and gifted painting instructor. Among Laurie's other passions are friends, walking, watching movies, and travel—all of which she partakes in as often as possible. She's also a thirty-year veteran of her favorite book club, which is now a bit like a wonderfully supportive group therapy.

## • 20 •

# Giving Voice to Those Who Suffer

### By Lynda Crane

Doug

For as long as I can remember, I wanted to be a mom. For all intents and purposes, I grew up as an "only" child. Having just one sibling (a brother who was eleven years my senior), I envied my friends who had large families. When I married at twenty, my husband and I saw no reason to wait to start a family, and my first child, Douglas Scott Marquis, was born nine months and two weeks later.

As an infant, Doug was a person of strong emotions, either crying his heart out or laughing out loud. As a child and teen, he became a person of wide interests and rare maturity. He played hockey from the age of six and continued through high school. He was musical and had a talent for playing trumpet. He was naturally insightful and had an uncanny ability to sense the reactions of others and adjust accordingly. He was friendly and could even be charming.

193

In the summer of 1980, when Doug was fifteen or so, a friend of mine remarked, "I can't wait to see the adult he becomes. He's such a neat kid now."

When I asked him to explain, he said that Doug was friends with both boys and girls and with those of other races, and that he fit in well with both kids and adults. He seemed confident in who he was, and relatively unworried about the approval of his peers. He was happy and fun-loving and didn't seem to worry about himself. In my friend's experience, these traits were relatively rare in young people of my son's age.

Doug's future showed promise in a number of ways. As a high school senior, he earned the Maryland Distinguished Scholar Award in Art and was courted by schools across the country. He drew and painted, but his real love was ceramics. He created fantasy landscapes from clay, and it was those creations that led to a scholarship at the Chicago Art Institute. The summer before Doug left for college, we were astonished to learn that he had made such an impression (during his visits over the years) on the manager of the apartments where his grandparents lived in Florida that she offered to help pay his expenses at college. Remarkably, this manager was an ex-army officer who was not known for an easy personality. It seemed to all who knew and cared for Doug that his future was bright.

In looking back, though, I can see there had been signs of my son's gradually developing mental illness starting from sometime in his seventeenth year. At that time, I was a PhD student working as an extern at a state psychiatric facility. Yet, I recognized no connection between the problems my bright, witty, talented son was starting to experience and the patients with schizophrenia that I assessed in the hospital.

Oh, I could see that something was wrong. Doug was obviously becoming increasingly more worried and anxious. And he had recently said some things to me that seemed odd. More and more often, I had a bad feeling in the pit of my stomach that I tried to ignore. I told myself that Doug was simply nervous about leaving for college, even though he insisted that he wanted to go.

In late August of 1984, still wanting to believe all was well, Doug and I packed his belongings and went to Chicago together. Once there, we found a room for him to rent in a house with two other freshmen at the institute, and I dropped him off to begin his new life.

For the first few weeks, Doug did seem (from all my husband and I could tell at a distance) to be managing all right. When someone called me from the art institute, however, and told me they were seriously concerned and that I should come to Chicago, I knew in an instant that something was very wrong. Everything I had been holding at bay and keeping from the forefront of my mind came crashing together. All the little signs and symptoms that I had written off and rationalized flooded back to me, and I knew my son was in serious trouble.

Doug desperately wanted to stay in school and to believe—in his words—that it wasn't "too late." Before the month was out, however, he was confined to a private psychiatric hospital and diagnosed with bipolar disorder. (That diagnosis was later changed to the even more severe schizoaffective disorder.)

As with most people who suffer from mental illness, Doug initially refused to believe the diagnosis and refused to take prescribed medication. Through a series of mishaps, professional mistakes, and general chaos that caused me constant stress, worry, and grief, it was a year before his dad and I were able to get Doug to take his first dose of medicine. When he finally began cooperating with treatment, the wild and dramatic nature of his life with schizophrenia calmed down.

At the same time, though, it was clear to our family, and to Doug as well, that the life he had envisioned, worked toward, and counted on, the "normal" life he had said so often that he wanted—one with a nice family, meaningful work, periods of accomplishment, friends, and happy social times—was not at all in his future. For Doug to accomplish any of those things would be difficult and uncertain. My own grief for him was intense, and in looking back, I believe it contributed to his own disappointment and despair.

For six years, between 1984 and 1990, Doug was in and out of hospitals. Every dream he had had, and that I had held for him, seemed destroyed. In the end, he asked to be readmitted to the hospital, after having just recently been discharged, and when his psychiatrist denied the request, Doug hung himself from a tree, facing the street, in front of his grandmother's house. His grandmother had a ranch-style duplex, and he had been living in one side of it. Maybe he chose such a public place in the hope that someone would see him and he would be stopped, or perhaps it was his way of demonstrating the failure of the mental health system in his life. Or maybe there was a reason in his mind that I could never imagine. I will never have answers to those questions.

No parent who has lost a child needs to be told of my devastation. Douglas was my firstborn child, my only son. And my grief was as great for what he had gone through and what he had lost as for his death. The heartbreak of seeing him disappear before our eyes and my constant preoccupation with his illness for so many years had destroyed my marriage. His three sisters' lives were in turmoil. All of us were permanently changed.

For a long time, I mostly focused on my remaining children and my career and worked to get beyond the daily anxiety and panic attacks. People said, "You're a psychologist. You could help others." I was afraid even to think of it. I taught abnormal psychology, and yet the wound in my heart went so deep, I was afraid to go near it, and I was unable to relate my own tragic experience even to the students in my classes.

At the time of Doug's death in 1990, I was teaching at a university in Michigan. In 1992, I married a kindhearted man who also taught there. David and I both had long-term interests in simple living and ecology, and in 1996 we moved to Ohio, bought a farm, and began to grow most of our own food. What we couldn't grow or derive from our hens, we bought from a food co-op.

We gradually built a demonstration facility for simple, ecological living, where classes from colleges and universities in Ohio and Kentucky came to spend a day or two, experience what we were doing, discuss what they saw, and consider its implications. Our days were full, and while the grief of my loss frequently still came over me (often when I least expected it) with the same intensity of the week Doug had died, I was able to apply what I had learned from years of practice in mindfulness, relax my muscles, allow the emotional pain rather than run from it, and allow it to pass through.

Then, in 2001, David was diagnosed with a malignant brain tumor. From that day, our farm project was over, and our lives were absorbed with his treatment and in living his remaining days together as peacefully and happily as we could. David died a few days before Christmas in 2002.

From the time of my son's death, my primary way of coping had been to find ways to be of service—to my students and my community. I stayed busy. I moved on. What I did not do was think very much about schizophrenia. Now that my farm project was over, and my husband was gone, I knew I was going to need another project, but I didn't want it to have anything to do with diagnosed mental illness.

For the next several months, I kept my eyes (and my heart) open for something to stir my interest. In the spring of 2003, I bought two nineteenth-century three-unit apartment buildings in an economically devastated area of Cincinnati. One had a storefront where I housed the Findlay Neighborhood Center, a 501(c)(3) designed to provide a sewing center that I hoped would act as a gathering place for women in the area to learn new sewing and craft skills or practice existing ones.

Because the center was across the street from a historic farmers' market, we set up a booth to sell items made by area residents. As fate and fortune would have it, two of the women who most regularly attended the center were living with schizophrenia. We became friends, and I became involved in their lives, as friends do. I began to feel that the easy friendship and acceptance that I had been unable to provide my son in my grief over his illness I could now give to others on his behalf.

Gradually, I became able to discuss my son's illness and his death, at appropriate times, in my classes at Mount St. Joseph University. A colleague, Dr. Tracy McDonough, who also taught abnormal psychology, asked me to talk about Doug in her class, and for the very first time, I told his story from the beginning of his illness to his death. I spoke about symptoms, health insurance, the involvement of law enforcement and the legal system, and psychiatric treatment and medication. I talked about the effect his illness had on his family and friendships.

While I spoke, pictures of Douglas, from babyhood to young manhood, were shown on a large screen behind me. Our students watched photos of the adorable baby; the cute, funny toddler; the Halloween clown; the teen with the golf trophy all flash on the screen as I spoke about my son's life. They saw a normal, healthy young person. They saw someone who had been like them.

The experience left me drained and shaken, but I could see our students' faces as I spoke. There was complete quiet in that room. Sometimes there were tears. As I finished, I told them, "The next time you see someone talking to himself, perhaps digging through a trash can for something to eat, I want you to remember that that person has a mother and a father someplace, and maybe sisters or brothers, and their hearts are broken. I want you to just be kind."

I wanted them to be unable to think of persons with schizophrenia as alien beings (as the public so often does), and to understand that illness, including mental illness, can happen to anyone. I didn't expect them to make it all right. I didn't expect their role to be one of either treatment or cure. I simply wanted them to react with empathy and human kindness, and I could see that my talk with them was not one they would forget. I saw, in that experience, the power of story.

I had long had an interest in oral history, and in the spring of 2010, I attended an Oral History Association meeting in Atlanta, Georgia, where I participated in a workshop to learn to design and carry through oral history projects. At a reception at that conference, I had a conversation with an editor of an oral history journal who, upon learning I'm a psychologist, suggested I was in the perfect position to devise a project involving persons with mental illness, something he said was rare and needed in the oral history field.

The idea of such a project with persons who have schizophrenia began to grow in my mind. Because of my experience in talking with students in Tracy's classes and my own at the university, I felt that I might be ready to take on such a venture, but I knew I didn't want to do it alone.

Through my experience in Tracy's class and through several years of working with her as a colleague, I had become familiar with her natural empathy, her commitment to and belief in the treatment of mental illness, and her work ethic. Tracy seemed the ideal partner for such a project, and when I approached her with my idea and the offer that we might work together, she graciously agreed.

Together we designed The Schizophrenia Oral History Project (TSOHP), which aimed to provide a platform for persons with schizophrenia—many of whom might not feel comfortable with public speaking themselves—to have their stories and their voices heard. We believed that in the process, their stories could have an impact in reducing misunderstanding and stigma among the general public, and therefore make the lives of those with schizophrenia easier and contribute to opening pathways to further social integration and fulfillment of purpose.

We began with the idea of gathering life stories from twenty to twenty-five people in the Cincinnati area who have schizophrenia, publishing excerpts of their stories in articles and presenting them at public talks, and eventually publishing them in a book. Today we have collected over sixty life stories, from narrators in several states.

Our narrators' life stories have been featured in articles in the *New York Times*, *Newsweek*, the American Psychological Association's *Monitor on Psychology*, and the *Oral History Review*, among others. They have been heard in podcasts. Their pictures and their stories have been shared in more than two hundred public presentations and on our website, www.schizophreniaoralhistories.com, which features audio excerpts from their stories and has been visited by thousands of viewers. Like almost everyone else, TSOHP has a Facebook page. So, our narrators' stories have reached the public well beyond their families and circles of friends.

My real hope, however, is that because of their stories, people will change their minds and attitudes about what schizophrenia is, and about the kind of people who have it. I want others to understand that schizophrenia happens to women and men around the world. It doesn't matter how well adjusted a family is, how much money they have, or how successful they have been in their professions; it can still happen. Persons with schizophrenia love their friends and family, and they have hopes, goals, and dreams, just as do the rest of us. They have the same need for purpose in their lives, too,

For many of our narrators, TSOHP has contributed to their own sense of purpose. Telling their stories often felt difficult and risky, and yet they told us they wanted to do so anyway, in the hope that it would help someone else, by either giving courage to another person with schizophrenia or by educating the public about the truth of their lives.

One way we have been able to tell if the impact on listeners was the effect we had hoped for was to invite written reactions to our narrators' stories from audiences at presentations. From that feedback, we have seen that almost everyone was surprised or impressed by something they heard, and this was true even for family members of those living with illness and for mental health professionals.

Many told us they had changed their minds and attitudes both about what schizophrenia is and those who have it. They spoke of their admiration for our narrators' courage in carrying out their lives in the face of such a challenge and for their willingness to share their lives with others. Especially impressively, some people said these stories would inspire them to take some action to contribute to better understanding, often by talking to others or by reaching out themselves to people with schizophrenia.

Because we make copies of audience remarks and give them to our narrators during subsequent visits, we know the effect these public responses have had on them in turn. Our narrators are quite pleased and gratified. They have tangible proof, in their hands, that their stories are reaching others and are making a difference. One woman became teary while reading what had been written and said, "I feel like I matter for the first time."

That our narrators are making a difference through TSOHP is a happy thing for me, and it does provide some comfort. I think Douglas would be well pleased about this too, and it helps me (in a way I don't completely understand) to believe that our suffering may have resulted in a project that eases the distress of other individuals and families. It is my fondest hope that the project will continue to grow and spread to have a real impact on public understanding of schizophrenia, and result in better treatment and a true reduction in stigma.

* * *

**Lynda Crane** is mom to Douglas and his three sisters, Sherri, Patty, and Nicole. She is professor emeritus at Mount St. Joseph University and holds a PhD in psychology. She is author of *Mental Retardation: A Community Integration Approach*, a textbook that promotes social inclusion of persons with disabilities; and numerous articles related to cognitive and clinical psychology. She is cofounder of The Schizophrenia Oral History Project (www.schizophreniaoralhistories.com), which provides a platform for individuals with schizophrenia to make their voices heard in the service of public education and the reduction of stigma.

# When Tragedy Brings Treasure

## By Michele Wollert

I loved the Boy with the utmost love of which my soul is capable, and he is taken from me—yet in the agony of my spirit in surrendering such a treasure I feel a thousand times richer than if I had never possessed it.

—William Wordsworth on the death of his son, Thomas, in a letter to a friend, 1812

*Jonny*

### OUR LOSS

*O*ur youngest son, Jonathan, took his own life in the early summer of 2005, when he was only twenty. He chose to surrender to the despair he felt over a newly diagnosed mental illness, most likely schizophrenia, at our quiet little cabin that rests peacefully among old-growth Douglas firs and cedars, on a secluded hill, on the northern Oregon coast.

"I feel safe there, Mom," Jonny told me, referring to the family retreat we liked to call our Cape Escape, before giving me the last hug we would ever share. His embrace

201

lingered, longer than usual, and I am certain now that he had already made his plan to hasten his final exit on his own terms.

While Jonny tried to engage in mental health treatment, the side effects of his medication were sometimes worse than the symptoms they were meant to treat. Often tortured by hateful voices who told him not to trust the people who loved him most, my son seemed unusually calm, unsuspicious, and at peace when he left our Oregon home earlier that day.

"I love you," Jonny offered, as he gathered up some belongings in a canvas bag.

"I love you more," I teased, and watched him get in his car and drive away.

The next time I held my son, he was mere ashes bundled up in a mulberry bark box. I was surprised at how much the compact container weighed, and worried that Jonny might have objected to the soft, feminine textures and pastel colors in which his remains were temporarily confined.

"Don't worry, Jonny," I whispered. "You'll be out of here soon. I promise."

## HIS ARRIVAL

His birth was quick and easy, but our newborn son emerged a little too relaxed and quiet for my comfort on that frigid February 1985 afternoon in Saskatchewan, Canada.

"He's not crying! Is he okay?"

I followed the doctor's movements and watched intently as he suctioned our little boy's nose and mouth, wiped his wet body quickly, wrapped him in a warm flannel blanket, and placed him gently in my outstretched and eager arms.

Tears filled my eyes as I reveled in the comfort of my newborn son's weight on my chest. Still quite anxious, I watched closely as he gradually awakened. My son took his first faint breaths ever so slowly and soundlessly, and I felt relieved as the puffs of breath from his nostrils warmed my neck.

But still, there was no cry, nor any large muscle movement.

"Shade his eyes with your hand and he'll perk up," the doctor suggested, in an attempt to ease my worry. "The lights are too bright in here."

I gently cupped the edge of my hand just above my son's tiny face in order to create a visor that cast a shadow across his eyes. Immediately sensing the shade, his eyelids opened, revealing beady eyes that were as dark as blackberries. When they squinted directly and intently in my direction, I could finally relax.

My son's hair was dark brown and abundant, and he inherited his father's forehead wrinkles and nose. His skin had a rosy glow, and as he grunted and stretched his little arms and legs, his gaze was fixed firmly on me, his overjoyed mother.

"Hello, Jonathan," I whispered, as I stroked his soft, round cheek. It was the name his father and I had chosen when we learned we were having our third son. Now that I had a chance to meet him, the traditional Hebrew name seemed to fit him well; he truly felt like a gift from the heavens and a higher power.

All new babies bring us surprises we cannot predict or imagine. But this child, resting quietly in my arms, was surveying his new world with what looked to me like the confidence, calm, and curiosity of a wise old man. No fear. No trepidation. This boy seemed more than ready for whatever life and fate would bring him, almost as if he knew what was coming.

Jonathan Peter Wollert, from the moment of his birth, set the tone for the way he would live and eventually end his short life two decades later: confidently, intentionally, and without fear.


## HIS GIFTS


By the time he was four, Jonny showed a natural athletic talent beyond his years that demanded an outlet, as well as some expert training. In T-ball, baseball, basketball, soccer, wrestling, and lacrosse, his coaches and teammates alike valued his skills, as well as his precocious nature. But it was soccer that Jonny loved most. He grew to be a fearless goalkeeper, playing on multiple elite championship teams from elementary through high school, and his skills were greatly admired. Jonny was of average height, but his quickness, agility, and ability to jump and fly were no match for most balls that came hurtling toward his net.

Jonny's bravery and ability to face risks—so valued in sports—had a downside, though. Speed was his middle name, and he took many spills from his skateboard and bike over the years which resulted in multiple injuries, like broken bones or cuts that required sutures. Once, after a brutal from-behind tackle during an intense soccer match, Jonny suffered a major concussion.

He wasn't cautious off the field either, which tested the patience of a few of his teachers, not to mention his anxious parents. Outgoing and popular, Jonny was regarded as a generous, loyal friend with an immensely big heart.

Jonny's lifelong attraction to adventure, coupled with his keen physical skills, led him to pursue a professional pilot training program in college. During his freshman year, he was well on his way to earning his license and flew under the guidance of a program instructor. He also joined the lacrosse team to keep active and fit, and made new friends easily wherever he went. After his first year of college, Jonny returned home for the summer armed with a future that seemed full of promise and great success.

*What could possibly go wrong?*

## HIS ILLNESS

Soon after Jonny had settled in back at home late that May, his father and I noticed some troubling changes in his mood and behavior. It was as if we'd sent one Jonny off to college and a total stranger—a Jonny we never knew—had returned. He was suspicious, accusatory, and angry. He withdrew from his friends and family and retreated to his darkened bedroom for most of the day, where he'd pound out angry messages to strangers from his computer.

Restorative sleep was elusive to Jonny, and sometimes he'd be awake for two or three days in a row. He wore heavy coats and layers of wool in hot weather and described odd somatic complaints in disturbing detail: a persistent bright white light flashing behind his left eye; a numbing on one side of his face creeping to the other side; and the terrifying, painful sensation that his muscles and bones were rearranging themselves under his skin.

We were quick to seek medical attention for Jonny, but a full neurological evaluation revealed no obvious physical reasons for the unusual symptoms he was experiencing. That left another option for us to explore—the possibility of serious mental illness.

Both my husband and I are mental health professionals and had cautiously recognized some signs of psychosis in our son's odd behavior patterns. When he refused to eat a meal I had prepared, accusing me of poisoning his food in collusion with the FBI, we realized Jonny needed immediate help, so we sought psychiatric assessment and treatment.

Thankfully, Jonny willingly engaged with a good doctor and followed the prescribed therapies, even though, as a legally independent young adult, he could have easily chosen not to. Relief was sporadic, however, and Jonny deteriorated further. He eventually suffered an alarming psychotic break that lasted an entire weekend, ending in a credible suicide threat that required involuntary hospitalization to keep him safe.

After Jonny's discharge from psychiatric care ten days later, he re-engaged in outpatient treatment and maintained that medical lifeline for nearly a year. Unfortunately, though, the side effects of his various prescribed medications seemed worse than the symptoms they were meant to alleviate. His blood sugar rose to pre-diabetic levels; he gained weight, became dull and lethargic, and suffered memory loss. And nothing seemed to quiet the incessant voices that demanded he reject and denounce everyone who ever loved and protected him.

The illness and medications prescribed disabled him and meant he could no longer pilot airplanes or play the sports that he loved so much. Life's adventures and joys were mostly lost to him, and all of his dwindling energy was focused on fighting the disease that was destroying the happy and competent young man he once was.

Helplessly witnessing the slow, punishing decline and ultimate death of your child is the worst kind of hell any parent can ever experience. How many times did I scream an angry and hoarse command to the Universe, or anyone within earshot who would listen, "Why Jonny? Take me! Give him his life back and give me his suffering instead!" I wanted so badly for this to be a nightmare from which I would soon awaken to find our youngest son healthy, happy, and whole again.

His doctor was reluctant to diagnose schizophrenia prematurely, even though Jonny's worsening symptoms pointed to this illness more and more as the weeks passed. Instead, he settled on a less-damning medical descriptor, one that might offer Jonny the hope of eventually escaping a permanent sentence.

So, in a compassionate gesture to do as little harm as possible, the psychiatrist settled on *psychotic disorder, not otherwise specified.* This general diagnosis was serious enough to give our son access to many of the critical services he needed without labeling him incurable for life.

And thus, with the simple swipe of a doctor's signature, our Jonny officially joined the ranks of the millions of Americans who are mentally ill. We wanted to shelter him safely in our quiet home, but he preferred to live most days in our secluded cabin on the northern Oregon coast, where the comforting rhythm of the ocean waves and whispers of wind through the trees helped muzzle the angry voices that tortured his peace and stole his sanity.

Jonny came back to us for doctor's visits and groceries, and to meet with his oldest and dearest friends, all of whom stayed by his side and continued their loving, loyal support in spite of all his puzzling behaviors. Sadly, the times that Jonny was at ease and engaged with his friends, family, and doctors decreased as time progressed and the disease worsened.

## HIS EXIT

During what would be his last time home with us, Jonny shared a rare lucid moment with me on a bright, sunshiny June morning. His sudden appearance surprised me as I was relaxing alone on our porch, sipping a steaming cup of freshly brewed coffee. He took a seat in the empty chair by my side, scooting it close.

I had learned to let him talk first, if he wanted to talk at all, so I acknowledged his presence by touching the back of his hand ever so gently. He did not reject my loving gesture and allowed my fingers to linger against his skin for a few seconds longer before he pulled away his hand and placed it down on his lap.

After a short pause, he turned and looked directly at me with a clarity of focus I hadn't seen from his tormented face in months. Jonny's unblinking, dark brown eyes stared as intently at me as they had two decades earlier, on the happy day of his birth.

Although I tried to return his gaze, I was briefly immobilized by an overwhelming rush of deep sadness, remembering how joyfully ignorant we all were back then, unaware of the trauma our precious new baby would be facing as a young man. Drawing in a deep, cleansing breath to smother my sobs before they could surface, I focused my blurry eyes in my son's direction.

His face was relaxed and expressionless. Blinking once, then twice, he drew his eyebrows together as if in solemn thought and spoke slowly, softly, in a soothing monotone that generated a hypnotic wave of calm flowing between us.

"Mom, I don't want to be the guy who stands on the corner downtown and screams at his demons."

I started to reply to offer some sympathy or reassurance, but he arose from the chair in a quick and decisive move and retreated to his darkened room once again, where he would stay for the rest of the day and most of the night.

Less than a week later, his devastated father, brothers, and I would be offering the ashes of our youngest son to the gently rolling waves of the secluded Pacific Ocean bay. After losing our sweet and brave son first to mental illness, we had lost him again, this time to suicide.

## OUR GOOD-BYE

There was never any question about where his final resting place would be. I joined my husband and Jonny's two older brothers in our small fishing boat and motored to his favorite crabbing spot, where we released the ecologically friendly box that held Jonny's earthly remains into the eternal care of that tucked-away coastal bay.

*Safe journey, my sweet son* was the only prayer my shocked and damaged soul could muster as I released the precious vessel into the ocean. It floated and bobbed, rocked gently by the waves, before it slowly sank out of sight and drifted down its long descent to the sandy bottom below.

Jonny would have approved of his simple send-off in the beloved boat that had given him such infinite joy over the years. We all sat in stunned silence for a very long time, each of us trying hard to digest the enormity of the act we had just performed. The water lapped at the sides of the boat and rocked it gently, as if soothing us in our collective grief.

Soon, however, the lull was interrupted by the sound of our motor starting and an insistent caw of one lone seagull that had suddenly appeared overhead, as if to guide us back to the marina. The bird swooped down and glided in front of the bow in large, oval arcs, dipping and diving in what looked like pure joy and unfettered ecstasy.

*Has Jonny's soul already commandeered this bird?* He was robbed of flying at the end of his life, but in death, perhaps, he had resumed his lost dream.

When we arrived at our destination, my husband struggled briefly to steer the boat into its tight docking spot and scraped the pier noisily. The minor collision he caused jolted us all up and out of our seats for a comical moment, everyone landing back on our seats askew, which would have surely amused any observer.

The only audience, however, was our feathered navigator, who by now had landed on the nearest piling overlooking the bow. Our new friend emitted a piercing staccato caw refrain that sounded more like the laugh an amused Jonny would have had at his family's expense.

Yep. Jonny now sported wings. I was certain.


## HIS VISIT


The days and weeks that followed our son's suicide were filled with loving messages and kindhearted gestures from friends, family, and even strangers. Jonny's friendships endured beyond his death as his pals rallied from their grief to adopt Edgar, his orphaned dog, and comfort his heartsick and broken family.

But I had fallen into such a bottomless pit of numbing, isolating grief that no one could reach me. The void left by Jonny's tragic death was a throbbing, breath-stopping pain that tortured me night and day.

Memories of our sweet son were everywhere: his final voice mail message that I've kept to this day; his smiling face in numerous family photos; his clothing and other possessions; Jonny's scent lingering on his clothes, bedding, and towels, and his various treasures.

I obsessed about what Jonny's desperate last moments may have been like and berated myself mercilessly for failing to save him. My attention was reserved exclusively for whatever would promote my personal pain and punishment. I ignored all the coping skills I had acquired as a mental health professional and instead wallowed in anger, self-pity, and sadness. I did not want to heal, let alone survive, this unimaginable loss. I felt like the perennial victim and surrendered to a bleak and hopeless future without my son.

Three months after Jonny's death, however, I had a vivid dream that helped change the course of my otherwise downward spiral. It was early morning on a crisp October day. Penny, our Australian shepherd mix, woke me up at her usual early hour, not at all caring that it was Saturday. I finally gave up trying to fend off her rude demands and arose in a fog. I took her out, hastily gave her some food, and returned to bed. At least I would grab a couple more hours of sleep, or so I thought.

It was then, in the twilight fog between wake and sleep, that Jonny chose to visit his heartbroken mother.

In my dream state, I was returning home alone after having had dinner with friends. As I walked into the yard, I noticed a little golden-haired terrier scampering, leaping over the grass, and exuding pure dog joy. Not thinking it could be our own sweet Terra, who'd died two years earlier, I assumed that my husband had adopted another dog as a surprise. In spite of the fact that this little creature was impossibly cute, I walked past her, ignoring her antics, and into the house. I was driven by a sense of urgency I did not understand.

My husband was busy in the kitchen, cooking dinner over the stove. He looked up as I walked in and greeted me with only a silent, solemn expression. He was not sad. But he was searching my eyes and trying to communicate something serious beyond words.

As I started to tell him about my dinner conversation, my story was interrupted by the familiar clop, clop, clop of cleats on hardwood coming from the end of the darkened hall. How many times had I heard that sound over the years, just before admonishing one or more sons, "Please get those soccer shoes off in the house . . . NOW!"

I turned toward the sound and gasped as Jonny appeared from the shadows, stepping into the kitchen light. I stopped breathing for a moment and my eyes filled with happy, hopeful tears. *Jonny is* not *dead! He is with us! What a cruel, wicked hoax! A terrible dream!* But there he stood, and I was so grateful to see my son's beautiful smile once again.

Jonny looked so handsome and strong. His face was tan, and he was dressed in dazzling soccer clothes: shiny white shorts with black satin trim that sparkled, black striped knit goalie shirt hugging his chest, knee socks, and those pesky cleats! *Where are his shin guards?* I worried. I reached out and pulled him close. *I'll never let you go again,* a silent promise I made to us both. His body was warm to the touch, and solid. We both started to cry, and Jonny declared, "Mom, I love you so much."

I told him how much I love him, too, and how much I've missed him. Reluctantly, I pulled away from his embrace. I held my son's head in my hands, and I got lost in his soulful, familiar eyes.

"So," I exclaimed, "you aren't dead?!" It was both a question and a command, prompted by hope and fear.

"No, Mom." Jonny said in a gentle whisper, reaching for my hand. "I died."

My elation disappeared. *So, it wasn't a nightmare, after all. Our gentle, brave boy is gone.* I took the truth in once again. When I found my voice, I offered a heartfelt plea.

"Please, *please*, Jonny, tell me you are in Heaven."

He looked at me and rolled his eyes, a familiar gesture he'd made hundreds of times. I could have just as easily been asking, "Please, please, Jonny, tell me you did *not* get another speeding ticket!"

"Yeah, Mom, don't worry. I'm in Heaven."

Hungry to know more, I pressed on. "So, tell me, Jonny, what's Heaven like?"

There was a long pause. He seemed to be struggling with his words, searching, perhaps, for an image or concept I might be able to comprehend. It felt like hours passed as I waited for a reassuring reply.

Finally, he offered this: "Well, Mom, Heaven is a hot pot of fun things to do."

*Huh? A hot pot of fun things to do. Hot pot? Hot pot?*

"Don't you mean 'hodgepodge,' honey?" Forever his mother, I'd felt compelled to correct him.

Then suddenly I awoke, and he was gone. *Too short! Too fast! Wait, please! I want more!* Jonny's latest words to me kept echoing in my ears. I rushed to write them down for fear I'd forget them.

*A hot pot of fun things to do.* He is playing soccer again, for sure, guardian of the goal in a game I cannot see. The clothes and cleats tell me this must be true.

*A hot pot of fun things to do.* Jonny returned to me in the company of his beloved little dog, Terra.

*A hot pot of fun things to do.* Yep, this sounds like the Heaven that Jonny would order up. No doubt about it.

## TREASURE

There is no rule book, playbook, or time limit to guide us in grieving the suicide death of a child. We are left on our own, to figure it out in our own way, and in our own time.

After Jonny's death, I tried to listen to what my body and brain needed and mostly ignored the well-meaning advice of anyone who still enjoyed the company of all their children. I slept when I felt like it, and for as long as I wanted. I ate when I was hungry and even sometimes when I was full. Or, I forgot to eat altogether.

I got dressed in the morning or chose to stay in a bathrobe all day. I ignored tasks that were critical and focused on those that were frivolous and unnecessary. Any routines I once honored were either abandoned or performed obsessively, like a life-giving ritual. There was no pattern, no reliable schedules for me. There was also no Jonny.

While I am not a person who follows one traditional spiritual path, I have borrowed comfort and wisdom from a variety of faiths over the years. I can't say for sure what happens after we die, but I am confident that the part of us that gives and receives love endures forever.

Love is definitely eternal and is the only thing capable of breaking through the impenetrable walls and impossible obstacles that grief and loss build to keep us isolated. Was Jonny's everlasting love energy able to reach out and steer me toward the light in that dream?

As my Buddhist friends often remind me, "The world we see is created by what we choose to focus on. It's never too late to adjust our lens." I decided, after what I believe was a life-changing nudge from Jonny, to get a new perspective on my future.

Tentatively, and oh so gradually, I took steps, unsteady and soft at first, to lift myself out of the depths of my self-imposed prison of grief. From the tragedy of my son's suicide came treasures of insight, action, and personal growth that I may never have otherwise known.

A return to the scene of Jonny's death was first on my healing list. One clear-skied evening under a brilliant full moon, a Native American friend and I visited the cabin where he died and performed a smudging ceremony to clean any negative energy. We lit the dry bundle of sage and let the smoke clear away all the pain and sorrow Jonny must have felt as he died. Then we guided the smoke out the upstairs window and into the night. We next lit fragrant sweetgrass to invite joy, love, and life back into our midst.

I joined an online support group for mothers whose children died by suicide and learned how to survive this shared and fragile sisterhood through their courageous examples. By helping each other, it was clear we were healing ourselves.

I volunteered to serve on the board of directors of our local National Alliance on Mental Illness (NAMI) chapter, and assisted other families in obtaining quality mental health care for their children and loved ones.

I learned to meditate; slow down; and be more patient, compassionate, and grateful. I surrounded myself with people who are positive and full of hope and rejected those that did not bring kindness and joy into my life.

The most helpful skill I have acquired, however, is mastering the art of stopping negative, painful thoughts before they take up permanent residence in my brain. Those thoughts do not promote my health or healing, and they certainly don't honor Jonny's precious life and memory. He deserves better from his mother.

I wish I could promise it's easy to break the harmful habit of perpetual grieving. Embracing victimhood can be a soothing addiction and protective escape. It's hard work to fight against its power. But with daily practice, mindful attention, and accepting the help of resilient survivors who can take your hand and lead the way, it can be done.

So, here's my favorite trick to keep me in the present and full of gratitude. When the everyday annoyances of living irritate or frustrate me . . . when painful memories become unwelcome visitors . . . whenever any negative or anxious thoughts rudely invade my peace . . . I ask myself one simple question: *Have I lost another child?*

If the answer is no, then it's going to be a very good day.

\*    \*    \*

**Michele Wollert** lives with her husband, Rich, and rescue dog, Annie, in the beautiful Pacific Northwest. In addition to Jonny, she is the proud mother of Zach and Jason and the devoted grandmother of Gracen and Remi. Michele is a theatrical costume designer turned school psychologist, now happily retired and eternally grateful. She has written about Jonny's life and legacy in a memorial blog: http://jonathan-wollert .memory-of.com.

# VI

# DRUGS

I fully understood that the only way out of the pit of despair was to go into the abyss and sit in the agony for as long as it took.

—Heidi Bright

# Waking Up Is Hard to Do

## By Heidi Bright

*Brennan*

Since the 1980s, I have written down my dreams and significant events in my journals. Both have helped me understand my life circumstances, have provided direction, and have even foreshadowed things to come. These chronicles contributed greatly to my waking up within my waking life and helped me manage what had been unbearable grief after I lost my nineteen-year-old son, Brennan, to a heroin overdose in 2015.

A couple years after Brennan was born, and shortly after his brother Jason's birth, I started seeing a psychotherapist to assist me with my marriage issues. She understood my primal wounding—I had become whiney after a difficult experience at age six, and around age eight I was told, "If you don't stop crying, I'll give you something to cry about." So, I stopped crying. For decades. And I covered up my emotions with habitual patterns of negative thought. Because I had been hiding many of my painful emotions from myself for years, the psychotherapist cautioned me to be careful to not rush our therapeutic process.

A few weeks later, on December 30, 1998, I read to my therapist a dream I'd had the previous night:

> I'm watching a bunch of people who are unconscious. A woman stumbles onto a way out, to being aware. It starts with an *X* under her tongue. She goes through the process but something isn't done right. She falls back into unconsciousness. She does it again and gets further but not all the way. She tries a third time, and knows enough this time to finish the process. She achieves consciousness and so do others.

My therapist was thrilled. "This is one of the 'biggest' dreams I've ever had brought in," she said—and she had been a practicing therapist for several decades, so that meant a lot.

As is commonly done with dream interpretation, we decided I was the woman in the dream. We concluded the *X* under my tongue was about speaking my truth, and it foreshadowed that I would go through a process of waking up, of becoming aware. She said, "This birthing process is not in your control, yet you are going to achieve consciousness."

The first event not in my control came three months later, when my then-husband Joe accepted a job offer in Cincinnati. With gratitude for his new opportunity, and with two preschoolers in tow, we packed up the house in Lexington, Kentucky, and made our way to Ohio. Shortly after we arrived, I set out to look for a therapist in our new hometown.

I soon found a Jungian dream analyst I liked, and I worked closely with him for several years. I came to him with many of my parenting issues and often received helpful insights. Yet, Brennan proved to be an extremely challenging child for me. Eventually I found out part of why being his mother was so hard—something else beyond my control.

When Brennan was five years old, he asked me, "Why does God make bad things like bacteria?" Why, indeed. It's a question people have debated since it was first conceived. I couldn't help but wonder how my son would know enough to ask this insightful question at such a tender age.

Brennan had recently taken an IQ test to see if he qualified for a gifted school in our area. To better understand him, I picked up the book *Guiding the Gifted Child* by Elizabeth A. Meckstroth and Stephanie S. Tolan, and read that gifted children ask such questions at ages eight or nine, while average-intelligence kids didn't formulate them until adolescence.

I had quite a challenge on my hands, especially because Brennan's IQ landed in the "highly gifted" range. This explained the disparity between what he figured out on his own and what other kids his age were not yet able to comprehend.

This discrepancy expressed itself one memorable time at Brennan's Montessori school. He used art materials to create "guns" to protect himself and his friends from imagined dangers. I was beginning to understand that my son was too smart to feel really safe, and yet didn't have the maturity or experience to deal with potential danger. Brennan became anxious, as expressed in repeated stomachaches, and he had difficulty trying to learn.

My son's anxiety continued. Joe and I took him to a psychologist, who determined that Brennan was almost obsessively afraid of losing us both. "He has problems coping with feelings of sadness," the psychologist added. "He bypasses them and goes straight to anger and acts out."

With such emotional intensity in Brennan, family therapy was recommended. Joe and I could not agree on next steps, however, so it never happened.

I placed Brennan in the gifted school and he thrived there for four years. Then Joe left his job abruptly and was unemployed for six months. That was the end of my dream analyst, which was a great disappointment. Also hard for me was placing Brennan in the public school, which was totally out of sync with his personality and academic abilities. He became so miserable that he cried himself to sleep most nights. For sixth grade, however, I was able to get my two boys back into the gifted school.

Just before Brennan was to begin high school, I was diagnosed with highly aggressive end-stage uterine sarcoma. Again, something beyond my control, as I had done everything "right"—eaten a healthy diet, maintained a good weight, exercised, and even meditated an hour every day. *Why does God make bad things like cancer?* All of us were traumatized. I had to quit my job, which meant Joe and I no longer had the financial means to send Brennan to private school. Now he would have to attend public high school. He despised it.

All of us went into therapy. I firmly believe that my third psychotherapist, a clinical psychologist, truly helped saved my life. She taught me a process called the Map of Emotions, which involves focusing only on the physical sensations of one's emotions as they move within our bodies.

Because I was still fairly disconnected from my body and living most of the time in my head, it took months for me to understand the process. Then it took years for me to remember to practice the process whenever a powerful emotion got triggered.

I had two years to practice, though, while I withstood forty-two grueling days of chemotherapy and three major cancer surgeries. At some point during that quite trying endurance race, I had the following dream:

> A Doberman grabs my left hand and bites. It's a firm, but not painful, grip. I feel dread, but remember that dogs who sense fear attack. I release the tension in my body and the terror ebbs. The dog releases my hand.

This dream told me I had not only faced my terror, but also learned to experience the emotion of dread in my body, even while dreaming. I processed my fear by staying aware of my body, accepting the tension, and allowing my body to dissipate it.

I was finally starting to wake up. Maybe my initiatory dream in 1998 was going to come true after all. I was now on my third therapist, and it had taken three tries to become conscious.

I wasn't quite there yet, though. Relentless, the cancer kept growing back. I felt completely powerless, though I did everything I could to survive. As I ran out of treatment options, I made one last-ditch effort to save my life. I moved into a separate apartment, and the boys took turns staying with me.

Within weeks of my move, I had my third major surgery to remove a tumor that was squatting on my pulmonary vein, next to my heart. During my post-op appointment, the nurse practitioner told me to get back on chemo.

"There is no more chemo," I said. "This is an orphan sarcoma, and all available chemos have failed."

The nurse practitioner, who had worked with cancer patients for more than three decades, looked directly into my eyes and said, "I see this all the time. If you can't get back on chemo, you need to get ready for hospice."

I was devastated. During the five weeks from discovery to removal, my tumor had grown from half an inch to a staggering two and a half inches.

During the next six weeks, I continued practicing the Map of Emotions, yet also spent a lot of time lying around, feeling depressed.

Miraculously, my next scan showed no cancer! Neither did the next one. Or the next after that. I have been free of cancer and free of all cancer treatment since 2011.

I had survived. Now I could more fully turn my attention back to my sons. By this time, Brennan was a junior in high school. Even though he hated being in class and had a lot of lifelong social anxiety, he still managed to make a few friends.

At a Halloween party in 2011, Brennan met and quickly fell in love with a young woman named Susan. And after talking with other students about some of their issues, he became convinced he had attention deficit hyperactivity disorder (ADHD), which I had actually suspected for years. I hadn't wanted to medicate him, yet felt it was probably time now because he needed to function better at school. After he started taking Adderall, Brennan's grades improved and he signed up for free college classes while still a high-schooler.

Unfortunately, people with ADHD, according to one report, are twice as likely to abuse substances as those without ADHD.

Without my knowledge, Brennan also began self-medicating; first with marijuana, and then with a variety of other drugs. He was trying to escape from his racing, obsessive thoughts that incited insomnia. Brennan later told me he sometimes only slept two hours at night, and then he had to spend the whole day in school. One day he fell asleep during class and no one could wake him. He was transported to the nurse's office in a wheelchair, fast asleep the whole way. He only woke up once he got there.

Based on what I now know, I suspect Brennan had been in a drug-induced stupor. But I had no idea then. None at all. Teenagers on drugs can go to great lengths to hide their usage. His sleep issues continued—sometimes severe insomnia, sometimes sleeping nearly thirty hours straight. The sleep doctor concluded Brennan just needed to adjust his sleeping patterns—go to bed earlier and get up earlier. *Are you kidding me?*

Despite his lack of sleep and growing drug use (of which I was yet unaware), Brennan managed to graduate from high school with a good GPA and was accepted into the local university's engineering program.

I was grateful to be cancer free and was proceeding with a divorce. I found a new psychotherapist for Brennan and they jelled well. I was relieved. Life seemed on track. Finally, I could take some deep breaths.

A few weeks later, however, the train crashed. On a night when Brennan was staying at Joe's while he was out of town, Brennan took Ambien (a sedative that, for some, can induce sleepwalking) from Joe's medicine cabinet and combined it with LSD. Shortly after midnight, my son went out of his mind on a bad trip. He entered a nearby family residence and was arrested days later on a felony charge. He spent the weekend in jail.

Jail! My brilliant son was in jail? *How could this be happening?* I cried on my bed. I cried in the car. I cried in the grocery store. The faucet turned off during childhood was flowing full force and I allowed it.

It was a terrible way to have to wake up. The pain seemed unrelenting, and I was grateful for my psychotherapist. She helped train me to always pay attention to physical sensations inside my body instead of automatically escaping into my head, as I had done for decades.

Life only got worse. Because of the serious charge, Susan broke off their relationship. Brennan had to complete a drug education program to get the felony dropped. To avoid issues on his weekly blood draw (checking for drug use), he switched to taking opioids because they left the body quickly. Brennan still felt a need to get high, especially to mask the pain of his breakup with his girlfriend. Even though he graduated from the drug program and his felony charge was dropped, Brennan got addicted to smoking heroin.

I had no idea. If my dreams had told me, they were too vague to wake me up to what was going on under my nose. Or I was in denial so deep, the reality could not penetrate my awareness.

Brennan said he wasn't ready for college, which I didn't quite understand. So, I took him to an emotional regulation course at a local substance abuse and mental health facility. He finished the class, yet two months later he shot up heroin for the first time. He overdosed and was left alone on a freezing sidewalk early in the morning while his "friends" fled and called 911. Brennan's life was saved and he was transported to the nearest emergency room.

At 8:30 a.m. he arrived back at my home as if nothing had happened. When I asked where he'd been, he said he overslept at a friend's house.

I believed him. Why wouldn't I? It seemed perfectly plausible to me. He had completed the drug abuse awareness program and he was seeing a great psychotherapist. I had no idea he was back on drugs.

And the lies continued.

Brennan became a raging addict, injecting daily and taking on some of the behaviors typical of many who live with the brain disease of addiction—lying, trading in drugs, and driving under the influence. At one point, he totaled my van. His out-of-control behavior deteriorated to the point that he shoved his brother, Jason, who fell and sustained a concussion.

While I felt powerless about Brennan's behavior, I did have one card left. In July 2014, I cut off his van insurance and told him he was not to come back onto my property.

Brennan went to live with his dad.

Two months later, he called me and said he was withdrawing.

"What from?"

After a lot of hedging, he finally told me.

"Heroin."

I was stunned. When that word finally penetrated my brain, I felt like the ground beneath me had given way. *Heroin is what addicts in inner cities without hope use, not bright suburban kids with opportunities and support.*

But I was wrong. Heroin and opioid addiction is not restricted to poor neighborhoods or families, nor to inner cities or street gutters. According to 2015 US government estimates, more than two million Americans are addicted to opioids,[1] and no one is immune. My son was a heroin addict and had already been addicted for a good year.

*What do I do?* My crazy world hadn't been patched up. It was decimated.

Brennan didn't want to get treatment . . . until Joe kicked him out. Then he was suddenly ready to try a residential detox program.

Brennan went in and out of drug rehabilitation centers from October through December, had another drug arrest, and in February 2015 finally completed a six-week rehab program in Florida. He returned to Cincinnati and moved into a sober living house. I got him enrolled in another outpatient program and urged him to attend twelve-step recovery meetings. He also needed to get a job so he could pay his rent after the first month.

None of it happened.

And then the sober living house closed in early April. Brennan had one other sober living option, but that rundown house had bedbugs, and he refused. *Why does God make bad things like bedbugs?* When Joe offered to let him move back into his house, Brennan accepted.

I felt punched in the gut because I was sure that without the support of a sober living community, Brennan would slip back into using. Brennan, however, could not pass up the chance to live in a nice suburban house near one of his drug suppliers.

I soon dreamt I saw a big white airplane flying low, coming in my direction. It passed by me and took a nosedive. The airplane turned dark yellow, then crashed and burned.

Perhaps the dream meant I was burning out. Or the airplane represented Brennan, who was trying to fly but not getting high and instead was crashing and burning.

Sure enough, by the end of May, Brennan got arrested again on felony drug charges. After all I had done to try to help my kid get and stay sober, he was back in jail. My chest sunk into my body with the weight of my shame and sorrow.

Brennan's situation felt completely hopeless, and I fell into despair. As I sobbed, I could barely breathe. *Maybe it would be easier on his tortured mind and emotions if he just overdosed and died.* I had to acknowledge and accept my absolute powerlessness in his situation. All I could control was my reactions to his behaviors.

My son may not have hit his bottom yet, but I had certainly hit mine. At long last I surrendered, and completely let go of my attempts to control his outcomes.

Brennan was released a few days later, on June 2, and returned to his dad's house. On Friday, June 5, Joe kicked him out of his house again. And my son was still not allowed back on my property.

I picked Brennan up outside his dad's house and drove him to the county courthouse to obtain a public defender. Then I offered to take him to a drop-in center so he could sleep indoors on a bed.

"No f****g way," he said.

He dialed a friend, hoping he could stay at her place overnight. Even after several tries, she never picked up. So at his request, I drove him to a fast-food restaurant near her house.

I dropped him off. "I love you," I said.

"I love you, too."

He closed the car door.

I drove home.

I never saw my nineteen-year-old son alive again.

The next morning, I woke up at 4:00 a.m. and felt like an elephant had stepped on my heart. I paid attention to the physical sensations in my body. And I repeatedly prayed, *Please, God. Help us.*

I texted Brennan later in the morning. He did not respond.

On Sunday, a deep sense of sadness about my son enveloped me. And I still had not received a response to my text.

By Monday, because I had not heard from Brennan, I felt sure he was using again. Whenever I entertained thoughts about him, I felt overwhelmed by sorrow. To obtain relief from my painful thoughts, I kept shifting my focus to the unpleasant tingling sensation throughout my body.

Tuesday afternoon, as I was sitting outside on our back porch, Jason (now seventeen) said, "Mom, there's some people at the door."

Curious, I walked through the house to the front door. Outside stood two police officers.

*What has Brennan done now?*

I stepped outside, not knowing I would be leaving my old life behind forever.

It took several minutes for my brain to register what the officers were telling me, over and over again. They had found a badly decomposed body . . . with a needle . . . and my son's court papers.

*No, God. No, God. No, God.*

I stumbled back into the house and told Jason the incomprehensible. We held each other and sobbed for what seemed like forever, through that dark, overwhelming night.

My dreams had shown me the crashing airplane. My body had known the unthinkable right after it happened. And I had allowed myself to accept the grief in my body without even knowing what it meant.

Waking up is so hard to do.

The therapeutic process I had been working since 2009 played a crucial role in my being able to sustain my sense of self through the ensuing days, weeks, months, and years. Because I'd had six years of good practice paying attention to the emotions in my body, and allowing them to lift, I was able to process and integrate my son's death.

I had learned that the only way to manage this grief was to go into the pain and fully embrace it. I allowed each wave of emotion to rise, I surrendered to the physical experience, I observed its course within my body, and I experienced the lift after ninety seconds. And then the next wave would hit, and I'd repeat the process again until it was gone.

I fully understood that the only way out of the pit of despair was to go into the abyss and sit in the agony for as long as it took.

To this practice, I added many options for managing my grief, including a practice I call Processing Grief Through Writing, along with guided visualizations and various hands-on healing therapies such as acupressure for depression. I also created a small memorial garden in my backyard, which soothed me.

My dreams around my son Brennan continue to bring me insights and help me grow in awareness. I once dreamt of a schoolteacher overdosing, signaling that I had more trauma to process. I also dreamt of Brennan floating away from me and I was unable to retrieve him, indicating the sense of powerlessness and yearning that I still needed to face and process.

Today, this trauma still lives in my heightened fears about Jason. Sometimes when he's away from my house, I ask him to text me, just so I can know he's still here. That behavior is not something I would ever have done had I not lost Brennan. Yet, now I know in my bones that terrible things happen in our world, and that they usually are beyond our control. We have bad bacteria, fatal cancers, and bedbugs, as Brennan pointed out long ago. And these are only a few of the bad things life can dish out.

Our children can pass on before us, sometimes under heinous circumstances. It is mystery and it is misery, and leaves our hearts shattered wide open.

Yet, just as a coin has two sides, our experiences can also have two sides—the traumatic and the tender. Because I cannot have my Brennan back in physical form, I will accept whatever gifts and graces come my way, including the wonderful gift of being awake and aware. It is one of the many gifts birthed out of my deepest wound.

Among other gifts have been so many beautiful dreams of my Brennan—giving him a solid hug, receiving a phone call from him, and him coming to my house to visit, all as if nothing was out of the ordinary. I will cherish these dreams always.

Perhaps the most telling experience I've had was on an unusually warm fall day in 2018, when I was lying on my deck swing after another difficult read-through of Brennan's story. His story will become a section in my upcoming book, *Grieving an Addict*, written as support for those who have lost a loved one to addiction.

As I lay there with my eyes closed, I heard songbird wings fluttering loudly. Then I felt a light touch on my left forearm.

I carefully opened my eyes.

OMG.

There was a yellow house finch perched on my arm! He looked around in different directions, then flew off.

I remained as still as possible.

A moment later he was back, gentle on my shoulder.

Waking up is so hard to do. Yet the extraordinary grace it imparts can be like a reassuring hand from heaven.

My Brennan's continuing love consoles me. I am alive, I am awake, and I am richly blessed.

## NOTE

1. Lenny Bernstein, "Opioid Prescriptions Dropped for the First Time in the Modern Drug Crisis," *Washington Post*, July 7, 2017, http://www.chicago tribune.com/lifestyles/health/ct-opioid-prescriptions-dropped-20170707 -story.html.

\* \* \*

**Heidi Bright, MDiv,** is intimately acquainted with grief. Because writing is the way Heidi shares her offerings with the world, she turned 250 options for managing cancer into the best-selling *Thriver Soup: A Feast for Living Consciously During the Cancer Journey* (2015) (www.thriver soup.com). Through her upcoming book *Grieving an Addict* (www .grievinganaddict.com), Heidi shares lifesaving gifts with others who grieve by showing them a way to process and integrate their emotions.

# Hunter's Hope

### By Tammy McDonnell

Hunter

Life doesn't always turn out the way you think it will.

My son Hunter, born in 1990, was full of spontaneity and fun, and his sparkly big brown eyes always showed his excitement and enthusiasm for everything. Although I loved him with all my heart, I wasn't a good mom—unfortunately, I was a cocaine addict off and on for about twenty years.

At least partially due to my drug addiction, when Hunter was four years old, my husband and I divorced. Shortly afterwards, my ex-husband and I both remarried. We rotated weekends and holidays with our son and maintained a flexible schedule.

Joe, my new husband, and I were both working, and we were able to buy a modest home together. When we had our daughter Keely, Hunter became a big brother at the age of eight, which he adored. However, it wasn't long after the September 11, 2001, terrorist attacks that Joe lost his job and we struggled financially. Soon, our home fell into foreclosure.

My parents lived in Florida, and we decided to move there and live with them until we could get back on our feet. Sadly, this meant leaving Hunter behind because I knew, in my heart of hearts, that Hunter (then thirteen) needed to be with his dad in Pennsylvania. They were very close, and I was still a mess, in terms of off-and-on drug use. On top of that, Hunter was my ex-husband's only child, so this plan made all the more sense.

Leaving Hunter behind to move to Florida was one of the hardest things I ever had to do in my life. I soothed myself by picturing vacations with all of us, visits throughout the year, and numerous phone calls. Still, I felt a lump in my throat as we packed up the U-Haul and left my son to establish ourselves in another state.

Joe and I were fortunate to get jobs right away, and we began building our new life in the Sunshine State. Then something happened I didn't expect. While we were still busy settling in, I would call to talk to Hunter and get no answer. I called and called and called, but with no response. I sent birthday cards and Christmas presents, but never received any reply of any kind. I had no contact at all with my son for seven years, and this left a gaping hole in my heart. Later I learned that Hunter's stepmom had taken control and thought it best that he have no contact with his drug addict mother.

I finally got clean in 2009. As soon as I got my bearings, I looked for Hunter on Facebook and found him. When I saw that little green circle on the right-hand side of my screen showing that Hunter was online, I was overwhelmed with happiness and excitement. *Oh my, I can finally talk to my son!* I typed him a message that said, "Hunter, it's Mom. I miss you," and included my phone number. It felt like only a second before the green light completely vanished.

When that little light disappeared, I thought I would, too. I kept telling myself, *He's busy. He'll read my message and call me later.* But sadly, that never happened.

After that, I was on Facebook 24/7 waiting for the green light to reappear next to my Hunter's name. Over and over again, I was letting him know how much I loved him and missed him, always sure to include my phone number. Much later on, I found out that his girlfriend had most often been logged on, under Hunter's Facebook account, and that he wasn't actually very big on social media himself.

Finally, in September 2010, I sent Hunter a birthday check bearing my phone number. I was desperately hoping he still lived at the same address and that he'd be the one to receive my check. At first, I was thrilled when he called, but my heart sank a few minutes into our conversation.

"Mom, I have something to tell you," he said. "I've been struggling with an addiction to opioids." Hunter told me he had been through an inpatient rehab and was taking Suboxone to help him get off of the opioids, and that he was working hard to get better. After that we kept in touch via Skype, telephone, and texting at least once or twice a week. I was glad that he had confided in me, but sad because I'd had no idea about his addiction and hadn't been there to support him or help him through it.

Although Hunter had known about my drug addiction, it wasn't something we ever discussed. I believe he was told different things from his stepmom and his dad, who told him, "I had to deal with your mother's addiction, and I am having a hard time dealing with yours."

After corresponding for about a year and a half, I flew to Pennsylvania and spent a whole week with Hunter. When we said hi and hugged, it was awkward for both of us, mostly because I didn't know him as an adult, and he didn't know me either. After all, we hadn't seen each other in several years and he was now twenty-three.

While I was there, Hunter and I shopped, went out to various restaurants, and just spent time trying our best to reconnect. It was hard at times, though. Once, I made a statement about something and his reply was, "Mom, you don't even know me."

His words pierced right through my heart because I knew, without doubt, he was right. Sad as it was, I didn't know my own son at all. Since I had been lost in my drug addiction for years, he had been kept from me. Now that I was finally clean, I wanted to make up for all the missed time and desperately longed to know the grown man who was my son.

After that visit, we kept in contact and everything seemed to be going well. Hunter filled me in on the "lost" years, telling me about certain times I had missed. He had graduated from a tech high school, where he had studied carpentry, as well as heating, ventilation, and air-conditioning (HVAC). This led to a great job that Hunter really enjoyed with a company that worked on HVAC for Amtrak in Philadelphia.

Unfortunately, after just a few years, Hunter's division at this company shut down and his job ended. Twenty-four years old by this time, he struggled to maintain himself financially. He moved in and out with his father as a cycle of beginning and losing various jobs began in earnest. He finally relapsed with opioids and went into inpatient treatment for a while.

It was during this same period of time that my dad had a stroke back in New York. Between the many trips from Florida to New York, I was totally overwhelmed caring for my father and being very concerned about my son and his addiction problem. On New Year's Day 2015, my dad passed away. Mourning the loss of my dad was compounded by the terrible worry I had for my son and the struggles I knew all too well that he was having.

Although I knew firsthand the ravages of addiction, Hunter's opioid addiction seemed even worse than what I had gone through with cocaine. Once he was out of treatment, we spoke with each other at least once or twice a week. Then, all of a sudden, all contact with him stopped—again. My calls to his cell phone went straight to voice mail and calls to his father's house were unanswered, just like when Hunter was young.

Eventually, I discovered that my son had relapsed again and was back in rehab for a third time, and we were all living the nightmare cycle of opioid addiction. I guess fortunately for me, I never saw my son in active addiction because he lived in another state. But what was so incredibly difficult was not hearing from him. I knew something was wrong but couldn't contact him. I would reach out to people who knew Hunter, including his father, but wouldn't hear back. I felt so completely helpless. I know what it is like to take the right instead of the left and be back in the same place you said you wouldn't ever go to again. I will be honest, though, for some reason I always thought he'd be fine. Maybe I was in denial and never really dealt with the severity of his addiction—even though I knew all about the insidious disease of addiction.

Then finally Hunter called, and I was ecstatic to learn he was sober. He was in outpatient treatment again and was staying in a sober living home in Lake Worth, Florida, where he ended up being a resident for quite some time.

In March 2017, I was grateful and pretty excited because, after renting for years, my husband and I had just purchased a home in Ocala,

Florida. It was an extra blessing for me because now Hunter was only four hours south of us. He had a good job doing landscaping, and by this time he'd been clean for a year and a half. I knew he still had some anxiety, though, and I believe that's why his temptation by drugs was so powerful. Plus, Hunter told me that his choice of friends was also a part of the problem.

In September of 2017, Hunter came up to stay with us in Ocala, to escape the direct path of Hurricane Irma. We'd had many other visits prior to this, and I was always overjoyed by the chance to spend more time with my beautiful son. He visited with us for a whole week, and we took pictures and enjoyed our time together, despite our lack of electricity.

During his stay, I mentioned to Hunter that I wanted to find a club, or something, to join in order to meet new people. "That would be great, Mom, but please not bar clubs like the Moose or Elks," he teased, peering at me with his infectious smile. "Look around and see what you'd like."

It was only a month later, on October 17, 2017, that I got the call that Hunter, then twenty-seven, was in the hospital, in a medically in-duced coma. They wouldn't give me any explanation over the phone as to what had happened. Joe and I drove in silence the whole four hours to south Florida. We had made that trip many times before with happy plans of fun things to do and restaurants we wanted to try when we visited Hunter, but this drive was unimaginable—full of fear, disbelief, and shock.

Immediately upon our arrival at the hospital at 6:30 p.m., we met with Hunter's neurosurgeon. He said he needed to warm Hunter's body, so they could do an MRI and learn the extent of any brain damage he might have incurred.

Staring at all the machines Hunter was hooked up to and hearing all the monitors beeping, I felt devastated. I wanted desperately to hold him and take him home, and I prayed to God for my son to survive.

The warming process was going to take a fair amount of time, so Joe and I left the hospital and went back to our hotel room to get some much-needed rest.

At 2:10 a.m., we got another call from the hospital, telling us Hunter had had a seizure and was in tachycardia, and they were check-ing him for a pulse. We raced to the hospital, only to find our son lying there all alone, with no machines and no monitors. Our precious Hunter was gone.

I had asked the doctor earlier that day about the toxicology report and he'd said it was negative. However, Hunter's autopsy report came back with *accidental overdose due to Fentanyl*, which is a synthetic opioid, as the cause of death.

What I now understand is that there are a number of fake pills being manufactured that look like various opioids and benzos such as Percocet and Xanax, and they are proving to be lethal in the tens of thousands. I believe Hunter was seeking Xanax, or something similar, to cope with his debilitating anxiety. I will never know for certain, though, until we are reunited in heavenly Paradise (but I don't think it will matter by then).

Gazing down at my now-deceased son, I was in shock. I was numb and felt like I wasn't even in my body. My mind was in a complete fog. It was pouring down rain when we left the hospital and went back to the hotel room. I told my husband, "I can't stay in this room."

I wanted to crawl out of my skin. I spent hours calling family, barely able to speak and sobbing uncontrollably, still not wanting to believe my precious Hunter was gone. I told Joe I needed a church, and he found one. Once there, I lit a candle and prayed to God to help me and bring me comfort. I wanted so badly to be with my son, and I sure as heck didn't want to be here on Earth, without him.

The next day Joe and I made the long, four-hour drive home in silence. I'm not sure how he even drove, he was so shook up. I vowed I would never stay in another hotel again; the reminders of this awful trip would be too hard. When we got home, I took off the shirt, sweater, and sneakers I wore while pacing that hospital and put them in a special place in my closet. I told myself, *They will stay there forever, and never be used again.*

I knew that I needed help right away, that if I didn't get it, I was going to slide into a dark pit of unbearable grief and pain and begin using again myself. In an effort to obtain some relief, I attended my first Grief Share meeting near my house.

These beautiful people embraced me, but couldn't believe I had just lost my son a few days prior. They said they had never had anyone come to their support group so soon after the death of a loved one. I explained that I knew if I didn't do something fast, I would go into a deep and scary abyss that I would never be able to climb up out of.

Although the Grief Share group helped me tremendously, I felt like I also needed a counselor to talk with one-on-one. I sought help through our community hospice, which allowed me to share my feelings of guilt, anger, and hopelessness, which I freely did.

These sessions, which lasted a few weeks, really helped me. My counselor validated the enormity of what I'd been through and gave me suggestions for ways to cope with my loss, like journaling and self-care, among others. I also purchased several books on grief, which were helpful, especially at night when I would retreat to my bedroom for some quiet time in an attempt to outsmart my insomnia.

The first couple of months following Hunter's death were difficult, to say the least. And it was a double whammy—I had lost Hunter during his growing-up years, and now I had lost him again. It felt as if the heartbreak would never let up. I spent a lot of time asking, *Why?*, *How did this happen?*, and *Why did I survive addiction but my son did not?* I would have taken his place in a heartbeat—he had his whole life ahead of him. I didn't care about our new home and wanted to sell it, get a divorce, and start a whole new life. Even though I had a wonderful husband and daughter (who was then twenty), family, and friends, I still longed for my Hunter. As much as some people who've not lost a child like to think otherwise, there's no replacing a child with your other children.

Once again, I knew I had to get busy to keep my own sanity and sobriety. One thing I hadn't yet found as a common denominator in any group or book was the loss of a child *and* that he suffered from addiction. I felt isolated and unable to talk frankly with anyone about my reality because it was always so different from theirs. Because of my fears around the stigma of addiction, I found myself telling some people that Hunter had passed away from a cardiac event, or that we hadn't yet discovered the cause.

I became so uncomfortable, I finally did some research online. I thought, *There has to be someone else in my situation out there.* I could hardly believe my eyes when I found a closed online group called Heroin Memorial. I read story after gut-wrenching story of the many that had lost a child, and in some cases two children, to addiction. Here I found the most compassionate, amazing people who understood what I was living through. I no longer felt the need to screen everything I said and felt, because I knew that they knew. Now I wasn't the only one who was enduring this kind of pain. I had spent months feeling I was unique, and I was dying inside a little each day before I found others who understood me.

I remember one of my last conversations with Hunter, when we talked about my wanting to join a club. Today, here I am, a member of a club that nobody wants to be in, including me. Sometimes I say to him, *Okay, Hunter, this definitely wasn't what I had in mind.* I have stopped asking why this happened; I believe now that I will never understand why until Hunter and I are finally reunited in heaven.

I have completely changed since Hunter's death. Something like this changes you down to your core, but it's hard to find words to describe how it does.

One day, I was in a restaurant with a friend, and I saw someone I knew, a person I've had some not-so-nice experiences with. I have never been mean-spirited, but I know a couple people who are, and this person I spotted happens to be one.

In the old days, I would have talked all about that to the friend I was with. I would have pointed out this other woman and told my friend something not nice about her. Now, I no longer have the desire to do such things. It doesn't change anything for me to complain about other people's behavior, and it robs me of peace if I spend my energy gossiping about someone else or complaining. It hurts *me*—not them. So, that is one way that I've changed.

Sometimes, I smile at people for no obvious reason—like when I see someone in the grocery store looking at the crackers that Hunter used to love to eat. I don't care what they might think of me. I find myself being more kind, and even more patient. More and more I see how one simple thing can change someone's day for the better.

I'm still angry about this, don't get me wrong, and I still cry a lot. I try to make sense of this every day. I will say, I thank God I was clean and able to be there for my son when he needed me most. For once, I felt I did something right in Hunter's life. How sad it is, though, that he should be graduating from trade school or getting married and having children or just doing something that makes him happy.

My loss is still very recent, only fifteen months ago as I write this. But I often feel Hunter with me, and hear him saying, *Mom!* He is calling my attention to something, and I am listening. He also sends lots of "signs" that comfort me and tell me I'm on the right track in ways that are both little and big.

Today, there are opportunities and situations put in front of me, like the wonderful invitation to write a chapter for this book, and I am choosing whether or not to act on each one of them. Hunter continues to make it clear to me that I'm supposed to be doing something to support others in my situation, to educate against this brutal opioid epidemic, and to work hard to spread the message of recovery that he had wanted to spread.

I have talked to so many other parents of children like mine. Their kids, who also died of addiction, were independent and not interested in a typical, nine-to-five kind of career or lifestyle. They didn't want to be locked into that. They weren't defiant, but they were not made for the kiss-ass board room life either.

Our children are trying to find their own way, and some of them wind up lost. They go to college and study, but then they come out and they can't get jobs. It's a crazy world today and our children are letting us know that, if we just pay attention.

These are kids who have died young, but when they were here, they lived a lot like Hunter lived. We were lucky enough to be with these amazing, beautiful children for such a short time, and how awesome is that? I believe that their compassionate, loving souls ultimately couldn't handle this world, and we have to pay attention to that message. We've got to work harder to spread hope, and that is what I'm striving to do for them, and for Hunter.

Sometimes, I can hear him saying, *Mom, you are supposed to be doing something about this!* I just keep listening to that, keep getting up every day and keep trying to make a real difference.

When we talked about the craziness in life, Hunter would often say, "Mom, it's just a shit show." I never really knew what he meant by that, but recently I looked it up online. It's defined as "a situation or event marked by chaos or controversy." Now, I think that's kind of funny, and kind of sad, because it describes so much of the world we live in today.

So, for Christmas this past year I ordered myself a T-shirt that says "I never wanted to be a part of the shit show," and I know Hunter appreciates that. Now, I can hear him again, and he's saying, *You go, Mom!*

My son is no longer here physically, but he is still by my side every day and continues to gently guide me. Because of him, I am active in a local task force here in my community. This task force has just started working for the education and prevention of drug abuse, with particular focus on the opioid epidemic. If I can help just one soul heal from this dreaded addiction, I will have made a difference, and I will be honoring my son in a way that is deeply meaningful. I pray that telling my story helps someone, just as I have been blessed with the kindness of so many others who have helped me.

When Hunter left our home after his last visit, the last thing he said to us was, "Don't let Keely get into drugs." This is Hunter's Hope, something that he wrote in one of his journals. It is what he wanted for himself, for his family, and for the world:

> May all beings be happy and free,
> and may the thoughts, words,
> and actions of my own life
> contribute in some way to that
> happiness and to that
> freedom for all.

I still have rough days, but they are softer and not so unkind. Next month, Joe and I are planning a vacation to Disney World for a week. And yes, I will be staying in a hotel again. We are celebrating our twentieth wedding anniversary, and I will break out the old sneakers and wear those as well.

I am looking forward to this joyous occasion, and I know Hunter will be joining us and saying, *Have fun, Mom! I am right here with you.*

\* \* \*

**Tammy McDonnell** lives in Ocala, Florida, with her husband Joe, their daughter Keely, and Gizmo their spoiled Peekapoo. As she tries to make a difference in the world, she is supportive of women in the online Facebook group #NotInVain and wants to help lessen the stigma of addiction so that it is talked about more openly.

# *VII*

# MURDER

We must do good in order for a bad circumstance to end in a good result.

—Rukiye Z. Abdul-Mutakallim

# A Single Tear

## By Rukiye Z. Abdul-Mutakallim

*Suliman*

*My* daughter, Khadijah, and I were seated in the courtroom, along with the family of the accused, when two of the three assailants who murdered my son were ushered into the courtroom.

*Boys! They are so young! Babies* . . . my heart said.

The younger, who was fourteen, was the taller of the two, and seeing his face for the first time was like looking into the face of a child who was lost and didn't know how to stop this horror he had somehow brought upon himself. The older one, sixteen, was shorter, and his face also was like a child's, only angry, hardened, and defiant.

This first court appearance was held in Juvenile Court, where evidence was presented for the boys to be remanded to Common Pleas Court, so they could be tried as adults.

As I looked at the mothers of the two boys, I noticed how young they were, both single moms, much younger than my son Suliman, who was thirty-nine on the day of his death. I noticed on each of their faces a look of regret and deep concern for their children. As we all listened to the evidence being presented against these boys, their mothers displayed a pain so deep that I know only comes from the heart.

Six months earlier, on Monday, June 29, 2015, my phone rang around 1:30 a.m. I remember the time well because I had been having a restless night. My daughter-in-law was calling. She said that my son Suliman had been shot half a block from their apartment, that a crowd had gathered, and the police were holding everyone back.

I sat straight up in bed, and I remember pleading to The Creator, Allah, *Let this be a dream.* I quickly woke my daughter and son-in-law, who were living with me, and within minutes we were all dressed and in the car.

As we arrived at Suliman's apartment building and saw all the police cars with their flashing lights, I flashed back to the first time I had visited my son and his wife shortly after they moved to this neighborhood. Imagine a place where even when the sun is shining, there is still a heavy feeling of despair in the air. This community has a high rate of adult unemployment. The hopelessness in his neighborhood was palpable from the moment I first stepped out of my car.

I remembered pulling my son aside and saying, "Suliman, how long do you plan to stay in this area? I sense nothing good can grow here."

He looked at me with his kind and gentle eyes and said, "*Ummi* [mother], I must try. I want to help people who feel that this life can't change for them. How better to encourage a person but to be among them, setting the example."

In the parking area of the building, I saw my son's wife talking with two detectives. They were questioning her when the three of us approached. I listened as the detectives explained that Suliman had been discovered about 10:30 p.m. Sunday night. He had been shot once only, from behind, in the nape of his neck. The assailants had shot him, robbed him, and left him to bleed to death in the street.

I could feel my heart pounding as I fought back tears. All I could think was, *Where is my son now? Where have they taken him? I must be with him!*

When we arrived at the hospital, my son was in the intensive care unit. The upper part of his head was wrapped completely in bandages, all the way around. I could see Suliman's face, but the swelling was so bad that his eyes were practically swollen shut. His coloration was dark from the blood that had built up in his head and neck from the gunshot. Yet, he was still alive when we arrived. It was as if he had been waiting for us . . . for me.

I leaned in close to my precious boy, speaking his name. My tears fell on his bandages, his shoulders, and his hands. I recited heartfelt Islamic prayers while I held his hand.

We called his older brother, Commander Hasan Umar Abdul-Mutakallim, a naval officer who was stationed at the Pentagon in Virginia, and held the phone up to Suliman's ear so he could hear the voice of his brother, whom he so cherished.

I sat by my baby's side, and as the hourglass of his life was trickling down to its end, I felt a strong urge to tell my sweet son about his birth. I said, "Suliman, you were born on a Tuesday, December 15, 1975, at 1:32 p.m. You were eight pounds, five ounces, twenty-one inches long. I carried you for ten months, because you were in no hurry to leave the warmth and safety of my womb. My labor with you was one hour only, and you were born in silence, as is the Islamic way. The first word you heard, pronounced in your right ear, was The Creator's name, *Allah*, and the next words uttered, pronounced in your left ear, were your name, Suliman Ahmed Abdul-Mutakallim."

I did not hold back my tears. I allowed them to fall as I kissed Suliman's hand and told him how very much I loved him, and that I was so honored to have him as my son.

As I looked upon him, I noticed a sudden glow emanating from his face, and I saw a tear run down the corner of his right eye. A single tear. And then his hands began to turn cold. I knew then, at that very moment, my baby boy was gone. His spirit and soul had vanished from his body forever.

I then said, "From *Allah* you came and unto *Allah* you have returned, as will happen to all who are born. Lord, please forgive us for any of our shortcomings while we were on this earth of Yours and grant us Your Mercy—*Amin!*" Then I let go of my son physically, but his Spirit shall always be with me in memory and in my heart.

As the weeks and months passed, the police filled in more details—information gathered by them, and what they had learned by watching footage captured on closed-circuit television (CCT) cameras that had been in place around Suliman's neighborhood. On the night of his death, my son had walked to an ATM near his home and withdrew sixty dollars from his account. Then he went to White Castle to pick up some carry-out dinner. Suliman was returning from the restaurant, walking under a poorly lit overpass, when he was brutally attacked. The amount of money the three assailants stole from his dying body was forty dollars. They also took his wallet, his cell phone, and the food he was bringing home to his wife for dinner, for them to enjoy.

Police were able to identify two of the three people on the CCT footage, so they were arrested. The leader, an adult male approximately twenty-five, remained free, leaving the teenage boys to take the fall for Suliman's murder.

It had been two years since the boys were arrested and bound over as adults to the Common Pleas Court. There had been no trial, because both boys confessed to the crime, and each entered a plea of guilty to a lesser charge. I was told that I would be allowed to speak in court when they were sentenced, but that they would be sentenced separately, at two separate hearings.

When the day of the sentencing came for the younger boy, Javon, I had not seen him or his mother in two long years. She looked changed—older and weakened. Her son was much taller now and more filled out. He appeared as a child in a man's body, not knowing what to do, or how to stop this horrible path he found himself on.

As the young teen entered his plea of guilty, I could not hold back my tears. I heard him say some words of regret, and then as the judge announced her sentencing, Javon's mother cried out in what no doubt was excruciating pain. As painful as it had been for me to lay my son down in his grave, knowing I can never touch him again on this Earth, I would never want to face the agony and despair Javon's mother will have to face for at least the next twenty years to come. She will see her son, but she can't touch him. To see your child in pain but be unable to comfort him, to see danger all around him but be incapable of reaching out and pulling him away from that danger, that is unfathomable, irreconcilable pain.

After the judge spoke to young Javon, I was invited to address the court. As if I was watching myself in a movie, I saw myself rise and walk up to the podium. The whole courtroom fell silent, and then, after a moment, I said these words to the young boy who stood before me: "My name is Rukiye Zathra Abdul-Mutakallim, and I am the proud mother of the man in this picture [I had a picture of my son in his naval uniform]. His name is Suliman Ahmed Abdul-Mutakallim. He comes from a long line of family members who have served this country honorably. He was raised with an Islamic understanding about how you live your life on this earth."

I looked directly at young Javon, still holding up my son's picture, and said: "You and your accomplices took upon yourselves to commit a horrible crime and showed no mercy to my son. Even as a child, he was kind and helpful to others. I have many stories of him calling me and asking me to help take someone to the doctor's office for an appointment, or take someone to the voting booth because they wanted to vote. This was the person you harmed that night. You shot him—all three of you pulled the trigger—robbed him, and left him dying in the gutter, mercilessly."

At that point I had to pause, fight back the tears, and take a deep breath. I addressed the young man by name, and said, "Javon, if you had just asked my son, he would have even given you the shirt off his back along with whatever money he had on him."

By the time Javon is released, he will be in his thirties. I told him I wanted to be in his life to help him, and his mother's life, too. To visit him and teach him how to read with understanding. To correspond with him. To help him focus on learning a trade so that when he is eventually let out, he could build a better life for himself.

Finally, I asked him, "May I be part of your life, to help you?" I was silent, and my tears were no longer flowing from my eyes.

Then Javon spoke, with tears in his eyes, and said, "Yes, please be a part of my life and help me." Then he broke down, sobbing.

I thanked the judge and turned to go back to my seat. As I was walking past the area where the boy was still standing, before the judge's bench, he turned towards me and said, "I really am so sorry for my part in hurting your son. I wish I could take back what I did. I wish that night had never happened. I will work hard to get away from such a life. Please come and see me. Please help me."

The sound of regret in his voice touched my heart deeply. I addressed the boy, the judge, and his mother, and asked for permission to hug him. In unison, they all gave me permission to do so.

Without hesitation, I approached Javon, and wrapped my arms around him as our tears fell simultaneously. As I recited a small prayer of forgiveness, mercy, and protection, I felt his heart—and I felt as if I was hugging my own son.

"I am here for you and your mother, *Fisabillilah*," I said. "Don't worry, I will come, *Insha'Allah*." (*Fisabillilah*—"for the pleasure of Allah." *Insha'Allah*—"if Allah wills.")

Then I went to his mother (she met me halfway) and we hugged. I recited the same prayer and said the same words to her.

Young Javon was then remanded over to the prison authorities, and court was adjourned.

A week later, when the time came for the older boy to be sentenced, he entered the room with the demeanor of someone carrying a badge of honor, because he did not "help the police" in any way, except to accuse Javon of being the shooter. His words of regret were hollow and insincere.

Regardless, I offered him the same forgiveness I had extended to Javon at his sentencing. But this boy just stared at me with an empty, unconcerned look, as if every word I was saying was a waste of my breath. He did not accept my offer of help, and I have often wondered why his mother was not present with him in the courtroom that day.

The court case is closed for now until more evidence can be brought to light concerning the third accomplice. Unfortunately, he is still out there, free to repeat this heinous crime. I pray every day that he is brought to justice before this happens again, and another family is robbed of their precious son or daughter.

Al-Islam teaches the meanings of true peace, forgiveness and love, and also mercy. It teaches us to look beneath the surface in all circumstances, underneath whatever might appear to be happening. Al-Islam says that before we can effect a cure, we must first know the disease, guard ourselves against that disease, and then administer its most effective cure, so the miscreant can be eliminated.

The cure for this infection/evil/disease is showing "true forgiveness, true mercy, and doing good"—and that starts with us first. Inside ourselves, with ourselves; then outside ourselves, which then spreads onto others like a wave, after wave, after wave.

In order for us to be effective, we must walk the walk and talk the talk of peace, forgiveness, mercy, love, and investigation, while being aware to safeguard ourselves. We seek all of this from Our Creator, the creator of everything. We must live the kind of life that brings light, not darkness and despair, so we can help others to change for the good. From good comes only good. We must do good in order for a bad circumstance to end in a good result. Good will conquer evil every time.

I have been asked if my son's death and the way he died have changed me. The answer is that I have not changed, as a mother or as a person. Mine is the Islamic Way, the way I have lived my life for decades. I believe in this "way" of life with all my heart, and I raised my children with this same understanding.

Today, we are losing our young people, who are the future of all humanity, to this disease of darkness and despair. As such, I'm now more determined than ever that we, as compassionate and awake human beings, must fight this disease that is infecting all our communities worldwide. I am resolved to encourage every person, every community, and every government to "Take a Knee, Join the Resistance" in order to eradicate this terrible hatred—this infection/evil/disease—once and for all.

Taking a knee, to Muslims, is an act of peacefulness. When we are down, we are surrendered. We are showing that we are no longer willing to fight, not able to fight, and we will not fight. In all countries, Muslims are on their knees at least five times a day. My family is not asking people to become Muslims; however, by asking others to "take a knee," we are encouraging them to act more humbly, and be willing to take a more peaceful approach to whatever difficult situation in which they may find themselves.

When we do that, we are more likely to come with peace in our hearts; to show forgiveness, mercy, love, and doing good. Then there is hope for humanity and for mankind. And then my son's death will not have been for naught.

\* \* \*

**Rukiye Z. Abdul-Mutakallim** is the proud mother of three beautiful children: Khadijah, Hasan, and Suliman. She lives in Cincinnati, Ohio, and retired from Citibank as a litigation officer in 1995. A dedicated student of Quran and Ahadith, Rukiye is a spokesperson and instructor for Islamic Affairs for The Crescent Moon Association (TCMA). She has lectured at the Arab Academy for Science, Technology and

Maritime Transport (AASTMT) Main Headquarters of Abukir Main Campus in Alexandria, Egypt. She is the centerpiece of a powerful viral video by Humankind, which has had over forty-four million views in the English language alone and has been translated into six additional languages worldwide. The video shows Rukiye in a Cincinnati courtroom, openly forgiving (and embracing) one of the boys who brutally murdered her son.

# VIII

# GOLD STAR PARENT

As one begins the healing journey after a passing, it is the child in spirit who is the Shining Light. It is their light that keeps us going.

—Suzanne Giesemann

# Celebrating Our Shining Light

## By Suzanne Giesemann

*Susan*

$\mathscr{I}$ have flown on Air Force One with the president. I have been catapulted off the deck of an aircraft carrier. I have met with kings and queens and sat in on top-secret meetings at the Pentagon and on Capitol Hill. Those moments make good stories, but they did not define my life. Not at all. It was the heart-stopping moment when I gazed down at the lifeless body of my stepdaughter in a coffin that turned out to be the defining moment of my life.

I recognized the immaculate dress blue uniform of a US Marine Corps sergeant laid out atop the white satin cushions, but little else resembled the twenty-seven-year-old wife and mother-to-be we had seen a few months earlier. "That's not Susan," I repeated several times as I tried to reconcile the image before me with the vibrant woman we all knew and so dearly loved. In that moment that remains etched forever in my mind, I felt certain that what I had read must be true: that the body is merely a vessel that houses the spirit. Susan had been so full of life, so full of love and joy. I knew intuitively that the spirit—Susan's spirit—had to have survived death.

I thought back to the moment seven years earlier when Susan had announced to her father and me, "I'm thinking of enlisting." I held my breath, aware of Ty's thoughts. She could have had a full Reserve Officer Training Corps scholarship to a big-name university, but she didn't want to go there. Always independent and feisty, she left college after one semester to find her own way.

Her father served for twenty-six years as a surface warfare officer in the Navy and had retired as a captain. I was still an active duty naval officer when she dropped this bombshell. We both knew the differences between how service members were treated in the officer and enlisted ranks. When I heard of her plans, I gave her some unsolicited motherly advice, born of my own years of experience as a woman in the military.

I described the Army, Navy, Air Force, and Marine Corps, and what a twenty-year-old enlisted woman could expect as far as types of jobs available, the amount of respect she might (or might not) garner from her fellow service members, and the lifestyle associated with each branch. I ranked the four services according to my personal observations from most to least desirable. Things have improved in recent years, but at the time of this discussion, I told Susan in no uncertain terms, "Whatever you do, don't join the Marines."

Susan listened to my advice, weighed it carefully, and promptly enlisted in the Marine Corps.

I had known Susan since she was thirteen. She changed her roles and costumes as deftly in real life as when acting in the school dramas she so enjoyed. She played the girly girl in skimpy shorts and camisole tops with equal finesse as the cocky, give-me-what-you've-got contender on the boy's wrestling team. Smart, sassy, funny, and a friend to everyone, her leading role was Daddy's girl—a part which required no acting.

Once she set her mind to something, Susan would always excel. She survived boot camp at Parris Island with no problem and thrived at the School of Infantry that followed. The Marines sent her to aviation training, where she qualified as a helicopter airframes mechanic. Far braver than I could have ever hoped to be, she earned her aircrew wings, an accomplishment that required several challenging physical and mental tests.

To qualify as an aircrewman, Susan was strapped blindfolded into the fuselage of a mock helicopter, which was then submersed in a swimming pool and flipped upside down. She failed in her first attempt to find the door and escape and had to be rescued. At that point, Susan said, "Put me back in there!" She successfully completed the test and went on to graduate third in the demanding Sergeants' Course.

Susan made two deployments to Okinawa. When her squadron asked for volunteers to deploy to Iraq shortly after she married in 2005, she raised her hand without hesitation. But her husband, Warren, a sergeant assigned to the same squadron, told her it was too dangerous to go to the Middle East. She honored her husband's wishes and stayed behind in North Carolina.

Staring at her lifeless body in the coffin, it was hard not to wonder how things might have turned out had she gone to the combat zone. On the day that Susan died, she had been on base hurrying from the parking lot to the hangar where she worked. It wasn't the impending storm that caused her to rush. She wanted to spend a few extra minutes with Warren, who had stood duty the night before.

A squadron-mate happened to be looking out an open window as Susan crossed the flight line. He pointed at the dark clouds in the distance and shouted that she should get inside. Moments later, a deafening crack accompanied the jagged bolt of lightning that struck Susan to the ground. A shout went throughout the squadron, "Marine down!" Warren was one of the first to reach Susan's side.

Fellow Marines performed CPR on Susan until medics arrived. Unable to rouse her, they rushed her to a nearby hospital, where medical personnel worked on her for seven hours. She never regained consciousness.

Convinced by my experience when viewing Susan's body at her funeral that she still existed in some form, I took Ty with me to visit a medium. He and I had each completed full careers in the United States Navy. Both of us had served as commanding officers; he as captain of a destroyer, and I as the head of a shore-based unit. I later went on to serve as aide to the chairman of the Joint Chiefs of Staff—the head of the US military.

No-nonsense by training, we were not about to be duped by a charlatan who claimed to be communicating with the dead. We provided the medium with no information about ourselves, including no mention of our last name. Upon meeting us, she calmly described the presence of a young woman in her twenties wearing a brown uniform who had died rather suddenly. The medium felt tingly, electrical feelings running up her arms and experienced what she referred to as "the headache of Zeus and Athena."

Well familiar with the mythological story of Zeus, we recognized him as the god often pictured holding a lightning bolt. To us, this information spoke directly to the bolt of lightning that had struck and killed our daughter. Other irrefutable evidence left us crying, but none so much as the medium's message that Susan had brought with her a baby boy who she wanted to introduce to us. The medium could not have known that Susan was six months pregnant with a son she had already named Liam Tyler at the time they were both struck dead.

The bubbly, loving personality that the medium described fit our Susan exactly. Susan loved being a new bride and she reveled in being pregnant. We were delighted that she and her husband had decided to give their first child a middle name in honor of Ty.

I recalled how the agony of Susan's death was compounded when our family received the urn containing her ashes. The small brass plaque contained not only her name but Liam Tyler's, for, of course, his ashes were intermingled with hers. When Warren placed the precious container on a shelf in their home, he propped a black-and-white photo of the ultrasound taken just days before his wife and child's death. It was our first and only view of the grandson we would know only in our hearts. That reading with the medium convinced me that Susan and Liam were not only in our hearts, but somehow present in the room with us.

I began meditating the week Susan passed in hopes of finding out if her soul still existed. Two years of this practice resulted in my unexpected discovery that we are all connected to a far greater reality than this physical plane, and that I can connect quite clearly and easily with those who have passed away.

Aware of the immense healing that our initial session with a medium brought to our family, I threw myself wholeheartedly into increasing the clarity of the connection and the depth of the evidence I receive. Communicating with loved ones who have passed became my new mission, along with increasing the credibility of mediumship. I allowed myself to be tested by several notable afterlife researchers and soon became the first medium ever to be invited to speak at reputable national afterlife conferences and those dealing with the study of consciousness.

Soon I began reading for other parents who had lost a child, as we had. What a joy it has been to discover that our children are not dead and gone, but still actively participating in our lives! Each time I connect with a loved one in the spirit world, I ask them to tell me something going on with their family here and now to show them that our connection is valid. I even put my own Susan to the test. I'll never forget the first time she dropped in on me personally. I heard her voice as if she had never departed. Knowing her father might doubt Susan's unexpected appearance, I asked her to tell me something current about her biological mother that I couldn't possibly know. True to her sassy manner, Susan put her hands on her hips and said, "Well, her cat is sick." Ty and I immediately called Susan's mom, who, much to Ty's amazement, verified that she had just brought her cat home from the veterinarian with a supply of pills.

Fast-forward to today, and I have added eight metaphysical books to the four I had already written on unrelated topics before Susan passed on. Being an author and a professional speaker allows me to reach a worldwide audience with the message that love never dies. I am heartened by the increasing number of people who have set aside their outdated fears and have come to discover that consulting an evidence-based medium provides a rapid path to healing. What those who have suffered the passing of a child want more than anything is hope. Signs and messages delivered personally from that child backed up with information (evidence) that the medium could not possibly have known take a grieving parent from merely hoping to deeply knowing that only the physical presence has been "lost" in the transition we call death.

Through my work over the past ten years, I have come to be involved with the grief support group Helping Parents Heal. This group of loving and dedicated volunteers assists parents, providing them invaluable resources to aid in the healing process. They go a step beyond other support groups by allowing the open discussion of spiritual experiences and evidence of the afterlife in a nondogmatic way.

This open-minded attitude results in parents being able to move beyond their grief. I recently spoke at the first conference held by Helping Parents Heal. There the assembled group of five hundred parents were introduced to and proudly embraced the term "Shining Light Parent" as one whose child has left the physical body, but whose light continues to shine as an ongoing presence in their family's heart and home.

The term is a positive replacement for the title of "bereaved parent," reflecting an awareness that the light of the soul cannot be extinguished on *either* side of the veil.

The term was given to me in meditation after two Helping Parents Heal board members decided they did not want to be saddled with the term "bereaved parent" forever. I thought of Ty's and my status as Gold Star Parents, indicating that our daughter was killed while on active duty in the US armed forces. Many people are not familiar with the term or with the Gold Star Parent logo, and we educate them proudly as a way of honoring Susan's sacrifice. With the understanding that we can help grieving parents heal by sharing the meaning of "Shining Light Parent," we explain that the term carries different meanings, depending on where one is in the healing process:

- As one begins the healing journey after a passing, it is the child in spirit who is the Shining Light. It is their light that keeps us going.
- Moment by moment, thanks to the unmistakable signs from those across the veil, the undeniable synchronicities, and the support from others, we begin to feel the light within ourselves once again.
- With the help of our Shining Light across the veil, we begin to serve as shining examples for those new to the journey, and our child rejoices in our healing. It no longer feels right to call ourselves "bereaved parents." We have graduated to full status as "Shining Light Parents."

If someone unaware of that which all the conference attendees had in common (the death of a child) had walked into the ballroom in the middle of the conference, they would have been stunned at the palpable love and joy—yes, joy—being expressed and experienced there. After a weekend of sharing signs from our children across the veil, of seeing that one need not remain bereaved for life once he or she realizes that their child is still very much part of the family—albeit in spirit—we celebrated life and love as we know our children want us to do.

I was honored to share at the conference the "Silver Lining List" that the Tampa, Florida, affiliate of Helping Parents Heal had compiled. These parents chose to look beyond the commonly held notion that losing a child destroys a parent's life forever and erases the possibility of joy and a fulfilling life. On the contrary, they discovered a multitude of ways that life has blessed us with profound gifts and life-changing insight into our lives. They confirmed that we move forward still bearing the scars of loss, but also shining a brighter light than we ever had before—a reflection of our children who live on, sharing their happiness and encouragement with us.

The Silver Lining List highlights five areas in which the parents' lives have been enhanced: faith, connection with others, self-awareness, sense of purpose, and personal growth. They acknowledge that those in the early stages of grief may find it difficult to fathom that this could ever be their experience. The authors of the list recognize that to embrace these gifts is to honor our children and the love they surround us with every day. They want us to feel joy and to realize the full potential of our lives until it is our turn to join them.[1]

Do Ty and I miss Susan? Yes. Do we grieve the grandson we will not watch grow up? Certainly. We miss their physical presence, their laughter, and their smiles. But Susan continues to send us signs that she is always around. Ty will never forget the day he was hiking along a trail that he and Susan had enjoyed together many times in years past. As he reviewed those precious memories in his mind, the press of two fingers on his arm caused him to turn around to see who walked beside him. Seeing no one there, he succumbed to tears, unable to deny that Susan had made her presence known to him in an unmistakable way.

My initial goal of connecting with Susan through meditation resulted in a daily spiritual practice that today is sacrosanct. As a result of sitting regularly in silence, I have far more patience, peace, and joy in my life than I ever had known was possible. I now know that we are never alone and that each of us is immensely loved. I have made it my goal to help others find their innate qualities of joy, peace, love, strength, and courage, and teach them how to make the connection with their loved ones themselves.

Ty and I had retired from the Navy and had gone off sailing the world's oceans when we received the phone call that changed our lives. Today, we have sold our boat and I am working harder than I ever did in the Navy. Ty married a naval officer, not a medium, yet he is my strongest supporter. We work year-round, traveling half of the year, sharing the message of hope that love never dies.

We have lost count of the number of people who have told us that their reading with me in which I connected them with their deceased loved one saved their life. I credit Susan with this honor. The daily messages I post online and the information I share in my books, classes, radio show, and presentations bring healing and comfort to multiple thousands. This work is a great responsibility and an equally great blessing. It is thanks to Susan and Liam Tyler that Ty and I are able to serve others and bring more love and joy into our world. For that we are eternally grateful.

## NOTE

1. To read the Silver Lining List, please visit www.helpingparentsheal.org/silver-lining-list.

*    *    *

**Suzanne Giesemann** is a spiritual teacher, an evidence-based medium, and the author of twelve books, including *Messages of Hope* and *Still Right Here*. She is a former US Navy commander who served as a commanding officer, special assistant to the Chief of Naval Operations, and as aide to the chairman of the Joint Chiefs of Staff. Suzanne's gift of communication with those on the other side provides stunning evidence of life after death and of our connection with the greater reality. She brings messages of hope, healing, and love that go straight to the heart. Her work has been recognized as highly credible by afterlife researcher Dr. Gary Schwartz, PhD, and best-selling author Dr. Wayne Dyer. Learn more at www.SuzanneGiesemann.com.

# · 26 ·

# Angel Wings

## By JoAnn Pohlkamp

*Mike*

$\mathcal{O}$n July 10, 1963, I gave birth to little twin boys at Fort Hood Army Hospital, in Texas. My husband Jack was a US Army officer and we were just starting our family. Although he was born sixteen minutes after Mike, our son Mark came home with us first by himself. Mike was only four pounds, eleven ounces and had to remain in the hospital until he weighed five pounds—which he finally did about ten days later. We were overjoyed at having not just one, but two children, and Jack and I felt truly blessed.

When the twins were less than ten weeks, Jack received orders to be stationed in Germany for three years. We were both excited and scared by this news, and in the end, it turned out to be a marvelous posting. We traveled all over Europe with the boys the many times Jack was on assignment to various special nuclear weapons trainings, and we met many wonderful people along the way—some of whom we are still friends with today. I enjoyed being an officer's wife very much, connecting with other Army wives, and felt blessed to be having such remarkable times with Jack and our young family.

Coffees, teas, luncheons, and hats and gloves were the mainstay of nearly every day, which was not easy with young twins as active as mine, but I managed to pull it off and I loved every minute of it.

About eleven months before we were to leave Germany, I got pregnant with another child, our daughter Sheila, and we moved back to the States with the boys and the baby when Sheila was just ten weeks old. Three years later we had Shauna, and six years after that our son Matthew. Our lives were so busy, as you can imagine with five children, and we prided ourselves in being a tight and very close-knit family.

We were members of Delhi Swim Club, in Cincinnati, and some of my fondest memories were made there, where the kids would swim and play together so well for hours. We had so much fun with the swim meets, our friends, and grilling out almost every evening at the pool, and we loved topping our dinners off with s'mores. I felt exceptionally blessed and always thanked God every night for my good fortune.

Like most mothers, I spent much of my kids' childhood taking them to play dates, music recitals, swim team practices, swim meets, and the like. I prayed they would benefit from their parents' hard work and attention and become upstanding citizens, and I'm proud to say this is exactly what happened. All five kids are college graduates now, and the four that remain are doing well in their respective careers, just as their brother Mike had.

Mike was a passionate child and loved spending time with his twin. Mike and Mark were inseparable and accomplished so much together, including excelling in swimming and school. It was clear since they were toddlers that they were each other's biggest fan, and it was fun to watch them at swim meets, where they'd motivate each other and cheer one another on excitedly.

Mike and Mark excelled at swimming in high school and for two years they also swam on a highly regarded American Athletics Union team called the Pepsi Marlins. The excellent training the boys received with the Marlins enabled them both to be awarded swimming scholarships at the University of Missouri, which they attended.

At college, both twins studied mechanical engineering. Mark often told us how he admired his brother's spirit and drive, and that the way Mike was in the world was contagious. I'm not sure how he did it, but Mike made everyone close to him become better people. He'd never boast about himself; he was too humble. But I don't think he minded so much when Mark did it for him. Likewise, Mike was Mark's biggest fan and loved to brag about his brother to anyone who would listen. Mike was a natural leader, and his teammates at the University of Missouri voted him captain of the swim team during both his junior and senior years.

After both our sons graduated with engineering degrees, the brothers went separate ways, but they always remained very close and in regular contact. Mike's dream was to fly for the Navy, so he enlisted, and Mark went to work for Boeing as a flight test engineer on the B-1/B-52 bombers.

After an exhaustive and thorough application process, Mike was accepted into Aviation Officer Candidate School (AOCS) in Pensacola, Florida. AOCS was a grueling program where very few make it to the end and even fewer go on to earn wings. In April 1987, after graduating first in physical training and third overall in his class, Mike was commissioned an ensign. After a few more months of flight training on the Navy T-34C, Mike proudly earned his wings in June 1987, and the whole family was there for the award presentation ceremony to cheer him on.

Mike and I shared a love of country music, and whenever I'd visit him in Pensacola, we'd go for long rides in his Mustang GT convertible. With the top and windows rolled down, we'd exuberantly sing along to George Strait songs, always belting them out at the top of our lungs. We had great fun together, Mike and I, and I felt blessed to have such a terrific son who was also my very dear friend.

In 1989, during the Iran-Iraq War, Mike was deployed to the Middle East and became the maintenance officer for the helicopter squadron aboard USS *Thomas S. Gates* (CG 51). The squadron consisted of five pilots and a few dozen enlisted sailors. Mike was the second-most senior pilot of that group of five.

When they deployed to the Caribbean Sea and Gulf of Mexico to interdict the flow of illegal drugs from South America, Mike's job, as one of their pilots, was to conduct maritime surveillance in search of boats smuggling those drugs. Once located, he would maintain covert tracking of them until their ship or another could move into a position to take the smugglers' boat down and seize the drugs.

Not even Mark knew the nature of these secret missions, and it wasn't until I was doing research for writing this story that the details were made known to any of us. I always thought Mike was joking when I'd ask what he was up to and he'd say, rather smugly, "I could tell you, Mom, but then I'd have to kill you." Perhaps he wasn't joking at all.

After seven-plus months overseas, Mike returned home from the war safe and sound and I prayed and prayed that he wouldn't have to go back, but he did. On August 2, 1990, Mike and his squadron were under way aboard USS *Thomas S. Gates* making their way back to Norfolk, Virginia, after a two-month counter narcotics deployment. They arrived in Norfolk on August 10, and were notified on August 11 that they'd be leaving to support Kuwait just ninety-six hours later.

Mike and his squadron set sail for Kuwait on August 15. His job as a pilot during that time was to provide surface surveillance of shipping around their carrier strike group to make sure there were no threats of any kind to the group.

I always knew Mike's life was in danger as part of the military, especially both times that he was deployed and stationed overseas during wartime. But again, it wasn't until I began writing this story that I found out how close to death he came every day.

It's ironic—and very sad—that Mike's death came about in such a ridiculous way. All those days he served on the *Thomas S. Gates*, when his life was in serious jeopardy, my son escaped without even a scratch. Yet, when he was back at a home base in Pensacola, he wound up dying from a midair collision with a buddy pilot in a way that was truly preventable.

Mike served on the *Thomas S. Gates* for 228 days and earned the Naval Air Medal for meritorious achievement while participating in combat missions. He mentioned to me once how the moon always guided his way whenever he had to maneuver a landing back onto the carrier after dark. Whenever Jack and I would relax in our backyard Jacuzzi at night, I felt comforted to know we were gazing up at the very same moon as Mike.

In August of 1991, a few months after the Gulf War had ended, I hoped and prayed that Mike would come home to begin a civilian career and be near his family. He loved flying so much, though, that he chose to continue his Navy career and quickly became one of the best naval flight instructors around—and that's not just a proud mother's judgment. Mike earned the honor of Distinguished Flight Instructor six times in less than two years.

Wednesday, May 13, 1992, began as any other day in my very busy life as a wife, working mom, and fitness enthusiast. When I woke up that morning, I could have never imagined, not for one minute, how that day would end. Around 10:40 p.m., my front doorbell rang. I was busy in the basement, so Sheila opened the door. When I asked, "Sheila, who is it?" she didn't answer, so I ran upstairs to see what was going on.

When I reached the door, I saw two nice-looking naval officers standing on my front porch. Dressed impeccably in their Navy whites and with unemotional faces, they informed me that our son had been in a plane crash in Pensacola and did not survive. Shock waves ran through my body, and for a moment, I thought I might faint. I couldn't even cry, though, because at that time I believed with every fiber of my being that Mike was somehow okay, and I was confused as to why these officers had come to see me at such a late hour.

I kept my eyes firmly fixed on both of them, and on their lack of expressions, and the truth of what they were saying finally began sinking in. My world collapsed all around me in that moment. *Please, God, can I freeze time or somehow reverse it?* I did *not* want to hear what these men were saying. I wondered, *Is my life suddenly over? How can I ever go on without my beloved son?*

The accident had happened earlier that day near Whiting Field, a large naval airbase in Milton, Florida, near Pensacola. It had been a beautiful day to be flying, with sparse puffy white clouds and blue skies in every direction.

This was Mike's favorite kind of weather, and he volunteered to fly a Navy pilot he knew up to another air base in Georgia. After the drop-off, the Navy cleared Mike to practice flight maneuvers for further training before heading back to Whiting. On his return and sometime during his descent, another flight instructor—his good buddy Sully—who was accompanied by a young flight student, was climbing into the sky after takeoff when the two planes collided in midair. The collision sheared off a section of the tail of Mike's plane, and then it crashed into a field and burst into flames near a residential area of Milton.

Witnesses said that Mike appeared to have regained control of his plane sufficiently to steer it away from the heavily populated neighborhoods below. However, the plane was too damaged for him to control a landing, and he crashed into the ground at precisely 4:44 p.m.

Just like that, my precious *Schweetie* was gone.

It was so hard during the funeral to see all the handsome young men in their Navy whites and all the officers, knowing that Mike was the naval officer they had brought home to me in that coffin, draped in a US flag. As an act of honor and great respect, after Mike's casket was lowered into the ground and dirt was being shoveled on top of it, Mike's fellow officers ceremoniously tossed their wings into the dirt, to be buried along with him. To me, it was symbolic of my feeling that when Mike died, he took a piece of all of us with him.

A few weeks after the funeral, my brother Ron drove his wife, Jack, and me down to Pensacola for a full military memorial at Whiting Field honoring Mike, and the rest of the kids joined us down there. I don't think a single word was spoken during that car ride, we were all so devastated and in shock. During the ceremony, Mark graciously accepted yet another naval award on behalf of his twin brother.

After the ceremony, in an effort to obtain some closure, I went to the hospital where Mike had been taken by ambulance right after the accident. I entered the emergency room and sat there for nearly an hour, sobbing, trying desperately to somehow connect with my son. I nearly collapsed onto the front desk when the nurse asked me what was wrong, because I needed so badly to speak to someone real and make a connection. When I explained who I was and why I was there, she said she remembered Mike being brought through the ER on his way down to the morgue.

Upon hearing those words, I became hysterical and I was, for a time, inconsolable. Other people waiting in the ER came toward me to bring comfort and sat quietly with me until the nurse walked me down the very hallways Mike had traveled on his final journey. I was completely distraught, yet I needed to make myself go where my son had, before being rolled into that cold, unfriendly mortuary. After all, I was his mother—and moms should stick with their kids till the end.

Following my trip to the hospital, an officer took me in his jeep to visit the crash site in the Emerald Forest, where we met up with the chief firefighter who had been the first to arrive on the scene. I couldn't help but notice that Mike had died surrounded by many trees of his favorite color, which had always been the same emerald green.

The chief was very emotional as he informed me that Mike died on impact, when his plane crashed hard into the ground. He was a very sensitive man, a minister as it turned out, and seemed eager to tell me there was an unusual number of butterflies flying over the crash site the day of Mike's death, and we marveled at how they were present again as we stood together looking on. The chief smiled warmly when he told me he felt the presence of angels strongly while he was watching the swarm of butterflies as they hovered.

Before I left the crash site, I pulled one of my favorite framed family photos out of my bag and buried it in the very spot where my son had lost his life just a few weeks before. I wanted Mike to know that his family was still with him, and that even in death he would never have to be alone.

Not long after Mike's death, we learned that commercial airlines had installed state-of-the-art anti-collision warning system (ACWS) devices on many of their airplanes. The Navy was aware these devices existed but had not yet installed them on their aircraft.

At first, I was furious with the Navy. Had they put those alarms on their planes once they had been made available, my beloved Mike would still be with us. But I knew how much the Navy had meant to my son and how much he loved living his dream of being a naval aviator—plus Mike had known all the dangers and accepted them gladly. I knew I could choose to stay mad at the Navy forever, but in time I chose not to disrespect what my son had stood for and deeply loved, so I found a way to somehow make peace with all of it.

When my father, Mike's grandfather, learned that the Navy had chosen not to install ACWS devices on their planes once the technology had become available, he petitioned to Washington, DC, to ask why these devices were not mandatory equipment on all Navy planes. When Dad learned they were not scheduled to be installed for ten years, he was outraged and fought a hard and furious battle with the Navy for their installation.

Finally, after two years of fierce nonstop advocating on the part of my father, the Navy accelerated the installation program and put the anti-collision devices on all the T-34Cs. They dedicated this effort to Mike after all the planes were equipped, and the Navy held a ceremony honoring Mike and our family for all of our efforts. As a direct result of this accelerated installation of ACWS devices on naval planes, there has not been a single midair collision since—not even one. For me, and for my dad, knowing that no other mother, father, sibling, or grandparent would ever have to grieve over losing a loved one in a midair collision gave some purpose to what had, heretofore, been such a senseless and useless death.

After Mike died, I was so brokenhearted that I wanted to die along with him. I didn't want to accept that he was never again going to be with our family, and there would always be an empty chair at our dining room table. It hurt so much to be without him that I felt excruciating physical pain.

I realized I had to somehow go on without Mike, but I couldn't begin to fathom quite how I'd do that. I had four other wonderful children, a granddaughter, and Jack. I knew how much we all needed each other, even though I had no real idea how we'd ever survive when such a vital part of us had just died.

I wanted so badly to be there for my children and Jack and my granddaughter Jacqueline, but in the beginning, it took everything in me just to get through the day. Although Jack is a man of few words, he was my rock—and always there to support me no matter what. I honestly would not have survived without all the love and unending support of my sister Angela and my other kids—Sheila, Shauna, and Matt.

Even though Matt was only sixteen when he lost one of his two biggest heroes, he had the wisdom of someone much older—and he, his two sisters, and Angela always knew just the right things to say to console me and help me go on. It was hard to receive, though, because my greatest desire was to make sure my kids were okay, and I tried my hardest to do that. Sheila worked and was going to college, and I was grateful to have lots of time alone with my nine-year-old granddaughter Jacque which brought joy again to my empty heart.

Sometime in the first months after Mike's death, I visited the local chapter of The Compassionate Friends, a support group for parents whose child or children have died. I loved the people a lot, and my heart ached for all of their losses. After two or three meetings, though, I realized my own grief was deeply personal, and I found that being with my family was far more healing for me than being with strangers. I went home, threw myself into my family, and cuddled up with my very first love—books—where I found great comfort for my broken heart.

I'd heard about a wonderful Catholic priest named Father Jim Willig and went to hear him speak one night with a friend at a nearby church. Father was still a young priest when he was diagnosed with terminal renal cancer and had suffered greatly. The inspiring pastor and priest had written a book called *Lessons from the Book of Suffering: A Young Priest with Cancer Teaches Us How to Live.*

In his talk, Father Willig shared lessons he'd learned from having cancer. I found this man enthralling and his message compelling, so I was thrilled when my friend Judy bought me a copy of his book some time later. In it, Father said that while suffering can crush a person into self-pity, it can also be an invaluable teacher. He said that if we fully learn the lessons that suffering brings us, they can transform our lives. I believe this book was his greatest sermon because he brought us through his suffering and into the heart of Jesus—which is where my suffering took me—and I found tremendous consolation in Father's words.

Another reason I loved Father Willig's book so much is because after Mike's death, I felt nailed to a cross like Jesus—and I also comprehended to my core the suffering of his mother Mary. The Blessed Mother is my sweetheart, God love her, and I don't know what I would do without her. When I lie in bed at night and pray my rosary, I see her so clearly in my mind and I know she knows the horrible grief of dying inside as I do—which is healing to me beyond measure. I wake up each morning feeling renewed and happy, ready to face another day.

Another mother I relate to deeply is St. Elizabeth Seton, who sadly buried two of her children during the course of her life. In her autobiography, *Elizabeth Seton*, she said she used to look out her side yard window at her daughter's grave and think, *If I had been obliged to, I would have died within her.* Elizabeth's words resonated intensely within me. She also cited one of my favorite psalms: "As the deer pants for water, so my soul pants for you, o Lord," which reminded me that in my thirst to be rejoined with my son, I was also longing for God.

One of the biggest lessons I've learned through Mike's death is it's vitally important to always be present—not just with myself, but with my family and everyone else with whom I ever come into contact. Little things are just little things, and mostly, I can let all the small stuff go now without much effort. But sometimes, when I catch myself being bothered by something trivial, it helps me to realize how far I've actually come—and I take a step back and laugh. After all, if I can survive my precious son's death as I have, I know I can survive anything life throws my way. If I've learned nothing else about myself, I know now that I am a survivor.

Jack and I have a beautiful pond in our backyard that Mike and Mark had been in the process of installing at the time of Mike's death, and Mark finished the project to honor his brother after he died. The pond has special meaning to me knowing that Mike was a part of its original design and creation.

I love sitting on the bench beside the water and watching the baby ducks swim, whether it's in silence or I'm watching my grandchildren or great-grandchildren play nearby. It's always such a healing place for me to be, and one where my soul often longs to sit and just pause. The pond rests in the midst of the very place where Mike and the other kids used to play for what seemed like forever, and I can still see Mike and Mark tossing a football or playing kick the can and ghost in the graveyard out there with their siblings.

When Mike died, Mark wrote a beautiful, heartfelt letter that, at his request, was read by one of the three priests saying Mike's funeral Mass. The whole letter touched me very deeply, but the final paragraph is what I'll share here:

> Mike, I am so proud. If you could only see the love, support and respect for you here today. Not only as a person but as a Naval Aviator. You are the best. Save me a place next to you, bro. I will live the best damn life for us, bro. You will always be here with me and people will know it. You will be proud. Tell God I am not afraid anymore. I'll take care of our family. I love you, Mike.

Mark continues to fulfill all the promises he made to his brother that day, and then some. As their mother, I couldn't be prouder of the extraordinary men my twins have grown up to be. Now, whenever I hug Mark, I feel both my boys hugging me back—and it's clear that Mike's spirit is ever present. For now, I'll settle for that, and celebrate all the joys of life for whatever time I have left on this earth.

I await, with great anticipation, the day Mike and I are reunited again in the loving embrace of our Heavenly Father, and I'll smother my little *Schweetie* with all the hugs and kisses in the world.

\* \* \*

**JoAnn Pohlkamp** is retired from UPS after twenty-three years, where she worked part-time while raising five children. Since retiring, JoAnn has been, at various times, a happy volunteer playmate to preschoolers and a volunteer aide for mentally ill adults and the elderly. Ever the student, JoAnn loves attending Life Learn college classes for people fifty-five and over. She travels a bit with Jack, her devoted husband of fifty-six years, but her favorite place to be is always home, where she loves spending time with her kids, grandkids, and great-grands. As JoAnn so often says, "We live in the Inn of the Sixth Happiness" (which is a snappy movie title that she has always loved).

# IX

# MULTIPLE DEATHS

I could remain burdened by a focus on sadness, or choose to feel joy and gratitude for the positive aspects of my life.

—Marla Grant

# An Intentional Journey

## By Marla Grant

*L*ooking back over the years, I can see that by comparison to many, my life has truly been uncommon. Certainly, outliving three of my five children would be considered a unique and harsh experience. Yet the real surprise is that I am at a loss to call this a tragedy or to assign myself the appellation "bereaved parent." I am not the victim of a harsh, capricious world in which divine blessings are bestowed on some, while trial, cruelty, and loss are given to others. I am the architect of my life and the arbiter between an ego world that wants to see me as a victim and a higher self that influences me every day with its call to awakening from this empty illusion we call life in bodies. I know it's not possible to die, and I have seen proof. But I didn't always believe these truths.

No doubt by heavenly design, I was blessed to inherit my mother's pragmatic approach to life and her ever-present optimism. So, when life's harsh lessons have appeared, I've been inspired to seek the wisdom and spiritual growth that always accompany challenges, to accept life as it is presented to me, and to just get on with the business of living.

Over time, I came to realize two things with certainty: first, that I came into this life equipped to handle whatever life handed me, and second, that the support I need on this side always shows up in some form—be it family, friends, a well-written book that speaks to me, or spiritual teachers and even strangers who lead me to new discoveries. I know also that I am under the constant guidance of my unseen spiritual helpers. Along the way I have also been gifted with some moments of grace and insight that I can only ascribe to a higher power.

As a young woman, I had a sense of curiosity about the world and a naive sense of self-confidence. Over the ensuing years, my curiosity would be fulfilled through extensive world travel, my unearned self-confidence broken down and deeply examined until it was finally legitimately acquired through some significant trials.

I owe both the world travel and much of my sense of self to my husband of twenty-seven years. He had an adventurous spirit which resulted in a life lived abroad for fifteen years in Australia, Iran, and Saudi Arabia, with many short-term travels in between. But it was also a life of great personal challenge between us, and difficulties I was thankfully able to mine over time for the raw materials necessary for profound self-discovery and inner strength.

My initiation into a life of future challenges began with the birth of my beloved first child, my son Brennan, in 1975. He was premature, but survived while I almost did not. Towards the end of my third trimester, I suddenly became very ill with what appeared to be a kidney problem. As it turned out, I had developed severe toxemia, and five weeks prior to my due date, I was rushed to the hospital. We lived in Sydney, Australia, at the time and, fortunately, I was at a very well-known teaching hospital with excellent critical care.

After being unconscious for two days, I awoke to learn that I had been given Last Rites, had an emergency C-section, and delivered a healthy, albeit tiny, premature son. I remembered nothing of the ordeal. When I got home, so grateful to be alive with my son, I stood on the balcony of our home, silently appreciating the hill below and a gorgeous view of the Pacific Ocean off in the distance.

I suddenly became aware that everywhere I looked, every single thing was shining brightly, like a diamond sparkling with a reflective brilliant light—rocks, the grass, buildings, trees—everything! It was amazing to see, and although I didn't fully understand what my eyes were taking in, I took this to be a sign that life inhabits everything we observe and that all would be well. This inspiration would contribute to my ability to deal with the challenge that followed within the next year.

In 1976, pregnant with our second child, I warily approached my delivery date, knowing that I was going to try for a natural delivery. The prevailing wisdom at the time was that having one C-section did not necessarily preclude subsequent natural childbirth. However, my baby was in breech position and additional unforeseen complications during the delivery resulted in a catastrophic outcome.

I was in a much smaller, private hospital that did not have robust emergency alternatives, and I was forced to endure a very difficult delivery. My perfectly healthy son, deprived of oxygen for too long while trapped in the birth canal, sadly did not survive. Shane's tiny body, never to have felt the tender embrace of his mother, was whisked away and buried in a common plot for stillborn infants. Both physically and emotionally, it was a horrific experience.

After Shane's death, I felt utterly and completely empty, a cavernous void replacing what should have been the transcendent joy of holding my child. All happy anticipation had been completely swept away in the agonizing hour-long delivery. In spite of my overwhelming sadness, I resisted repeated attempts by well-intentioned hospital staff to keep me sedated with sleeping pills. I knew that sooner or later I would have to face the reality before me, and I didn't want to prolong the inevitable. Even then, at the age of twenty-four, I knew that the only way I could survive difficulties was to move through them without denial.

As soon as I was able to be up and around, I went to the hospital's tiny chapel and sat quietly. Raised Catholic but not being a faithful devotee of the theology, I nevertheless silently spoke to Jesus's mother, Mary, as I wanted to commiserate mentally with a mother who had also lost a son she had loved. I asked how she had dealt with her loss and sought her help. The moment I did, I was immediately overcome with a tangible sense of calm, then relief, and my tears ceased.

I was stunned! Was Mary really there listening and heard my prayer? I knew in my heart that she had and that soothed me. It was an early affirmation that something greater and beyond what I could physically sense was accompanying me and supporting me through this earthly journey.

Just twelve weeks after my little one was laid to rest, I learned the happy news that I was pregnant again. Exactly one year and one week after my second son had come briefly into this world and gone, I welcomed my third child with open arms, a cherished boy we also named Shane.

It was evident from the beginning that we shared an uncommon emotional bond. From the time my son was barely more than a toddler, we were close confidants and able to talk candidly about almost anything. It wasn't long before I was overcome with the strong feeling that Shane was the same little soul I had given birth to previously. This belief became a deep knowing as I watched my boy grow into adulthood. Many years later, to my surprise, my all-grown-up, agnostic, very left-brain son told me he wholeheartedly agreed.

The final confirmation came thirty-seven years after Shane's birth when I sat for a reading with the highly respected and internationally renowned evidence-based medium Suzanne Giesemann. She had already channeled two of my children on the other side with undeniable proof they were present when she suddenly asked, "Is there a twin?" She had known no details about my children, so when I divulged information about the infant Shane who had died during delivery, she said, "That's why I can't read him on the other side. He's here!"

In the intervening years before the birth of my fourth child, my beloved only daughter Nicole, I began to understand that although I had experienced tragedy, life was bringing good things to me as well. Though I will never forget the pain of having my infant son die before he'd been given a chance to live, knowing with increasing certainty that he has come back in the body of my third son gave me great comfort. I also began to see that I could remain burdened by a focus on sadness, or choose to feel joy and gratitude for the positive aspects of my life.

Four years after my second Shane was born, my fourth child arrived. As I began to emerge from the foggy haze of anesthesia, I was told I had delivered a baby girl. I was giddy with gratitude—finally, a little girl! From the beginning, Nicole charmed everyone she met. Her light, effervescent personality was a joy to experience and is reflected in the many photos I have of her as a young girl. Even candid photos show a beautiful, authentic smile that beamed her intrinsic joy. Later in life, I would reflect how Nicole so perfectly fit the concept that old souls don't have many spiritual lessons left to learn and often live short lives.

A few months after Nicole's seventh birthday, we were shocked to learn that what we thought was possibly a stomach flu turned out to be a tentative diagnosis of something much worse—chronic myelogenous leukemia, an adult leukemia rarely seen in children.

We had been living abroad at the time but returned to the United States to confirm the diagnosis. Under the care of her excellent pediatric cancer team, it was determined that Nicole's only chance for survival was a bone marrow transplant. Testing of immediate family members soon followed, and Shane was determined to be a perfect match—a near miracle since there is only a 25 percent chance of finding a family member who is a match.

Nicole's treatment was arduous but throughout she remained upbeat and courageous, and after her transplant and a year of post-recovery therapy, she settled into a normal and active life. For six years Nicole was the picture of health until suddenly, just months before her fourteenth birthday, she experienced a relapse, this time with a more aggressive form of leukemia.

Shane, who had donated stem cells previously, donated again, but after six very difficult months of struggling to recover, Nicole succumbed not to leukemia but to the devastating side effects of the cell transplant. Her short life in the world of form was over, but her passing served to escalate my spiritual learning.

Nicole had said to me once in a moment of quiet reflection, "Mom, I think the reason we are all here on Earth is to help each other." She certainly did that for me and for many others who came into contact with her. The ways in which she helped me cope with her passing and gain peace and understanding about the nature of life and the false notion of "death" began before my little girl ever left her body.

Nicole was a wise, very thoughtful child who gave me a lifelong gift of love and release when she said to me one evening, as she sat contemplating her impending passage, "Mom, I know this is going to be hard for you, but please don't let it ruin your life."

Her gift in that moment became my mantra.

There is nothing like witnessing a spiritual phenomenon to shift one's awareness and inspire a desire to learn more. On Tuesday, January 31, 1995, the day before she passed—and in spite of being sedated with a massive amount of morphine—Nicole sat up in bed completely unaided, and spoke to someone in front of her that none of the rest of us in the room could see. With a gesture of her hand, she said, "No, no, not today, not today!" and then quietly lay back down to sleep.

Nicole had been receiving friends and family for two days and doing the best she could to say her good-byes, but there was one special friend who had been the director of a cancer camp she had attended several times who was not able to arrive until the following day. Once the young woman came to visit in the early afternoon on Wednesday and they said their final good-byes, Nicole's breathing began to slow, and it was apparent she was ready for her transition.

We had known that moment was imminent, but I asked her in a whisper if she could please hang on a few more minutes until her brother Brennan returned. He had been caught in rush-hour traffic on his way back to the hospital.

Five minutes after Brennan arrived, Nicole's spirit left her body. She passed with ease, cradled in my arms as I lay next to her, her father and brothers nearby.

There is simply no way to relate in words the desolation one feels upon the passing of their own child. We are so accustomed to the physical presence of our children and the notion that we are their protector that to realize they have evaporated into apparent nothingness leaves us bereft, stripped of any place to anchor our feelings. We become adrift in a sea of sorrow with no shore in sight, no destination that does not include an overwhelming sense of crushing emptiness.

After Nicole died, it was the sunny days that were the worst, probably because they reminded me so much of her joyful personality. It took me a long time to stop getting that catch of dread in my heart and throat when thinking about her passage because for so long it felt like a nightmare that I would suddenly realize had materialized into reality. It took me well over a year to integrate that experience into my new reality and accept it as my new normal.

I've learned that if we can open our hearts and minds even a little with the willingness to consider a new way of thinking, we can slowly begin to embrace a more enlightened way to perceive the cessation of life in a body and the truth of our eternal nature.

The night I left Nicole's body at the hospital, I slept in her bed at home. Immediately upon turning the lights out, I heard the distinct sound of what I could only describe as a marble rolling around and around in a bowl. I knew there was nothing in the room that could have possibly made that noise, so I lay transfixed—and slightly on edge—as I contemplated what it might mean. I turned the light on to confirm that there wasn't a logical physical explanation and saw none. Nicole had a cheeky, clever sense of humor, and I later concluded that it was her way of telling me she was "around."

I returned to my daughter's bed, and as I began falling off to sleep, awash in sorrow, I felt the distinct presence of an open portal of sorts between the bed and the other side of the veil where I knew Nicole's spirit had gone. There was no fear, only a feeling of peace, serenity, and closeness.

I would experience this even more intensely in subsequent dreams in which I was able to visit her. On the day of Nicole's funeral, I had an experience that made it crystal clear to me that her loving, vital spirit lives on. I was at the funeral home, where we were having an open casket viewing. My dear son Brennan, then nineteen, was with me and asked if I wanted to see her. I was very hesitant, as I had not seen her body since we left the hospital several days before, and I was not sure I had the strength to see her again.

Fortunately, Brennan encouraged me to go with him to view her body, and as I glanced down at my girl, I had such a striking realization that it took away my breath. I exclaimed, "That's not Nicole!"

She had been so full of life and joyful, loving energy that the contrast between that reality and the lifeless shell that was in front of me was unmistakable. The experience made it forever clear to me that everything I knew and loved about my Nicole lived on.

Years later, Jennifer Farmer, an intuitive, medium, and spiritual teacher who during one reading correctly identified the obscure name of Nicole's favorite childhood doll, remarked to me about Nicole's joyful energy, "When Nicole shows up, the stars begin to twinkle."

I have had many dreams over the years, but two stand out as being particularly vivid. When I say vivid, I am describing a level of dreaming that is akin to the experience of reality we usually ascribe to our waking moments.

In the first, I was with someone who appeared to be a loving guide, who took me by the hand and led me through a narrow, dimly lit passageway. As we rounded a curve, we entered a sort of antechamber in which there was a variety of people—souls who were in the process of transitioning from the world of form back to their spirit form. I knew this because of the various emotional and physical states they were in. I somehow realized where we were but there was no fear, only a strong sense of wonderment.

My guide took me to an open area in the room we had entered and asked if I was ready to see her, already knowing that I understood where we were. As soon as I uttered an excited "Yes!" in rode Nicole, looking just as she did when she was seven, dressed in her jammies and happily sitting astride Clifford, the Big Red Dog!

Nothing could have been more apropos of Nicole. She was absolutely in love with animals, especially dogs, so to see her in that setting was perfect. We wordlessly embraced (curiously, Nicole has never spoken to me in dreams), and before too long my guide told me it was time and asked if I was ready to go. I reluctantly said yes, and thus ended my first encounter with my daughter.

In the second dream, one that showed me how utterly close we are to our loved ones, there was no guide assisting us. As in my previous dream, I was both the observer of the dream and the participant. This one found me sitting in a void—not a room, but an empty, dark space with nothing else in it but Nicole, who was sitting in my lap in a rocking chair. No words were spoken but she was snuggled against my chest, completely relaxed in my loving embrace.

At one point Nicole gently reached up and cupped her hand against my cheek in a gesture of love. The instant that happened, I awoke and could still feel the warm imprint of her hand upon my cheek. I was spontaneously awash in tears, as I knew that moment with her had been as real as my awareness of being awake in my bed.

Experiences such as these two dreams brought me a measure of peace in spite of Nicole's absence, certain in those moments that she lived on at another vibrational level that I could not yet tap into. But there was more that was happening for me in occasional subtle ways over the years—occurrences that convinced me there was so much more to our true lives than what we experience while in human form. I refer to these as "moments of grace" since they were spontaneous, brief, and occurred without any request on my part other than allowing myself to be in a general state of mind that was willing and open. Both of the revelations I share lasted only seconds, yet what they revealed to me changed my understanding forever.

The first happened one day when I was outside, walking on the streets of Tehran, where we lived for a year. Something caused me to stop in my tracks and look around my environment. I saw palm trees, buildings, billboards, cars—nothing out of the ordinary—yet quite suddenly, I knew with certainty that none of it was real. I don't mean that I had a passing moment of imagination in which I thought everything was made up. I was given the understanding that what I was seeing was nothing more than an imaginary, temporary image. It was as if God said to me, "Consider an alternative to what you perceive as reality." That instant opened my mind to further spiritual growth.

The second moment of clarity came to me in an even more mundane setting years later. I was passing through a very short hallway in my apartment and was literally stopped dead in my tracks by a very lucid image planted in my mind. It was of such short duration and was so esoteric that I hardly know how to relate it in words, but I was given the clear knowing that the concept of time is a fabrication, that all that exists is this moment.

For an instant my mind was opened, and I had an experiential understanding that there is no such thing as future or past, only the present. I would be lying if I told you that it was a moment of permanent enlightenment, for like everyone inhabiting a body on planet Earth, I still struggle with aspects of life, casting behind me in the "past" for causation and looking into the "future" with anticipation and sometimes anxiety. But it did ground my thinking and gave me a reference point to return to time and again during life's difficulties. It informed my understanding that nothing of what I perceive as happening in the past needs to drive my state of mind or decisions in the present.

What that means for overcoming the passing of three children is that their present existence is real and nothing that appeared to happen to them is of any consequence. For anyone committed to traditional religious beliefs about death, I understand this will be a foreign if not heretical concept. Yet, it is what I have come not only to believe, but to know from my personal experience.

Other concepts within the framework of the world we know may be acceptable to others, and I would not argue against that. All paths up the mountain lead us to awaken in the same home of our Creator, just from different directions and perhaps with more or less difficulty along the way. I do not have the same understanding of life and spiritual matters as I did years ago, and years from now I will no doubt have gained greater, more enlightened insights.

This brings me to the most recent, unanticipated transition of my youngest son, Ryan. The fifth of my children and soul companion to his slightly older sister, he was born just sixteen months after Nicole. She was so petite and he so robust that by the time he was two, they were often mistaken for twins.

They were inseparable as children. Nicole was like a little mother to Ryan—attentive, protective, and loving—and I know her transition to her spirit state was very difficult for him. I only discovered years later how much of his grief he had withheld from me, fearing it would be too upsetting for me to discuss. This was surprising, as I spoke of Nicole often and never shied away from reminiscing about her, but I think he was unable to articulate how deeply her loss had affected him.

There was something else about Ryan I couldn't quite identify. From the time he was a small child, he had a faraway look in his eyes, as if he were distracted and not really here. I remember on occasion asking him to look at me, really look into my eyes, so I could bring his focus "here." It was almost as if he had one foot in this world and one in the other.

Ryan was a spiritual, though nondogmatic, person who often told me how he could feel energy and move it between his hands and could often see orbs of light. I would later come to believe that he had come into this life too soon, unprepared for its challenges. This proved to be true, for even though Ryan had recently become a father to a little girl he adored, life's demands and what he perceived as his inadequacies collided, and he completed suicide just a few months before his thirty-second birthday.

As I write, I'm sitting just feet away from the doorway where I was standing almost five years ago when I received the phone call from a police officer telling me of my beloved son's untimely death. I can still hear the heart-wrenching sounds of my daughter-in-law screaming in the background as she listened to the officer reveal the horrific way in which Ryan had died.

I could easily choose to let that be a constant reminder of the desolation and sorrow I felt in that moment, agonizing about how desperately alone and confused my youngest child must have felt at the moment he pulled the trigger.

Strangely, that thought was the motivation for my own emotional recovery in the weeks and months following his death. I knew that in a very real way, Ryan's spiritual recovery after passing from this life would be immensely helped by my own ability to stay out of deep sorrow, so I sent him my love and comfort instead.

Fortunately, having been through significant loss such as this twice before, I had the emotional strength and sufficient spiritual resources to rise above devastation, at least most of the time. Even now, I still have moments when Ryan's physical absence seems unreal to me, when accidentally coming across his wallet or a note to me from his childhood will send a wave of sadness through me and tears flow. But mostly I focus on happier times, when we shared a love of cooking or a good laugh about life's ridiculous moments, or the memory of a tender moment with his daughter. I know these thoughts and the love that surrounds them is healing for both of us.

I am generally reluctant to reveal to people that only two of my five children are still with me, not because it's disturbing for me to discuss, but because of others' reactions. For most people, the passing of even one child is tragic, but the passing of three is unfathomable. It elicits an undue amount of sympathy and pity I find uncomfortable because I am not mired in permanent grief, living a desperate life of devastation in the wake of these losses.

On the contrary, I am so confident that my children remain alive and well and happy in their true spirit state that our physical separation does not leave me thinking of them as "dead." In fact, many people find it puzzling when I tell them that I often feel Nicole and Ryan are closer and more available to me than my two sons still on this side.

In a real sense, the ones on this side—subject to the laws of the human condition—cannot hear me or communicate with me unless there is a device that makes that possible. I have to somehow get their attention, and then arrange a means of verbal communication or plan physical proximity. One lives out of state and the other internationally, and we all have busy lives so there are often long delays in connecting.

Nicole and Ryan, on the other hand, can hear me instantly and at times will let me know they are near if I ask them for a sign. In one recent extraordinary example, I had been talking to them one morning as I sat in my backyard, and I mentioned that it had been a while since I'd heard from them. I asked them to send me a sign that they were listening and hear me whenever I talk to them. Early the following morning, a close friend, who was away on a trip with her daughter, sent me a text message with this picture, sharing that she saw this sign just outside their rental home. I know I had asked for a sign, but I didn't expect to get an actual *sign*!

*Street sign*

I have immense empathy for parents who have experienced the transition of a child from this world of form. I understand the pain and heart-wrenching constant reminder of their absence. But I know this, too: The ability to move out of the immobilizing stages of intense grief and to reengage the life we are blessed to experience is possible when one is willing.

We don't have to be victims of an event that would falsely have us believe our children don't still exist, nor the victims of the popular notion that life has ended for us, too. I still periodically have moments of deep sorrow, but there is too much joy and growth and love for me yet to experience to want to stay there.

The memory of my children is etched in my heart forever, and I want that heart to resonate joy and peace and love, so they feel it, too.

\* \* \*

**Marla Grant** founded the Tampa affiliate of the national organization Helping Parents Heal (HPH) in 2016 and served as national affiliate director in 2018. She feels privileged to help grieving parents rise from the early shattering effects of child loss to a place of peace and even joy. With a degree in organizational studies and human development, Marla has lived and worked in the United States and abroad, currently as a community relations director in Tampa, Florida. She was engaged in fundraising for marrow donor testing and pediatric cancer research for twenty years through the all-volunteer nonprofit she founded in 1995, Kickin' for Kids. Marla has continued volunteering as an international and domestic courier for the National Marrow Donor Program, transporting lifesaving cells from donor collection centers to transplant patients. She engages in her lifelong passion for travel and dance as well as visits to see her two beloved sons and two grandchildren whenever possible.

# Epilogue

## An Editor Reflects

*By Mary Langford*

*H*ow do I begin to thank all the angel kids who have shown up for me in this editing process? I got to know all of these gorgeous souls intimately through the loving eyes of their parents, and every single one of them melts my heart. So many beautiful souls sat beside me on my couch, where I work, and whispered just the right words for me to type as I edited their heartwarming stories.

Tina's darling Ryan jumped into my heart and stayed there from the day I first read her story—which was only the second story I edited for this book. We were both so new in this process, so it took us spending countless hours together on the phone, laughing and crying as we worked, in order to get Tina's chapter written and rewritten and tweaked to where we were both finally happy. Ever since, I've experienced the joy of giving many Pay It Forwards in Ryan's honor.

When I first came to know Sharon, she told me that her niece, Tamara, was also writing a story for this book. It wasn't until Sharon's own son Gabriel died that she could fully comprehend the enormity of Tamara's loss over her daughter Janna, who had died a decade before. To hold the space for both women as they confronted some challenging family dynamics in each of their stories was a unique and beautiful experience. While they have been close, again, for years now, I'm sure that being twin contributors to this book has solidified their bond even more.

Tamara's organization, Healing Hugs, provides funeral-related (and other) expenses for bereaved parents. When Tamara learned that, for a number of complicated reasons, one of the children in this book did not yet have a headstone, she offered to provide one for his grave. Tamara had mentioned to me that it's sometimes tough for parents to receive gifts like hers, so I knew to expect some resistance initially. She sealed the deal, though, when she told the boy's dad, "Think of it as a gift from my daughter to your son—she always loved giving people presents. Besides, they're probably the ones who concocted this scheme in the first place!"

I wish there was enough space for me to mention every contributor by name, and every incredible experience we've shared. There were far too many to recount. Each parent has touched me deeply and enriched my life beyond measure. Some, I'm certain, I will be friends with for as long as I live, and I am richly blessed by all of these wonderful new relationships.

I felt Divinely appointed to edit this book. Of the nine categories of losses, I have experienced firsthand at least half of them. I have no children of my own, but I was molested as a young teenager and lost that child, and I was never able to conceive again. Suicide, mental illness, and addiction have shown up in my life very personally, as well as the murder of my first love, at the age of sixteen. All of these experiences have been tremendously painful and a source of great grief off and on throughout my life.

I'm so grateful for the many suggestions for dealing with grief by the contributors, especially SourceTapping, EFT, and the Map of Emotions, since they have helped me process and release my own pain that has come up for me in the process of reshaping these stories.

I've been reminded, by the words of these brave parents, that grief comes in waves—and even when I'm decades past a loss, it can still show up out of the blue at times when I least expect it. But when I can allow myself to be in the feelings and fully embrace them, I'm able to quickly process the loss and release it—energetically, emotionally, and spiritually.

I've been down in the trenches with everyone. Sometimes it was hard nudging the moms and dads to dig a little bit deeper into their grief. For most, that was a very scary endeavor. But I made the same vow to everyone—that if they trusted me and allowed me to take them down to the depths of despair, I'd bring them back safely, and that the sorrow people would feel in the midst of reading their story would be far surpassed by the hope and inspiration they would feel in the end.

I hope I have fulfilled my promise.

\*    \*    \*

**Mary Langford** worked so closely with the 27 Contributors herein that she has become known as the "Bereavement Editor." In the very intimate process of crafting and refining their stories, Mary fell head over heels in love with each brave Contributor, as well as their adorable Spirit Kids. Prior to launching her business, The Write Mary (TheWriteMary .com), Mary spent 18 years in Los Angeles as an actress, stand-up comedienne, and personal assistant/scribe for many international luminaries. For five years, she worked at the right hand of *New York Times* bestselling author and Emmy-winning producer, Sidney Sheldon. Mary worked very closely with Sidney on his last two books: his 18th and final novel, as well as his memoir. The two formed an indelible bond that has deeply affected the trajectory of Mary's career. Later, she assisted world-famous hairstylist and entrepreneur, Vidal Sassoon, in the writing of his autobiography. In addition to her work as a freelance writing coach, ghostwriter and editor, Mary is currently writing her first book, inspired by her 44-year (and counting) friendship with her best friend, Linda Mallory: *Everybody Needs a Linda: A Girlfriends' Guide to Friendships that Last a Lifetime.* In so doing, she's keeping a promise she made to her beloved Sidney in 2005 – that she would one day follow in his footsteps and write books of her own. Mary feels Sidney's spirit with her as she works, and loves declaring to her clients: "Sidney Sheldon is helping us write your book!" And she's not kidding.

# Tools and Techniques
# We Used on Our Grief Journeys

**Are You Addicted to Misery?**
*Contributed by Meryl Hershey Beck*

The following questions I've asked myself, as well as clients. For some individuals, feeling miserable has become a part of their identity and they don't know how to let go of it.

Here are some questions to ask yourself:

- Do you keep telling and retelling your story, over and over again?
- Do you feel guilty if you start to feel happy?
- When others offer support, do you reject it?
- Do you only remember the good times and push away memories of the challenging times with your child?
- Do you know that even though you've had a major loss, it's possible to have a worthwhile, fulfilling life?

If you answered yes to any of these questions, I invite you to sign up for our newsletters, updates, and messages of hope at www.Loss SurviveThrive.com.

**Ask and Receive**
https://askandreceive.org
*Contributed by Shoshana Garfield*

This is intentional work that at its most effective requires either careful intuition/self-awareness or muscle testing. Like EFT tapping, it is deceptively simple and is easily learned and so flexible. There are five statements that you can find on the website for free with some examples on how to use it. It helps to slow down your breathing and allow your-self to be a bit meditative and focused when you do it.

## The Awakened Way—A Path to Knowing Who You Are and Why You're Here

www.theawakenedway.org

*Contributed by Suzanne Giesemann*

The Awakened Way is built upon three basic truths:

1. You are a beautiful soul—an eternal being—who walks in both worlds at once.
2. You are part of one big web connecting all that is.
3. You find your way Home through the heart.

The Awakened Way is not a system, not a process, not a religion. It is an awakened approach to living a consciously connected and divinely guided life.

## The BLESS ME Method

www.suzannegiesemann.com

*Contributed by Suzanne Giesemann*

BLESS ME is a memory device and each of the seven letters represents a specific stage of the meditative process.

**B:**  Breathe. By taking several slow, deep breaths, you automati-cally begin to slow your brain waves and induce a state of relaxation. Always breathe deeply, drawing the air down into the abdomen.

**L:**  Lift. In this stage, you utilize one or more mental tools, as de-sired, to raise your personal vibration. Thoughts that focus on love and gratitude are optimum for creating a coherent state.

**E:**  Expand. Take in a deep breath, and as you exhale, imagine your human energy field in the shape of a sphere expanding at the speed of light in all directions. This imagery takes your focus off the human body, providing awareness of the limitless nature of the soul.

**S:**  Surrender. Silently state the words "I surrender." This inten-tion-filled statement asserts your willingness to remove your focus from the ego's "story" and identify with your true nature as a soul.

S:  Shift. This crucial stage shifts your focus from the physical world to the world of no form, no time, and no space. You may choose any keyword or imagery that helps you to shift your awareness from form to spirit. I use the verbal command "Shift."

M:  Merge. Through intention, merge your energy field as a soul—your etheric body—with that of any other being of light that will serve the greater good. This could be a loved one who has passed, a higher being, or your own higher self. Use a phrase such as "Come now."

E:  Experience. During this nonguided stage, spend as much time as you need to experience whatever is supposed to happen. This is the time to practice quieting the mind. Alternatively, it is the optimum state for asking for insight and guidance from loved ones who have passed.

Guided meditations using this process are available for free and for purchase.

### Blue Diamond Healing
www.philmollon.co.uk
*Contributed by Shoshana Garfield*
Phil Mollon's Blue Diamond Healing is an advanced method for those who know how to muscle test and are willing to go deep, deep, deep down the rabbit hole. You emerge into a beautiful world that is well worth the journey. It requires a calm, loving state of mind and an open heart. It is incredibly effective when you can allow the presence and focus the method requires.

### Courageous Mothers
www.courageousmothers.com
*Contributed by Jo-Anne Joseph*
This site includes categories such as: Comfort & Inspiration, Courageous Fathers, Faith & Spirituality, Holidays, Infertility & TTC, Life After Loss, News, Pregnancy & Parenting After Loss, and Stories of Loss.

## CranioSacral Therapy
www.upledger.com
*Contributed by Vickie Bodner*

This gentle hands-on technique works with soft tissue structures and the flow of cerebrospinal fluid in the body to relieve tension and/or trauma in these areas as well as deeper tissue such as the brain, nerves, central nervous system, etc.

## Emotional Freedom Techniques (EFT Tapping)
www.eftinternational.com
*Contributed by Shoshana Garfield*

Emotional Freedom Techniques, often known simply as "tapping," helps people relieve distress with or without speaking through details. It also helps shift longstanding, complex, and unwanted behavior and belief patterns when you work with it persistently; for example, complex money issues, over- or undereating, being angry or indecisive, and, of course, complex grief. The evidence base for this way of working gets stronger year by year, and in 2018, for the first time in world history, a government (United Kingdom) made EFT a national research priority for the treatment of post-traumatic stress disorder. EFT uses manual stimulation on the end points of meridians while saying a targeted phrase. The main sequence is fairly easy to learn and, like all of these modalities, takes persistence and training to master. Lots of free resources.

## Energy Psychology
www.energypsych.org
*Contributed by Shoshana Garfield*

The website of the Association for Comprehensive Energy Psychology (ACEP) is well organized and incredibly informative, particularly their free research materials. They have their own modality, a way of combining meridian, chakra, and biofield work that I highly recommend. The annual conferences are world class and attract the authors of many books you have probably read, as well as practitioners and energy explorers from all over the world.

**Facebook Groups**

• **Grieving Parents Healing Hearts Child Loss.** A closed group where we can talk about our children and focus on healing our hearts by helping one another.

**Five Element Acupuncture**
*Contributed by Alice Adams*

Five Element Acupuncture is a unique and profound form of Chinese acupuncture. It is several thousand years old and is different from other forms of acupuncture because it focuses on diagnosing and treating the root cause of the patient's body (physical) and mind (mental/emotional) complaints, like overwhelming grief. It is described as "body/mind/spirit" medicine because it addresses the patient's physical and mental/emotional challenges and supports the patient's "spirit." To find a Five Element acupuncturist, contact the Maryland University of Integrative Health (www.muih.edu), Academy for Five Element Acupuncture (www.acupuncturist.edu), or Institute of Taoist Education and Acupuncture (www.itea.edu).

**Glow in the Woods**
www.glowinthewoods.com
*Contributed by Jo-Anne Joseph*

A site for babylost mothers and fathers.

**griefHaven**
www.griefhaven.org
*Contributed by Meryl Hershey Beck and Tim deZarn*

griefHaven (aka The Erika Whitmore Godwin Foundation) is a 501(c)(3) nonprofit foundation dedicated to providing grief support and education to those who have loved and lost, those who want to know how to support someone who is grieving, and professionals who work within the arena of death and dying.

**GriefShare**
www.griefshare.org
*Contributed by Tammy McDonnell*

GriefShare is a friendly, caring group of people who will walk alongside you through one of life's most difficult experiences.

## Heart Assisted Therapy (HAT)
www.heartassistedtherapy.net
*Contributed by Shoshana Garfield*

This deceptively simple technique arose from years and years of experimentation and practice by Dr. John Diepold, a psychoanalytical therapist in the United States. It focuses on, as you can probably guess from the name, the heart chakra. Dr. Diepold has been working on stripping down and simplifying the procedures of energy psychology. His book with the easy-to-find name *Heart Assisted Therapy* is a delightful read and comes with appendices for procedures.

## Ho'oponopono
*Contributed by Meryl Hershey Beck*

Meryl had the good fortune of studying this forgiveness method with Joe Vitale and Dr. Ihaleakala Hew Len. A mental institution in Hawaii for the criminally insane hired Dr. Hew Len. It was a frightening place to work, very high turnover, with nurses and doctors scooting along the walls to protect their backs from attack. The inmates were either drugged or shackled to manage their violent tendencies. Enter Dr. Hew Len with an unorthodox method. He stayed in his office and did not see patients individually, but rather perused their charts with care, and used the mystical Hawaiian healing method of Ho'oponopono. As the good doctor read the charts, he'd have feelings about the events.

The Ho'oponopono method is the repetition of these four phrases in any order:

1. I love you.
2. I am sorry.
3. Please forgive me.
4. Thank you.

Dr. Hew Len refers to this process as "cleaning," and as he did it with each of the inmates, the person got better. It seems so simple, but in the four years of his tenure, patients gradually had no further need either for the shackles or the sedation. Staff started staying as the people got better, all inmates were eventually released, and the ward was closed. Dr. Hew Len gives an excellent description in a short video: www.youtube.com/watch?v=U7T1h7loFME.

• **HOPE ASAP—Grief Support After Substance Addiction Loss.** A closed group offering help, encouragement, support, and a shoulder to cry on for those who suffered the loss of a dear loved one due to substance abuse.

## Inner Guidance and a Course in Miracles
https://facim.org
*Contributed by Marla Grant*

I have often been asked how it is that I'm living such a joyful life in spite of having three of my five children leave their existence in this world of form. My response is partly that I feel I came into this life already prepared for the immense challenge of watching my children transition. I also feel I am constantly attended by my guides on the other side who lead me, through quiet introspection, to find the right books, messengers, and teachers who inform my understanding of life in a human body.

In large part, A Course in Miracles has been my source for the wisdom and insight that helped me perceive the truth about life, time, and our true existence as Spirit. I understand the inalienable and eternal continuity of life and the principle that we are all one and not truly separate from one another or our Source. I am merely experiencing a dream state of separation but as the Course teaches, "You are at home in God, dreaming of exile but perfectly capable of awakening to reality." Through the practices of forgiveness and acceptance, sorrow has fallen away and been replaced with patience, faith, and love.

## Integral Breath Therapy
www.integrationconcepts.net
*Contributed by Vickie Bodner*

Created by Carol Lampman, Integral Breath Therapy is an experiential process using specific breathing techniques to remove blocks or stress, induce a relaxation response, release negative emotional energy, and channel vital life-force energy. It works on the principle that there is a direct connection between the psychological, emotional, spiritual, and physical well-being and the openness of the breath.

## Journaling
*Contributed by Sandy Peckinpah*

One of the best tools to walk your emotions through the grieving process is to write in a journal. The very nature of writing opens the brain and allows it to form words of emotion onto paper, and then it releases them. It creates space in between the hurt and the sorrow in order to heal. (More on this in the book *Writing to Heal* by research psychologist James W. Pennebaker.) Your journal is a safe place to be *you*. You get to share your true feelings, your fears, your weaknesses, and your daily struggle with the loss of your child. Don't worry about spelling or grammar. This is for you and no one else. Your journal also provides a framework to monitor your resilience. After a while, an amazing thing begins to happen. You see *hope* rising up from the pages. Someday, you'll look back on your writing and be astonished at how far you've come.

For more writing and articles from Sandy, visit www.Sandy Peckinpah.com.

## Map of Emotions
*Contributed by Heidi Bright*

Emotions are simply e-motion, energy in motion. The Map of Emotions, developed by David Berenson, encourages you to experience your feelings as they are happening without managing or manipulating them. By not attempting to control, act on, rationalize, or think about your feelings, you will feel a deeper sense of control over your situation. The task is about awareness and sensing in your body, as opposed to thinking.

The process involves giving your emotions your undivided attention. When you are emotionally triggered yet not thinking about your reaction, you allow the energy in your body to move around, intensify, and dissipate. If you simply sit with your emotion, feeling it inside your body, it will lift.

## Mindfulness Healing
*Contributed by Lynda Crane*

The practice I found most helpful in enduring the intense waves of grief that I experienced in the years following my son's death (and sometimes still) is the mindfulness exercise of acceptance. I found that tensing my muscles and emotionally running from the pain (both natural in such circumstances) only served to intensify the experience. If, instead, I simply acknowledged it and allowed it to happen, it seemed to ease my distress a little, and it also shortened the time before the agony passed through me and allowed me to breathe easier.

One way of testing this is during extremely cold weather. When the temperature is approaching zero, and the winds are bitter and strong, it is natural to tense the muscles and run for cover. However, if one makes a conscious effort to relax every muscle, breathe evenly, and walk at a steady pace, the pain of the cold (while certainly still there) is more bearable, and the experience emotionally easier to take. This practice holds true for any unpleasant thought or emotion: Notice it, let it pass through without judgment or comment, and move on.

### Pay It Forward
*Contributed by Tina Zarlenga*

Small acts of kindness allowed me to share my son's gentle spirit with others while filling me with a joy I had forgotten existed. Each kind act lifted me in a way nothing else had since his death, creating the Pay It Forward movement that I had never imagined. Now every year at Ryan's birthday I wake early with a plan to share the love of Ryan as a community of family and friends joins with me to scatter kindness with small gifts to strangers.

### The Prayer Registry
http://www.sheriperl.com/the-prayer-registry
*Contributed by Janice Crowder-Torrez*

A free website service dedicated to all families who have lost children, whatever their age when they passed. The Prayer Team, an online community, will honor your child's legacy, connecting with other bereaved parents, and participating in a world-wide group prayer for every registered loved one on the anniversary date of their passing.

### Processing Grief Through Writing
http://grievinganaddict.com
*Contributed by Heidi Bright*

When we lose a loved one to addiction, we have powerful feelings, such as rage, sorrow, guilt, and shame. Writing down our stories can help us reconnect with our loved ones and ourselves, weave ourselves back together, and give our lives meaning and purpose.

You can begin your process with a guided visualization. Select an unpleasant yet not traumatic event that occurred with your deceased loved one. Then completely relax your body, allowing muscle tension to dissipate. Try to keep your spine straight, and take some slow, deep breaths. When you are relaxed and ready, imagine you are back in that situation with your child. Observe without judging. Take note of your thoughts, feelings, and words. Ask your inner writer and healer to assist you with your writing. When you feel complete, return to full waking consciousness. Then write about the experience. Pay no attention to grammar, just write. Describe what happened, how you felt about what happened at the time, how you feel about it now, and any insights you might have gained.

Carefully select a trusted friend or counselor and ask her or him to simply listen without judgment or comparison as you share what you wrote. Through deep, honest writing and sharing, our emotions become more manageable and we are better able to process and integrate our grief.

## Receiving Messages
*Contributed by Laurie Mathes Arshonsky*

Anything can be a message: a song on the radio, a billboard, finding a card from your child, seeing a bird or animal, something someone says that your child may have said. Setting an intention to dream about your child or receive a message is very helpful. Before you go to sleep, ask your child to communicate with you. After my son passed, I encouraged his siblings to put a blanket over their heads and ask for a message. Sometimes it works, sometimes it doesn't.

Writing letters to a deceased child is a helpful practice. Try using your nondominant hand to receive an answer. Sometimes it's illegible, but you can pretend to know what your child said. It's probably true! Meditation classes help calm your mind to receiving messages. I sometimes sit with a notebook and write what comes to me. Once I felt like I was channeling a poem from my son, and I illustrated it and framed it. In the middle of the night sometimes words come to us that do not make any sense. I write these words down and try to discern them in the morning. Anything that gives us comfort is ours. Other people don't have to believe it.

# Reiki
*Contributed by Vickie Bodner and Lucia Maya*

Reiki is an ancient channel of intelligent, universal, and Divine energy. This technique is used to promote relaxation and relieve stress, which enhances the body's ability to heal. It works with the body, mind, heart, and spirit and can help to relieve physical pain, mental/emotional pain, and anxiety. The ability to use Reiki is transmitted through a simple initiation, which allows practitioners to channel it through their hands both in person (including on oneself) and at a distance. The patient's body determines how much energy is distributed in the session.

• **Resolving Grief and Feeling Lighter.** Support and resources to resolve the grief that weighs you down and feel like yourself again.

• **The Schizophrenia Oral History Project—TSOHP.** An archive of life stories of persons with schizophrenia co-founded by Lynda Crane and Tracy McDonough.

# Sending Energy Exercise
*Contributed by Meryl Hershey Beck*

1. Sit comfortably with your spine straight.
2. Focus on your breath. No need to change it, just be aware of the inhale and the exhale as you continue to breathe in and breathe out.
3. Imagine a large brilliant light above your head. As you inhale, image bringing the light in through your crown and down into your heart. Exhale. Continue breathing in this light through the top of your head and into your heart, filling yourself with light, love, and energy.
4. Now imagine a large bright light in the earth beneath you and visualize a cord connecting your tailbone to this light. Now as you inhale, bring the light up through the cord, into your body, and then into your heart. Continue to breathe in this earth energy, filling your heart.
5. Next, if you are able, breathe in the light from both heaven and earth—in through your crown and also up from the earth. Continue filling up with light, love, and healing energy.

6. Now . . . inhale this delicious energy in (from above and/or below), and as you exhale, imagine sending this light, love, and energy to any part of your body that is tense or tight or in pain. Repeat five times.
7. Continue inhaling the energy, and now as you exhale, send the breath to all your organs and cells. Repeat five times.
8. Continue breathing in this light, and as you breathe out, send it to specific people or places, wherever it is needed. Repeat five times.
9. Sit for a few moments and enjoy the feelings of relaxation plus heightened energy.

Note: When you send energy to someone else, your body takes what it needs first before sending it on. It's important to not use your own finite energy, but to be the conduit and tap into the infinite resources of Mother Earth and the Universe.

Want to hear this exercise? Go to www.stopeatingyourheartout .com/sendingenergy.

### Service Work
*Contributed by Tamara Gabriel*

What I found to be most helpful during my grief was service work and helping others. By making other people's lives better, I was able to take myself out of myself. This gave meaning to my loss so it would not be in vain. Some examples of my service work include leading twelve-step recovery meetings at the county jail, as well as state and federal prisons, and working with abused women. I also lead a women's spiritual empowerment group, Women's Original Wisdom (WOW).

### Silver Linings List
www.helpingparentsheal.org/silver-lining-list
*Contributed by Marla Grant*

In late 2017, the parents of the Helping Parents Heal Tampa affiliate enthusiastically took part in sharing some of the surprising and unexpected blessings they have experienced since their children transitioned. This is a transformative tool for parents who are ready to begin exploring the gifts of growth and meaning that grief can present.

**Still Standing Magazine**
www.stillstandingmag.com
*Contributed by Jo-Anne Joseph*

Founded in 2012, Still Standing Magazine, LLC, shares stories from around the world of writers surviving the aftermath of loss, infertility—and includes information on how others can help.

**SourceTapping**
www.SourceTapping.com
*Contributed by Meryl Hershey Beck*

Are you familiar with EFT (Emotional Freedom Techniques), or "tapping"? These energy psychology techniques involve touching or tapping certain acupressure points to release pain, ease grief, manage stress, heal trauma, curb cravings, and more. SourceTapping is an evolved form that I created over twenty years ago. It brings in a spiritual component, includes a script, uses the Pleasure Breath, and anchors in a positive state of being. After my son suicided, I used SourceTapping daily just to feel like I could breathe. I also used it to clear the trauma—receiving the phone call telling me that Jon was dead. Whenever I felt like I was sinking, I did SourceTapping on myself to move stuck energy and feel calmer. You can do SourceTapping with a qualified practitioner for deep traumas (go to the website for a list of practitioners), or you can do it on your own to decrease the feelings of deep grief. The grief won't necessarily go away, but tapping will make it more manageable. Get your copy of the script, "SourceTapping for Grief and Loss," by going to www.sourcetapping.com/grief-script.

**The Work of Byron Katie**
www.thework.com
*Contributed by Laurie Mathes Arshonsky and Lucia Maya*

According to the website, "The Work is a simple yet powerful process of inquiry that teaches you to identify and question the thoughts that cause all the suffering in the world. It's a way to understand what's hurting you, and to address the cause of your problems with clarity. In its most basic form, The Work consists of four questions and the turnarounds." There are free worksheets on the website and many YouTube videos of Byron Katie doing The Work.

## Writing as a Tool
*Contributed by Tina Zarlenga*

When immersed in grief the only thing I could force myself to do was write. I would cry and scribble into journals, asking why, writing to Ryan, my son, as if he would hear me, while begging for an answer. In time, the answers came to me through my own writing. Gradually, I saw the small improvement as I did the work of grief. My days included waking, writing, and tears as I pushed to survive one more day. And that was enough. As my writing grew into poems and stories, I found a place of comfort. I found immense solace in blogging, being witnessed and connected with a community of others who were familiar with grief and loss. I can pour my emotions into words, knowing that our story has touched countless others.

# Resources

**American Foundation for Suicide Prevention**
www.afsp.org
*Contributed by Michele Wollert*
The American Foundation for Suicide Prevention (AFSP) raises awareness, funds scientific research, and provides resources and aid to those affected by suicide.

**Be SMART**
www.momsdemandaction.org
*Contributed by Kelley Ireland*
Be SMART is the education arm of Moms Demand Action for Gun Sense in America. It is a program designed to be nonpartisan, and helps families to understand how they can be proactive with guns and safety in households with children or those at risk for suicide. Be SMART educates families, teachers, doctors, first responders, clergy, and the general public about how important it is to follow the acronym SMART:

S: Secure guns in the home and in vehicles. Just telling kids not to touch guns is not enough.

M: Model responsible gun behavior. Guns are not toys, and education about the dangers of them should begin as early as possible. Children and even teens don't have the ability to truly understand the ramifications of accidents with them.

**A:**    Ask about the presence of unsecured guns when your children or grandchildren are visiting other homes, even those of family members. Many unintentional shootings occur this way.

**R:**    Recognize the risks of teen suicide. There are many subtle things we may not tie to risky behavior in our child or teen. Learn what they are.

**T:**    Tell your peers to Be SMART. Often, people don't even think about the risks of their children being injured or killed by the presence of guns in their or others' homes. They consider them devices for the safety of their home and hearth, not as threats to their kids, but kids and teens see things vastly differently than adults.

You can invite Be SMART presenters to give programs that are tailored to your home, church, or workplace. Contact a local Moms Demand Action group for more information.

### Children's Hospital Family House, Oakland, California
*Contributed by Robert (Bob) R. Burdt*

When a child is ill, parents want to stay with them. Some hospitals, however, do not offer accommodations for family members. When my son was hospitalized, I spent each night sleeping under his crib to stay close to him. Other parents did the same, or slept in the waiting room or in a corner of their child's room. With heartbreaking misery, they needed a place to cry and rest. I met with a few other parents at the hospital when I was there with my very ill son, and together we decided to raise money for a type of Ronald McDonald House, so parents would have a place to stay close by. We held many fund-raisers and meetings with hospital executives and local businesses, and in the early 1980s we raised enough money to purchase a three-story Victorian home near Children's Hospital in Oakland, California.

After some renovations, the Children's Hospital Family House opened its doors. With sixteen bedrooms, two kitchens, a common living room, playroom, exercise room, and laundry room, it provides a very low-cost place for families whose children are under care at Children's Hospital. Now, more than thirty-eight years since first opening its doors, it is still going strong. Call (510) 428-3100 for more information.

## The Compassionate Friends

www.compassionatefriends.org

*Contributed by Meryl Hershey Beck*

With over five hundred chapters throughout the United States, The Compassionate Friends has been providing support to bereaved families for over forty years. Their goal is to provide friendship, understanding, and hope to those who have lost a child (any age, any cause).

## Facebook Groups

*Contributed by many*

Tammy McDonnell commented: "The closed online groups have been a lifesaver for me. Here I have met some of the most amazing compassionate people. There is no judgment, and I have always felt I could express myself openly."

**The Compassionate Friends/USA.** Provides support to every family experiencing the death of a child, sibling, or grandchild.

**From Surviving to Thriving Support Group for Suicide Loss.** Its goal is to offer support to the bereaved and provide a safe and compassionate place for survivors to share thoughts and feelings with fellow survivors.

**Grace for Grieving Moms.** This is an online closed faith-based group for moms who have lost their children due to substance abuse disorder.

**Grieving an Addict.** Created by Heidi Bright in memory of her son, this page offers hope to other parents who have lost a child due to drug addiction.

**Grieving Dads: To the Brink and Back.** Kelly Farley created this page (and book) to bring awareness to the impact that child loss has on fathers and to let them know they are not alone.

**Healing Hugs.** This page was created by Tamara Gabriel, who posts healing messages that now touch over two million people daily.

**Helping Parents Heal Online Support Group.** An open group for parents and siblings with the goal of celebrating the lives of our children and to ultimately heal as a group.

**Heroin Memorial.** An online closed group for anyone that has lost a loved one due to heroin or opioids. Unfortunately, it seems that fentanyl is being mixed with everything, so many of our loved ones aren't getting what they think they are.

**Loss, Survive, Thrive.** An online closed group for anyone who has experienced profound grief *and* has not just survived, but is thriving. Also invited is anyone affected by the loss of a child—siblings, grandparents, etc. Use this group to post inspirational quotes, as well as your own tips and tools.

**#NotInVain.** An online closed group for moms who have lost children due to substance abuse disorder.

### Grieving an Addict
www.grievinganaddict.com
*Contributed by Heidi Bright*

*Grieving an Addict* is a soon-to-be published book for those who have suffered great loss. Discover what I, other bereaved people, recovering addicts, and involved professionals have learned that can go a long way in easing heartbreak:

- My story: A suburban mother and her son journey through addiction, rehabs, overdoses, and death, and find along the way that when we are most powerless, we receive unspeakable gifts.
- Fifty-six reflections that demonstrate how to allow the agony, process the pain, and integrate the loss. Each includes a personal story from a bereaved family member.
- Answers to burning questions about this storm of epidemic proportions with compelling confessions that recount the perils of addiction and its aftermath. This section also includes actable suggestions for slowing the hurricane down.

Visit the website to receive your free copy of "Seven Ways to Cope with Loss" and a weekly blog.

### Grieving Dads Project
www.grievingdads.com
*Created by Kelly Farley*

The Grieving Dads Project was created to provide support for all of the grieving dads out there that feel alone and lost in their grief. It was designed to help men realize that they are not alone in their pain after losing a child. The Grieving Dads website and Facebook page provide a place for men to "Tell Their Story" to others without the fear of being looked upon as weak by those in our society that have had the luxury of not knowing the pain of burying a child.

## Healing Hugs
www.healinghugs.net
*Created by Tamara Gabriel*

Healing Hugs raises and donates money for funerals, counseling, and any other expenses for those who have lost a child. In addition, Tamara developed a Facebook page for Healing Hugs and posts healing messages. It now touches over two million people daily.

## Helping Parents Heal
www.helpingparentsheal.org
*Contributed by Ernie Jackson, Marla Grant, Janice Crowder-Torrez, and Laurie Savoie*

Helping Parents Heal (HPH) is a nonprofit organization dedicated to assisting bereaved parents, giving them support and resources to aid in the healing process. HPH goes a step beyond other groups by allowing the open discussion of spiritual experiences and evidence for the afterlife, in a nondogmatic way. Affiliate groups welcome everyone regardless of religious or nonreligious background and allow for open dialog. This is the mission of HPH, and its purpose has connected with many. The group has grown exponentially over the past seven years, with a membership of over eleven thousand members.

## National Alliance on Mental Illness
www.nami.org
*Contributed by Michele Wollert*

The National Alliance on Mental Illness (NAMI) is the nation's largest grassroots mental health organization dedicated to building better lives for the millions of Americans affected by mental illness through education and advocacy.

## The Schizophrenia Oral History Project

www.schizophreniaoralhistories.com

*Contributed by Lynda Crane*

The Schizophrenia Oral History Project (TSOHP) aims to provide a platform for persons with schizophrenia—many of whom might not feel comfortable with public speaking themselves—to have their stories and their voices heard. We believe that in the process, their stories could have an impact in reducing misunderstanding and stigma among the general public, and therefore make the lives of those with schizophrenia easier and contribute to opening pathways to further social integration and fulfillment of purpose.

We began with the idea of gathering life stories from twenty to twenty-five people in the Cincinnati area who have schizophrenia, publishing excerpts of their stories in articles and presenting them at public talks, and eventually publishing them in a book. Today we have collected over sixty life stories, from narrators in several states. Our narrators' life stories have been featured in articles in the *New York Times*, *Newsweek*, the American Psychological Association's *Monitor on Psychology*, and the *Oral History Review*, among others, and have been heard in podcasts. Their pictures and their stories have been shared in more than two hundred public presentations, and our website, which features audio excerpts from their stories, has been visited by thousands of viewers. Like almost everyone else, TSOHP has a Facebook page.

## Strength in Mothers

*Led by Laurie Arshonsky, laurie.arshonsky@gmail.com*

This is a closed support group composed of thirteen women who all lost children ages nineteen to twenty-five from various causes. There are shared agreements such as confidentiality, compassion, and respect. The group meets monthly in a private home, in a Cincinnati suburb, on Thursdays from 7:00 to 9:00 p.m. At the onset of the meeting, the leader lights a candle, which is passed in silence. At the end, the leader blows out the candle and passes it in the opposite direction in silence. A heart-shaped stone is held by the person whose turn it is to speak and is passed to the next participant when she is complete. Topics have included holidays, anniversaries, sharing pictures, quilts made in memory, sibling issues, what helps, our most intense feeling (such as longing, depression, loneliness), making a scrapbook, and things to do to remember and honor our children. No charge.

# Books We Recommend

Alexander, Eben. *Proof of Heaven: A Neurosurgeon's Journey into the Afterlife*. New York: Simon & Schuster, 2012.

Beck, Meryl Hershey. *Stop Eating Your Heart Out: The 21-Day Program to Free Yourself from Emotional Eating*. San Francisco: Conari Press, 2012.

Botkin, Allan L., and Craig Hogan. *Induced After Death Communication: A Miraculous Therapy for Grief and Loss*. Charlottesville, VA: Hampton Roads Publishing, 2014.

Bradshaw, John. *Creating Love: The Next Great Stage of Growth*. New York: Bantam, 1994.

Browne, Mary T. *Mary T. Reflects on the Other Side*. New York: Fawcett Columbine, 1994.

Buscaglia, Leo. *The Fall of Freddie the Leaf*. New York: Slack Incorporated, 1982.

Cacciatore, Joanne. *Bearing the Unbearable: Love, Loss, and the Heartbreaking Path of Grief*. Somerville, MA: Wisdom Publications, 2017.

Crane, Lynda, *Mental Retardation: A Community Integration Approach*. Belmont, CA: Wadsworth Publishing, 2001.

Delts, Bob. *Life after Loss: A Practical Guide to Renewing Your Life After Experiencing Major Loss*. Boston: Da Capo Press, 2017.

Dyer, Wayne. *The Power of Intention*. Carlsbad, CA: Hay House, 2004.

Farley, Kelly, with David DiCola. *Grieving Dads: To the Brink and Back*. Aurora, IL: Grieving Dads, 2012.

Giesemann, Suzanne. *Messages of Hope: The Metaphysical Memoir of a Most Unexpected Medium*. The Villages, FL: One Mind Books, 2011.

———. *Still Right Here: A True Story of Healing and Hope*. The Villages, FL: One Mind Books, 2017.

Greaves, Helen. *Testimony of Light*. Saffron Walden, UK: Neville Spearman Publishers, 2004.

Hay, Louise. *You Can Heal Your Life*. Carlsbad, CA: Hay House, 1984.

Hickman, Martha Whitmore. *Healing After Loss*. New York: Perennial, 2002.

Hicks, Esther, and Jerry Hicks. *Ask and It Is Given: Learning to Manifest Your Desires.* Carlsbad, CA: Hay House, 2004.

Jackson, Ernie. *Quinton's Messages.* 2nd ed. Self-published, 2016.

James, John W., and Russell Friedman. *The Grief Recovery Handbook.* New York: HarperCollins, 2009.

Joseph, Jo-Anne, and Brian Joseph. *Footprints on the Heart: A Remembrance Anthology—A Collection of Poetry and Prose by Bereaved Parents.* Self-published, Amazon, 2017.

Joy, W. Brugh. *Joy's Way. A Map for the Transformational Journey: An Introduction to the Potentials for Healing with Body Energies.* New York: J. P. Tarcher, 1979.

Kagan, Annie. *The Afterlife of Billy Fingers.* Charlottesville, VA: Hampton Roads, 2013.

Katie, Byron. *Loving What Is: Four Questions That Can Change Your Life.* New York: Harmony Reprint, 2002.

Kelly, Ellin. *Elizabeth Seton: Selected Writings (Sources of American Spirituality).* New York: Paulist Press, 1987.

Lupo, Lesley Joan. *Remember, Every Breath Is Precious: Dying Taught Me How to Live.* Hove, UK: White Crow Books, 2018.

Martini, Richard. *Flipside: A Tourist's Guide on How to Navigate the Afterlife.* Santa Monica, CA: Hormina Publishing, 2011.

McCormack, Jerusha Hull. *Grieving: A Beginner's Guide.* Brewster, MA: Paraclete Press, 2010.

McGill, Ormond. *Grieve No More, Beloved.* Bancyfelin, Carmarthen, Wales: Crown House Publishing, 2003.

Medhus, Elisa. *My Son in the Afterlife: Conversations from the Other Side.* New York: Atria Paperback, 2013.

Meissner, Susan. *A Fall of Marigolds.* New York: Penguin Group, 2014.

Neal, Mary. *To Heaven and Back: A Doctor's Extraordinary Account of Her Death, Heaven, Angels, and Life Again.* Colorado Springs, CO: Waterbrook Press, 2012.

Neimeyer, Robert A. "Correspondence with the Deceased." In Neimeyer, *Techniques of Grief Therapy,* 259–61.

———, ed. *Techniques of Grief Therapy: Creative Practices for Counseling the Bereaved.* New York: Routledge, 2012.

Newton, Michael. *Destiny of Souls: New Case Studies of Life Between Lives.* St. Paul, MN: Llewellyn Publications, 2001.

———. *Journey of Souls: Case Studies of Life Between Lives.* St. Paul, MN: Llewellyn Publications, 1994.

O'Neill, Derek. *More Truth Will Set You Free.* San Antonio, TX: Bianca Productions, 2010.

Ornish, Dean. *Love and Survival: The Scientific Basis for the Healing Power of Intimacy.* New York: HarperCollins, 1998.

Paladin, Lynda S. *Ceremonies for Change: Creating Rituals to Heal Life's Hurts.* Boston: E. P. Dutton, 1991.

Peckinpah, Sandy. *How to Survive the Worst That Can Happen: A Parent's Step by Step Guide to Healing After the Loss of a Child.* Bloomington, IN: Balboa Press, 2014.

Perl, Sheri. *Lost and Found: A Mother Connects-Up with Her Son in Spirit.* New York: Perl Publications, 2011.

Peterson, Jerre. *Heart Works: A Father's Grief.* Ashland, OR: Take Five Books, 2003.

Pitstick, Mark. *Soul Proof: Compelling Evidence That No One Really Dies and How That Benefits You Now.* Self-published, 2016.

Puryear, Anne. *Stephen Lives! My Son Stephen: His Life, Suicide, and Afterlife.* New York: Pocket Books, 1996.

Savoie, Laurie. *The Ripple Effect: Invisible Impact of Suicide.* Self-published, CreateSpace, 2015.

Schiff, Harriet Sarnoff. *The Bereaved Parent.* New York: Crown Publishers, 1977.

Schwartz, Robert. *Your Soul's Gift: The Healing Power of the Life You Planned Before You Were Born.* Chesterland, OH: Whispering Winds Press, 2012.

———. *Your Soul's Plan: Discovering the Real Meaning of the Life You Planned Before You Were Born.* Berkeley, CA: Frog Books, 2009.

Starr, Mirabai. *Caravan of No Despair: A Memoir of Loss and Transformation.* Boulder, CO: Sounds True, 2015.

Sutphen, Dick, with Tara Sutphen. *Soul Agreements.* Charlottesville, VA: Hampton Roads, 2004.

Tipping, Colin. *Radical Forgiveness: A Revolutionary Five-Step Process to Heal Relationships, Let Go of Anger and Blame, and Find Peace in Any Situation.* Boulder, CO: Sounds True, 2009.

Tolle, Eckhart. *The Power of Now: A Guide to Spiritual Enlightenment.* Vancouver, BC: Namaste Publishing, 1997.

Vanderbilt, Gloria. *A Mother's Story.* New York: Alfred A. Knopf, 1996.

Weiss, Brian. *Many Lives, Many Masters: The True Story of a Prominent Psychiatrist, His Young Patient, and the Past-Life Therapy That Changed Both Their Lives.* New York: Fireside Book, 1988.

———. *Messages from the Masters: Tapping into the Power of Love.* New York: Warner Books, 2000.

Williamson, Marianne. *A Return to Love.* New York: HarperCollins, 1992.

Willig, Rev. Jim, with Tammy Bundy. *Lessons from the School of Suffering: A Young Priest with Cancer Teaches Us How to Live.* Cincinnati, OH: St. Anthony Messenger Press, 2001.

Wolfelt, Alan. *Understanding Your Grief.* Fort Collins, CO: Companion Press, 2004.

————. *The Understanding Your Grief Support Group Guide: Starting and Leading a Support Group Guide.* Fort Collins, CO: Companion Press, 2004.

Worden, J. William. *Grief Counseling and Grief Therapy.* New York: Springer, 2009.

Zuba, Tom. *Permission to Mourn: A New Way to Do Grief.* Rockford, IL: Bish Press, 2014.

# Final Words from
# Some Contributors

**Alice Adams:** It's difficult to put into words the myriad effects that continue to evolve as a result of contributing to this book. When I was first invited to contribute, I was quite surprised. My son's story (his life *and* death) had taken place over three decades ago! I wasn't sure anyone would be interested in events I felt were no longer "current."

Then I started to write! It has truly been a labor of love, particularly self-love, and an honor to be asked.

Of course, I remembered the magnitude, the tumult of emotions I felt after Lucas's death. And I knew intellectually that the direction my life had taken, particularly my career choices, was directly related to my grief experience. But I was unprepared for the torrents, not only of emotion, but of newfound inspiration I've received during the process of telling this story!

Now I'm exploring with deepening purpose my work with those experiencing loss and grief. And the process of recording this story has renewed a long-held interest I've had in writing.

I can only hope that like all good stories, the reading of this story will not only engage the reader's attention, but also reward them with some small yet meaningful gift to support them in their own healing.

**Michelle Barbuto:** The path of grief is extremely difficult, and there is never a correct answer to our feelings, moods, or meaning. Emotions come in waves, never knowing when panic will leave us unable to face the day, or when hope enables us to take that next step forward. Writing my chapter for this book helped me to tell a story about my special son John, who entered my life, stayed a while, and continued on his journey, where he now waits for me. John taught me about love, laughter, and hope. God willing, you have been able to have a small glimmer of light shine on your path through my words. I am forever grateful to be able to share my experience, although not one of us would have chosen to be here.

**Vickie Bodner:** If I allow myself to live more and more in the present moment without controlling outcomes, life brings me exactly what I need. When asked to write my story for this book my immediate feelings were mixed. I had truly grieved appropriately, but in writing my story found even different levels of grief that needed to be addressed. A book like this is needed in our society because death of a loved one is not honored the way it was in indigenous cultures or other older cultures. Three days or even a week is not enough time off work to grieve a loss so deep. This book helps honor the feelings that our society tends to ignore. Oftentimes I see this manifest as pain in the body. I am grateful for Meryl and her strength to put this book together to help others. It has helped me greatly to let go, to move on, and to find peace in my life even deeper than I could have imagined. I now hope to work with premature babies and help them while they help me.

**Heidi Bright, MDiv:** Throughout history, parents of deceased children have worked for tremendous positive change. When I read about Joan of Arc, the fifteenth-century French saint who was burned at the stake for heresy, I always wondered where her mother was during Joan's imprisonment and subsequent execution.

In 2018, I went to Rouen, France, where Joan spent her final year. I toured a museum that re-created Joan's second trial, which was conducted about fifteen years after her death. I learned that Joan's court case was reopened because her mother, Isabelle Romée, had spent the intervening years working to clear her daughter's name, even petitioning the pope for a new trial. Joan, who had been stigmatized, misunderstood, and killed, finally was vindicated—and eventually declared a saint.

When I was asked to participate in Meryl Hershey Beck's book, I was delighted to add to the body of work that celebrates what parents have done in honor and recognition of their deceased children. These life-shattering events do not have to destroy us. Instead, they can turn us into fiercely compassionate pioneers who bring about tremendous positive change in society. I am honored to be counted among them, as

I work to assist others with processing and integrating their grief after losing a loved one to the brain disease of addiction. Thank you, Meryl, for the opportunity, and thank you, Mary Langford, for your editing skill, making the stories even more readable and powerful.

**Janice Crowder-Torrez:** It is with (much) heartfelt gratitude that I thank Meryl Hershey Beck for asking me to contribute a chapter/story about my grief journey after my son "passed" at the age of thirty-one. Having known Meryl (a true "healer" in every sense of the word) for several years, I am honored.

There is something to be said when our paths cross with another soul who has shared a familiar experience. I have nothing but deep admiration and respect for Meryl as a healer, teacher, and role model who has given so much love to those of us lucky enough to share her presence. (I recently mentioned to a close friend how much the process of "writing my story" provided healing. Even if "my story" was not selected by the publisher, the many gifts were well worth the effort.)

This experience of writing my story blessed me with two gifts: (1) the real-time vision of my son walking down our front hallway as I completed writing my chapter, and (2) the beauty of additional healing that has come about in being so honored to share space with others who have experienced soul growth as a result of their losses. Thank you, Meryl.

**Tamara Gabriel, LMT:** I wanted to take the time to share my feelings about being a part of such a healing project. I think it's always important to share my story to help inspire H.O.P.E.—Hold On Pain Ends—in others. We are an abnormal club that nobody wants to join, and the fact that we can share our grief truly means a lot to me, especially knowing we are not alone. The most important part of participation has been bringing my aunt Sharon into this project to share her experiences as well and collaborating with her. I have felt so all alone and I'm sorry to share this club with anyone, let alone my aunt, but it has helped us to talk about our loss and bond in a way that no one else could ever understand. She has brought some reality where I walked in the family of delusions. I pray to bring peace, comfort, and insight to our community of Angel-parents for them to follow in our difficult but life-enhancing footsteps. There can be life after death!

**Shoshana Garfield:** How it had been to contribute:

> Cold rain on grey beach
> Grief rinsed clean as shining stones
> All is deeply well.

**Marla Grant:** I could never have imagined in the first third of my life that my most meaningful work would manifest in the final third of it. That work has been informed not only by the passing of three of my five children over a period of thirty-eight years, but also by the love that we shared, the spiritual lessons learned, and the willingness to see the infinite, eternal nature of life. I've had abundant support from family, friends, my spiritual guides, and now Meryl Hershey Beck. She has kindly allowed me a platform to help others see they have the power to survive life's greatest challenges, and for that gift, I am so grateful. It is my hope that in sharing my story as other inspired contributors to *Loss, Survive, Thrive* have done, readers will begin to experience what they thought was impossible: living a joyful, fulfilling life that acknowledges adversity but isn't defined by it.

**Kelley Ireland:** I would like to thank Meryl for her invitation to write my story. I must admit my surprise at being asked to share it. I loved the idea that the book would highlight people who had survived terrible loss and who had made the hard choice to not just live, but to thrive again afterward. I looked in vain during my initial grieving period for a book or a guide to help me learn how to rebuild my life. I read so many books on grief, loss, suicide, and dying but they didn't give me the tools I needed to cope, let alone survive loss that was so profound. I sought connections with people who were a month, six months, a year into grief and wanted to learn how they were managing. I believe *Loss, Survive, Thrive* will do just that. It will show not only how people survived, but how they gave meaning to their grief in all the unique ways they did. Again, my deepest gratitude to Meryl Hershey Beck for allowing my story, and my son's story, to be told.

**Sharon Gabriel Rossy, MEd:** When I first heard about the book *Loss, Survive, Thrive,* from my niece Tamara, my thought was that more of our stories needed to be told, and what a brave and marvelous endeavor. I immediately asked if my story could be included, and was so excited to be a part of this project. Our voices and our unique experiences needed to be shared with others, not merely with those who have unwillingly joined this journey, but also for those who work with the grieving, and for anyone who knows a grieving parent. It is so important to truly understand the nuances and the loss that knows no boundaries for those of us that have lost a child. Sadly, grief is still greatly misunderstood and I believe remains an uncomfortable area for most people, in particular the unspeakable grief of losing a child.

My story was initially shared at a conference several years ago at a workshop on what one learns from loss—any type of loss. It was four years after the death of my son Gabriel, and parts of me were still on autopilot. This time around, revisiting the story and really going into much more depth about my personal journey hit me in a deeper and more profound way. Twelve years after his death, I was asked to recall deeply personal memories—listening to a recording that he had left on his girlfriend's phone, remembering the active little boy with his bright blue eyes—and to write about it. My emotions were all over the place, and I cried like I hadn't cried for a long, long time. At the same time, I felt enormous pride to be able to tell Gabriel's story and felt that it was truly a privilege to share it with others.

Both Mary Langford and Meryl Hershey Beck have been incredibly supportive through this process. Mary and I have laughed and cried together over the phone—a lot! The experience of this book goes beyond the writing of the story. It's the connections we have made—each one of us kindred spirits in so many ways—all of our stories and experiences. All are unique, and all are connected.

From the bottom of my heart, thank you to those angels who have contributed to this book. Thank you to Meryl for her courageous journey through her own grief and life struggles. And thank you to Mary and others who have hung in there and worked so hard to make this happen.

And most importantly, thank you to our darling children—angels who have enriched our lives and taught us about unconditional love and what it means to live in honor of their memories.

# About the Author

**Meryl Hershey Beck,** MA, MEd is a teacher—whether facilitating a workshop, one-on-one with a client, or through the written words of her books. She began her career as a high school English teacher and became a licensed professional clinical counselor (LPCC) in 1989. In addition, Beck

- is an Amazon #1 bestselling author—*Stop Eating Your Heart Out*;
- created and developed a meridian therapy technique, Source Tapping®, and offers classes as well as certification training for professionals;
- has presented numerous times at the international Association for Comprehensive Energy Psychology (ACEP) conferences;
- develops and facilitates workshops, seminars, and teleclasses; and
- has been a frequent guest presenter at online summits and has been featured on radio and television.

Beck unhappily joined the Bereaved Parent Club in October 2011 when her only son Jonathan ended his life. Since that time, she has written articles and teaches workshops on grief and loss. Living in Tucson, Arizona, she enjoys spending time with her daughter Alison and her grandchildren and great-grandchildren.

She can be reached through her websites www.SourceTapping .com, www.StopEatingYourHeartOut.com, and www.LossSurvive Thrive.com

"*Meryl Hershey Beck is a shining example of how wisdom and light can be harvested from the darkest tragedy. As a friend and colleague, I've seen her battered by waves of anguish after the suicide of her son, yet she retains her natural buoyancy in the ocean of a mother's undying love. If you've ever wondered if it can be possible to reclaim a whole and joyful life after unthinkable loss, Meryl offers proof.*" ~ Kate Hawke, director, Trauma Transformation Network

# About the Contributors

**Rukiye Z. Abdul-Mutakallim** (story p. 239)

*Rukiye shocked and astounded everyone in the courtroom when she came face-to-face with the teens who murdered her son, offered to hug them, and made plans to visit them regularly in prison to help them become better people.*

Rukiye's son Suliman was a Navy veteran and a gentle, law-abiding soul living in a 'rough' neighborhood (by choice, trying to help the people there by his example), when he was shot, robbed, and killed a half block from his apartment building. Rukiye has attracted much media attention after the court appearance where she hugged her son's killer and his mother, such as a video produced by Humankind (over 44 million views and translated into several different languages), with thousands of positive responses to her story. In addition, a second Humankind video, which answers the question, "Why did you do this?" will be released in 2019. "The Power of Forgiveness," a documentary that chronicles Rukiye's story, was the 2019 Webby People's Voice Award Winner in the Internet Video -Documentary: Shortform category. Rukiye lives in Cincinnati, Ohio. She is a spokesperson and Instructor for Islamic Affairs for TCMA (The Crescent Moon Association) and has lectured at the Arab Academy for Science.

**Alice Adams, Lac** (story p. 45)

*After Alice experienced the tragedy of losing her young son to congenital heart disease, she helped heal her grief by receiving Five Element acupuncture, which led her to becoming a Five Element acupuncturist, so she could assist others in a similar fashion.*

In the early 1980s, Alice was working as a registered nurse in a large East Coast hospital when her 7-year-old son died suddenly of

319

congenital heart disease. After this life-changing event, Alice entered graduate school and became a licensed acupuncturist in 1990. She also continued part-time work in hospice nursing for over twenty years. Alice is currently in private practice as a licensed Five Element acupuncturist and Qi Gong instructor in Tucson, Arizona and is passionate about helping others.

**Laurie Arshonsky, artist** (story p. 181)
*Laurie's beloved son Austin struggled with Attention Deficit Hyperactive Disorder (ADHD) and learning disabilities as a young child, and then mental illness as a later teen, which sadly cost him his life at 23.*

Laurie is a busy mother of five, grandmother, watercolor artist and instructor. "During the 1999 Cincinnati tornado," Laurie shared, "I almost lost my life when my home was destroyed and my next-door neighbors were killed. My husband and I were injured, but grateful to be alive!" Her best tribute to Austin is to live her life joyfully and give service to others. Laurie founded "Strength in Mothers," a support group, six months after her son's death in 2005. At these monthly gatherings, she inspires and supports the members who continue to heal and thrive.

**Michelle Barbuto, RN** (story p. 85)
*Although Michelle lost her 18-year-old son, John, in a motorcycle accident, she discovered that love transcends time and the physical.*

Michelle has been in the nursing industry for 32 years, starting as a Licensed Practical Nurse in geriatrics and is currently a Home Health Registered Nurse, working with the frail elderly. Prior to that, she had specialized in Rehabilitative Nursing for four years. Michelle's passion for helping people live life to their fullest led her down the path of becoming a personal trainer and yoga instructor. She specializes and is a Master Trainer/Mentor for the T-Tapp method of fitness.

**Vickie Bodner, LMT** (story p. 7)
*Vickie transitioned from an incredibly sad loss (a miscarriage) that was compounded by divorce, cancer, and depression, to a level of acceptance and surrender that she is certain will last a lifetime.*

Vickie Bodner, a Reiki Master, has been a licensed massage therapist in private practice since 1996. Her specialties include therapeutic and relaxation massage and craniosacral therapy. Vickie specializes in energy bodywork that increases awareness and relationship of the body, mind, spirit and emotions.

**Heidi Bright, MDiv, author, and national speaker** (story p. 215)
*The brain disease of addiction claimed the life of Heidi's teenaged son when he fatally overdosed on heroin in 2015. Even as it happened, Heidi understood fully that the only way out of the pit of despair was to go into the abyss and sit in the agony for as long as it would take.*
Heidi is intimately acquainted with grief. Confronted with a diagnosis of end-stage uterine cancer in 2009, Heidi consulted with a psychologist for assistance in grieving the impending end of her life—and learned a highly effective process for managing emotions. In October 2011, during her post-op appointment following her third cancer surgery, Heidi was told to get her affairs in order. Amazingly, six weeks later, she learned she was cancer-free. Heidi has been free of any evidence of disease and free of cancer treatment ever since. Because writing is the way Heidi shares her offerings with the world, she turned 250 options for managing cancer into the best-selling book, *Thriver Soup: A Feast for Living Consciously During the Cancer Journey* (Sunstone Press, 2015). Within one month of *Thriver Soup*'s release, Heidi's life was turned upside-down again by an even more painful grief: the death of her beloved 19-year-old son Brennan to a heroin overdose. She continued using the Map of Emotions© process and it shifted and lifted her grief. Through her upcoming book *Grieving an Addict* (grievinganaddict.com), Heidi is sharing this and other life-saving gifts with others who also grieve by showing them a way to process and integrate their emotions.

**Robert (Bob) R. Burdt** (story p. 52)
*19-month-old Brandon died from an incurable congenital heart defect, leaving his father with gifts about life and love that he will cherish for the rest of his life.*
Robert, known to friends as "Bobby," became a father for the first time in August 1977, with the birth of his son Brandon. Tragically, Brandon died of heart failure before his second birthday. In order to create meaning from his loss, Bob joined with other parents (whose children also received care at Children's Hospital in Oakland, California) in raising funds to purchase a home where families can stay while their

child receives lifesaving treatments at that hospital. Bob was President of the Board of The Mourning Star Center for grieving children and their families, and he continues helping others through his volunteer work with hospice. His philosophy is "We're not here for a long time but we're here for a good time."

**Lynda L. Crane, PhD, professor of psychology (retired)** (story p. 193)
*After her son Douglas developed schizophrenia and took his life as a result, Lynda turned to advocacy in the hope that others might avoid that despair.*
    Lynda is mom to Douglas and his three sisters, Sherri, Patty, and Nicole. She holds a Ph.D. in psychology and is Professor Emeritus at Mount St. Joseph University in Ohio. She is author of *Mental Retardation: A Community Integration Approach*, a textbook that promotes social inclusion of persons with disabilities, and numerous articles related to cognitive and clinical psychology. Lynda is co-founder of The Schizophrenia Oral History Project that provides a platform for individuals with schizophrenia to make their voices heard in the service of public education and the reduction of stigma. Most recently, Lynda has teamed up with her two oldest daughters (Patty Marquis and Sherri Marquis Schneider) who are opening an exciting and innovative Reggio-inspired charter school in St. Cloud, Florida, where Lynda will be Director of Psychology and Behavior. www.schizophreniaoralhistories.org and www.cijsstcloud.org

**Janice Crowder-Torrez, MS, CNM, RN (retired)** (story p. 152)
*Much to her surprise, Janice's 31-year-old son Anthony decided he was done and chose to end his life, and although devastated with overwhelming grief, his mother understood his choice.*
    Janice's professional career in health care began as an RN in Critical Care and Labor & Delivery, followed by her decision to become a Certified Nurse Midwife (CNM). After losing her son, Janice discovered the Helping Parents Heal (HPH) meetings in Scottsdale, Arizona, which focused on honoring her son's spirit, courage, and the many gifts he had left behind. So impressed with the meetings, Janice started an HPH chapter in Tucson where she lives. Janice is currently writing a book about her son's amazing life and the many challenges he faced while on the earth plane.

**Tim deZarn, actor** (story p. 95)
*After losing his first wife in less than 48 hours to a fatal virus, Tim was left to raise their two-month-old son Travis alone. When Travis was seven, Tim remarried, to a wonderful woman named Janine and the family moved to Culver City, California. Four years later, they had a beautiful daughter Emma, who was the apple of her big brother's eye. Tragedy struck again when eighteen-year-old Travis was killed on a foggy night in a head-on collision.*

Tim is a well-known and respected character actor who has played over 150 different roles in film and television, and has also appeared on the professional stage in more than 40 plays. Although he felt suicidal after losing first his wife and then, eighteen years later, Travis, in time Tim managed to climb out of the depression and PTSD that had plagued him. Travis lives on in spirit, especially at his alma mater, Palisades High School, where he was a star lacrosse player. The Most Inspirational Player title is awarded each year for a senior lacrosse athlete in honor of Travis, who is known for being one of the most inspirational lacrosse players of all time. The award also includes receipt of the Travis deZarn Memorial Scholarship.

**Kelly Farley, author** (story p. 14)
*Losing two babies over an 18-month period changed Kelly's perspective on life and continues to guide him along his journey.*

Kelly was caught up in the rat race of life when he experienced the loss of two babies over an eighteen month period. He lost his daughter, Katie, in 2004, and son, Noah, in 2006. Like many men, during these losses and the years that followed, he felt like he was the only dad that had ever experienced such a devastating loss. Kelly spent several years trying to put his life back together. He realized during his journey that society, for the most part, feels quite uncomfortable with an openly grieving male. That realization inspired him to start the Grieving Dads Project and write his book *Grieving Dads: To the Brink and Back.* (Kelly has personally shipped his book to 23+ countries on 5 continents, not including Amazon purchases). His Facebook page, "Grieving Dads: To the Brink and Back," has over 4000 followers. In November 2018, the Today Show produced a video highlighting Kelly and his story—https://www.today.com/video/one-dad-s-mission-to-help-men-cope-with-pregnancy-loss-1368691779998/. Kelly has a passion for helping people "pick up the pieces" after the death of a child and often conducts workshops on the subject. www.GrievingDads.com

**Tamara Gabriel, LMT/spiritual mentor** (story p. 108)
*Tamara's life took a downward turn following her motor vehicle accident, which resulted in the death of her 9-year-old daughter Janna. After several years, Tamara turned her pain into a project and began a non-profit community Healing Hugs—which now has over two million members.*
Tamara is married to a wonderful supportive husband, Dr. Richard Barnes, a psychiatrist. They have a holistic psychiatric clinic in Tucson, where Tamara runs women's empowerment classes and practices massage. Her non-profit organization, Healing Hugs, raises money for funeral and other expenses for parents who have lost a child. Throughout her twenty years of recovery, Tamara has brought 12-step meetings into local jails, as well as state and federal prisons. Tamara is a firm believer that the best way to heal ourselves is to help others by paying it forward because serving others lifts us out of our own pain.www.HealingHugs.net

**Shoshana Garfield, PhD, author** (story p. 20)
*Shoshana endured the devastation of her baby son's death by sinking deeper and deeper into her spiritual practices, aided immensely by energy psychology and angels on earth (friends and colleagues), and says she "continuously experiences increasingly expansive acceptance, peace and joy, right here, right now, no matter what."*
Shoshana considers her greatest and most important accomplishment to be that she is abidingly happy, despite having lost her son. Mother to Aiden and his big sister Aliyah, Shoshana lives in England with her best friend and belovèd, Sasha. She is a frequent keynote speaker and also teaches internationally on 100% responsibility for self-leadership. Her first book is cheerfully titled *The Smart Person's Guide to BIG FAT LIES on Stress, Suffering and Happiness.* Shoshana volunteers for two international charities and is a consultant for MISSING, a charity in India doing public education to reduce abduction of teenage girls into the sex slave trade. She has scores of videos on YouTube and you can visit her websites www.shoshangarfield.com and www.notjustacontract.com

**Suzanne Giesemann, spiritual teacher, author, and evidential medium** (story p. 249)
*Coming to grips with the sudden death of her stepdaughter Susan changed the career path of this Gold Star Mother—from being a Navy Commander and the Chairman of the Joint Chiefs of Staff's top aide to a world-renowned evidence-based medium.*

Suzanne is a spiritual teacher, an evidence-based medium, and the author of twelve books, including *Messages of Hope* and *Still Right Here.* She is a former U.S. Navy Commander who served as special assistant to the Chief of Naval Operations and as aide to the Chairman of the Joint Chiefs of Staff. Suzanne's powerful gift of communication with those on the other side provides stunning evidence of life after death and of our connection with the greater reality. Suzanne delivers messages of hope, healing, and love straight to the heart. Her work has been recognized as highly credible by famed afterlife researcher Dr. Gary Schwartz, Ph.D., and best-selling author Dr. Wayne Dyer. For more about Suzanne's work, visit www.SuzanneGiesemann.com

**Marla Grant, Helping Parents Heal affiliate leader** (story p. 271)
*The uncommonly harsh experience of losing three of her five children set Marla on a journey of profound spiritual discovery. Through it she has acquired a deep understanding of the grief process and its unexpected gifts that distill life down to its most essential elements—the greatest of which is love.*

Little did Marla realize at the time it happened that the death of her second-born infant son, during a tragic delivery, was just the beginning of her training ground in grief recovery. Baby Shane's death prepared Marla for the passing of two more children; her daughter Nicole (age 14) from leukemia nineteen years later, followed by her youngest son, Ryan, by suicide nineteen years after losing his cherished sister. Marla's abiding belief in the eternal nature of life has inspired her to help other parents realize that it's possible to return to a life of joy and fulfillment, even after the devastation of child loss—and even three. Marla is the founding Tampa Affiliate Leader for Helping Parents Heal and a Certified Grief Recovery Specialist. She is also a volunteer courier for the National Marrow Donor Program, delivering life-saving bone marrow to patients at transplant centers.

**Kelley Ireland, Tai Chi/Qigong teacher** (story p. 162)
*After losing her 18 year-old son Leslie to suicide, Kelley became a reluctant "student of grief." Her son's unexpected death suddenly placed Kelley into "The Club Nobody Wants To Be In"—to which her most profound and immediate reaction was "How do people even begin to live through this?"*

Kelley founded a non-profit grief/loss group in rural Arizona, called Good Grief, which she facilitated for several years. She worked for a suicide crisis line as a volunteer at Tucson's "Help on Call" center, and now works as a volunteer and activist with "Moms Demand Action for Gun Sense in America." Her role is in the education arm of the organization, called "Be Smart," which teaches gun owners about safe storage of firearms and also focuses on raising awareness and the recognition of the signs of teen suicide. Kelley has spoken before the Arizona Senate as an advocate for gun sense laws. She also goes to the Arizona state legislature when dangerous gun bills are being presented and debated as to whether they should become law, to not only protest them, but also speak out about the need for strengthening gun safety laws. Kelley still operates a grief and loss page, "Good Grief," on social media.

**Ernie Jackson, author** (story p. 118)
*The transition of his 9-year-old son Quinton in a tragic accident opened up Ernie's perception to a whole new world.*

Ernie and his wife Kristine have two children, a daughter, Cheyanne, here on the earth plane, and a son, Quinton, who has transitioned. Quinton's passing changed Ernie's life in ways he never expected. Ernie and his son continue to have a very strong connection, which Ernie shares in his two books, *Quinton's Messages* and *Quinton's Legacy*. Ernie's role on the board of directors for Helping Parents Heal (www.Helping ParentsHeal.org) allows him a broad base for sharing his two greatest passions: the divine message of 'There is More' and to be of service in any way he can. www.QuintonsMessages.com

**Jo-Anne Joseph, author** (story p. 31)
*The greatest tragedy to befall Jo-Anne's world was losing her full term daughter to birth asphyxia.*

Jo-Anne Joseph is a career woman, freelance writer, and a multi-genre author who has published over ten novels since 2017. She's an artist, poet, and a believer in the greatness of humanity. Jo-Anne lives in South Africa and is married to her best friend, Brian. She is above all, mother to two beautiful children, Braydon who she has the honor of sharing her days with, and watch grow into an incredible little man; and her daughter Zia, who she holds in her heart. Love and a deep passion for helping others are what drive her to participate in the loss community. She writes regularly and voluntarily for online forums, *Glow in the Woods* and *Still Standing Magazine*. She contributed to the anthology book, *Our Only Time: Stories of Pregnancy/Infant Loss with Strategies for Health Professionals*, as well as published a remembrance poetry anthology entitled *Footprints on the Heart*. Connect and find out more about Jo-Anne on her website www.joannejosephauthor.com

**Lucia Maya, spiritual teacher and healer** (story p. 58)
*After Lucia's 22-year-old daughter Elizabeth died of non-Hodgkin's lymphoma, Lucia discovered the transformational process of grief.*

Lucia is the proud mother of two daughters. Her older daughter, Elizabeth Blue, who was 22 when she died of cancer, continues to be a loving presence in Lucia's life. Lucia's younger daughter, Julianna, lives in New York City, and includes stories of her sister's life and death in her standup comedy. Lucia lives and works on Maui and Molokai, Hawaii, with her loving and supportive wife Zelie. Lucia's work as a Reiki practitioner/teacher and intuitive guide brings her great joy and peace, as she supports others in their transformation and healing. Lucia has been interviewed on Upworthy.com and Arizona Public Media about Elizabeth's death—the journey they took together in life and in death, and the transformational process of grief. Her blog includes Elizabeth's writing and poetry, and her own intimate journey of living with loss and transformation: www.luminousblue5.com and Lucia's work website is: www.luminousadventures.com

**Tammy McDonnell** (story p. 226)
*Although Tammy's son Hunter had been clean and sober for a year and a half and seemed to be doing well, Tammy received the call that would change her life forever.*

As a believer and follower of Jesus, Tammy trusts in the promise that He made to mankind of eternal life. Her precious son's drug addiction ended young Hunter's life, and Tammy says, as a result, she has met the most broken compassionate people since then. She wants to change the stigma of addiction by educating and finding help for those who struggle with this awful disease. Having received many heavenly signs from Hunter, Tammy knows that her son continues to place people in her path to help her and others who also need help.

**Sandy Peckinpah, author and certified Grief Recovery Specialist®** (story p. 68)
*Sandy's 16-year-old son Garrett woke up with a fever and was dead 24 hours later of bacterial meningitis, changing the way Sandy pursued life, love, and the future.*
Sandy is the author of four books, including the multi-award winning, *How to Survive the Worst that Can Happen: A Parent's Step-by-Step Guide to Healing after the Loss of a Child.* Her articles on resilience are featured in *Huffington Post* and "Thrive Global." Sandy is a frequent Livestream broadcaster, sharing her passion for helping people rise up and transition through life's difficult challenges. She is also a Certified Grief Recovery Specialist®, as well as a real estate agent in Southern California. www.SandyPeckinpah.com www.How ToSurviveTheWorstThatCanHappen.com

**JoAnn Pohlkamp** (story p. 257)
*Although JoAnn's husband had been an Army officer, her son Mike's dream was to become a pilot and fly for the Navy. Mike, who was by then an aviation instructor, was killed in a mid-air collision on his way in for a landing at his Naval air base. After Mike's death, JoAnn says one of the biggest lessons she learned is to be present with herself, her family, and everyone.*
As a military wife, JoAnn loved living in Germany with her husband Jack, and traveling all throughout Europe with their twin baby boys, Mike and Mark. Upon returning to the States, they settled in Cincinnati Ohio and raised five children. JoAnn's family is the center of her world and she loves spending time with them—husband, kids, grandkids, and even great-grandkids. JoAnn credits her family and faith in a loving God with helping her to survive the devastating loss of Mike, her beloved son.

**Sharon Gabriel Rossy, MEd, psychotherapist** (story p. 125)
*Although Sharon suffered tremendous grief when Gabriel, the eldest of her four sons, died, she made a conscious decision to live and openly shares the lessons she has learned as a grieving mother.*

After Gabriel's death, when a large tree fell on his car during a rainstorm, Sharon and her family took legal action against the municipality for allowing rotting trees to line major roads. They also created a fund in Gabriel's name and held three major fundraisers for underprivileged children in his honor. Three years later, Sharon returned to university in Canada to finish her master's degree and continue to obtain her permit as a psychotherapist. Now, as a therapist, Sharon works primarily with grief and bereavement, and most of her clients are grieving parents. Having gone through the loss of Gabriel, she feels it's her mission to help others navigate the very difficult journey of grief.

**Laurie Savoie, author** (story p. 172)
*After Laurie's 19-year-old son ended his life, Laurie turned her profound grief into a life-changing passion for helping others.*

Laurie, mother of three, was living a normal, happy life until November 17, 2010, the day her 19-year-old son Garrett took his own life. Laurie turned her grief and sadness into a life-changing passion for helping others and is spreading the message of Hope and Love in her book, *The Ripple Effect: Invisible Impact of Suicide.* Profits from the book are donated to purchase additional books, which have been shared across more than ten countries. In addition, Laurie is actively involved in Helping Parents Heal, HOPE ASAP, and has been a frequent guest speaker in the Arizona Prison System.

**Michele Wollert, MA, MS, school psychologist (retired)** (story p. 201)
*From the tragedy of her son Jonny's suicide came treasures of love and insight that brought healing and hope for Michele and others.*

Michele lives with her husband Rich and rescue dog Annie in the beautiful Pacific Northwest. In addition to Jonny, she is the proud mother of Zach and Jason, as well as a devoted grandmother. Michele is a theatrical costume designer turned school psychologist, now happily retired. She is also eternally inquisitive. Michele has written about Jonny's life and legacy in a memorial blog: http://jonathan-wollert.memory-of.com/

**Tina Zarlenga, writer** (story p. 74)

*When an unknown virus extinguished the light and life of her rambunctious five-year-old son Ryan, Tina discovered that giving back would actually save her.*

Tina shares stories of inspiration, hope, and her journey through grief with emotional essays of survival on her website. And through a campaign to pay it forward for Ryan, she uncovered JOY. Published essays of Tina's can be found in *Bella Grace* magazine, The Compassionate Friends' *We Need Not Walk Alone* magazine, *Tiny Buddha*, and many other inspirational online communities. Tina shares stories on subjects from grieving to grateful on her blog: http://www.unraveling myheartthewriteway.com